12 July 1971

THE NATIONAL INSTITUTE OF
ECONOMIC AND SOCIAL RESEARCH

Occasional Papers

XXIV

THE ECONOMIC IMPACT OF COMMONWEALTH IMMIGRATION

A

The National Institute of Economic and Social Research is an independent, non-profit-making body, founded in 1938. It has as its aim the promotion of realistic research, particularly in the field of economics. It conducts research by its own research staff and in co-operation with the universities and other academic bodies. The results of the work done under the Institute's auspices are published in several series, and a list of its publications up to the present time will be found at the end of this volume.

A2

THE ECONOMIC IMPACT
OF
COMMONWEALTH IMMIGRATION

BY

K. JONES and A. D. SMITH

CAMBRIDGE
AT THE UNIVERSITY PRESS
1970

PUBLISHED BY

THE SYNDICS OF THE CAMBRIDGE UNIVERSITY PRESS

Bentley House, 200 Euston Road, London, N.W.1

American Branch : 32 East 57th Street, New York N.Y. 10022

©

THE NATIONAL INSTITUTE OF ECONOMIC AND SOCIAL RESEARCH

1970

Library of Congress Catalogue Card Number : 70-118064

Standard Book Number : 521 07917 9

Printed in Great Britain by Metcalfe, Cooper & Hepburn Ltd., London, E.C.2

CONTENTS

LIST OF TABLES

TEXT TABLES

LIST OF CHARTS

SYMBOLS AND CONVENTIONS

.. not available

— nil or negligible

Fiscal years are indicated by a stroke between two dates, e.g. 1964/5. A hyphen between two dates, e.g. 1964–5, means an average over the years given.

Details in tablets may not add to totals because of rounding.

AUTHORS' PREFACE

This study on immigration was made possible by a grant from the Department of Economic Affairs, which the National Institute gratefully acknowledges.

In the early part of the study, officials in the Departments of Economic Affairs, Education and Science, Employment and Productivity, Health and Social Security, and in the Home Office, provided both helpful advice and some unpublished material. Staff at the Survey of Race Relations helped us in various ways. We are also grateful to Professor Brinley Thomas, Mr Duncan Burn and Dr E. J. Mishan for reading and commenting on drafts. But the authors alone are responsible for the uses to which the data have been put and for the conclusions drawn.

At the Institute we are particularly indebted to the Director, Mr G. D. N. Worswick for his helpful advice and comments. We are also grateful to Mr C. A. Blyth for reading and commenting on the manuscript, Mrs P. Garzon who assisted in the preparation of the material and Mrs G. I. Barlow for carrying the paper through the press. The manuscript was typed by Mrs A. Pethig whom we also thank.

K. J.
A. D. S.

London, December 1969

CHAPTER I

INTRODUCTION

Compared with the research effort devoted to the social implications of recent migration to this country, the economic consequences have been rather neglected. This is surprising, for not only have questions of economic performance and management been very much to the fore during the past decade, but also contemplation of the social aspects of immigration can yield misleading conclusions if their interrelationships with economic consequences are ignored. This study seeks to redress this imbalance.

Almost automatically, in the context of British economic development and policy in the past decade, interest is directed towards the impact of immigration on four issues: structural economic adjustments, growth, the rate of inflation and the balance of payments situation. Any costs and benefits of immigration under these headings need to be considered alongside the social costs and benefits before a general assessment of the advantages of migration for Britain, if not for the immigrant groups themselves, can be made. Indeed, the ties between social and economic impacts are at some points so close that it is virtually impossible to treat social and economic impacts separately. Housing standards constitute one such focal point: the accommodation of immigrants obviously has a major influence both on their social integration and on the (possibly inflationary) expenditure on the stock of social capital. Much attention has now been paid to the former aspect.[1] The purpose of this study is to consider the latter question and others like it. In fact, instances of possibly close interrelationships between social and economic impacts abound. Another that has been considered to be potentially very important is that, while the most significant economic advantages of recent immigration are widely thought to derive from structural changes that it facilitates, the social problems raised by immigration could well be due to the concentration of immigrants—in jobs, industries and areas—which such a contribution requires.

A further distinction between this and other recent immigration studies is that it attempts to direct attention to national aggregates. Very important studies devoted to the impact of immigrant workers in individual

---

[1] See, especially, E. Burney, *Housing on Trial : A Study of Immigrants and Local Government,* Oxford University Press, London, 1967 ; and for a wider study of the social conditions and impacts of immigrants, J. Rex and R. Moore, *Race, Community and Conflict : A Study of Sparkbrook,* Oxford University Press, London, 1967. See also E. Butterworth (ed.), *Immigrants in West Yorkshire,* Oxford University Press, London, 1967.

factories have now appeared.[1] A good part of these studies is taken up with industrial sociology, but they also yield economic information complementary to the essentially macro-economic analysis attempted in this book. Quantitative consideration has been paid to some economic consequences of immigration in the Greater London and West Midlands conurbations, and some general conclusions drawn, in the wide ranging study of migrants recently produced by the Institute of Race Relations.[2] The present study is concerned throughout with the determination of the economic characteristics and impacts of immigrants at the national level. Whilst, however, it seeks to fill some of the gaps in the study of the economic aspects of migration to this country, it does so in the hope that these impacts, whatever they may prove to be, will be considered alongside the social costs and benefits. Moreover, we have been at some considerable pains throughout to draw attention to those areas where economic and social factors are especially closely connected.

The study is concerned with the economic impact of coloured immigration to this country. Not only has the stream of coloured immigrants been far and away the largest of any group in the 1950s and 1960s, and as such of major interest in any survey of recent immigration to Britain, but also, like certain earlier migrant groups though to a greater degree, it has posed special social problems. Since the primary objective is to provide an economic picture that complements the surveys of the social consequences of immigration, it naturally became focused on this group of migrants. However, throughout the study an attempt has been made, wherever the relevant data were readily available, to set the macro-economic variables relating to coloured immigrants in perspective against the magnitudes of total immigrant flows. Fortunately, granted the quantitative and qualitative importance of coloured immigration, it is a development about which considerable information now exists—a statement that is not equally valid for other immigrant communities within the British Isles.

To be more precise, the study is for the most part concerned with immigrants from the New Commonwealth, that is from Commonwealth countries other than Australia, Canada and New Zealand, and at many points it surveys this body of migrants in terms of three groups: migrants born in India and Pakistan, in the British Caribbean and in the other New Commonwealth. Though we refer to immigrants from the New Commonwealth as coloured, they include arrivals from certain Mediterranean areas and some Indian-born offspring of British civil servants. Of

---

[1] Sheila Patterson, *Immigrants in Industry*, Oxford University Press, London, 1968 ; P. L. Wright, *The Coloured Worker in British Industry*, Oxford University Press, London, 1968.

[2] E. J. B. Rose and Associates, *Colour and Citizenship, A Report on British Race Relations*, Oxford University Press, London, 1969.

greater significance is the extent to which the definition excludes some coloured members of the British population—those born in this country. This latter distinction has conceptual as well as statistical implications. Bearing upon them is the consideration that, rather than dealing with the economic impact of all coloured members of the population of Britain at any one moment of time, our aim has been at many points to gauge the major economic consequences of the sharp *change* which has recently taken place in the size of the coloured community in Britain. More precisely, attention has frequently been directed to its growth as a result of further immigration between 1961 and 1966. These terminal years have the advantage that, on the one hand, they embrace the period during which most of the coloured influx occurred[1] and, on the other, they are years for which population censuses provide much useful material. Our aim, especially in chapters 8 and 9, has been essentially to trace the short- and medium-term economic consequences of the arrival of new immigrants in this period, although where they are thought likely, longer-term impacts have also been mentioned. Concern with an immigrant definition that relates to people born abroad not only suffers the analytical disadvantage of including some white immigrants, but also means that, on occasion, less information is available than exists for households—including children born in this country—whose head was born in the New Commonwealth. In some instances, therefore, use has been made of the latter information.

A less important point relates to the comparisons made in this study between characteristics of the New Commonwealth population and of the total British population. Strictly such comparisons are not between coloured immigrants and the indigenous population, for (even neglecting the inclusion of non-coloured immigrants) a figure for the total population itself includes the New Commonwealth community. However, given the fact that the New Commonwealth population still constitutes only a small percentage of the total, the approximation involved, yielding in each instance a slight understatement of the true indigenous-immigrant difference, will not generally lead to major errors. Exceptions to this, however, are those cases where developments between 1961 and 1966, in population and labour force, are being examined. Because of the more important role played by New Commonwealth immigrants in changes during this period, identification of the indigenous change with the total change would be misleading and, accordingly, indigenous changes—which for convenience have been identified as total changes less changes for New Commonwealth immigrants only—are specifically computed.

---

[1] The sharp rise in immigration from the New Commonwealth actually got under way in 1960.

Chapters 2 to 7 are largely devoted to the measurement and description of certain demographic and, especially, economic characteristics of New Commonwealth immigrants: their contribution to population changes in this country, to quantitative and qualitative changes in the British labour force, their income and expenditure characteristics, demands on the social services and capital requirements. Other writers have considered certain of these features, especially in relation to the provenance and migration motives of New Commonwealth migrants,[1] but nothing comparable appears to have been attempted on such a general basis and with the emphasis placed so specifically on the economic characteristics and implications of New Commonwealth immigrants in the setting of the British economy. The nature of chapters 8 and 9 is rather different. Whilst the earlier chapters inevitably contain sections concerned with assessing the impact of the immigrants' economic characteristics on British economic development, the latter two chapters are almost wholly taken up with this task. Chapter 8 concentrates on the impact of New Commonwealth immigrants on economic growth; chapter 9 deals with their effect on inflation and the balance of payments.

[1] See R. B. Davison, *West Indian Migrants : Social and Economic Facts of Migration from the West Indies*, Oxford University Press, London, 1962 ; R. B. Davison, *Black British : Immigrants to England*, Oxford University Press, London, 1966 ; and C. Peach, *West Indian Migration to Britain : A Social Geography*, Oxford University Press, London, 1968.

CHAPTER 2

THE IMMIGRANT POPULATION

THE GROWTH OF THE IMMIGRANT POPULATION

The immigrant population of Great Britain was something over 2 million in 1961 and of the order of 2½ million in 1966; as such it represented approximately 4 to 4½ per cent of the British population in 1961 and about 5 per cent of the total in 1966. It is impossible to be more precise than this. For the primary source of statistics relating to the size and composition of the immigrant population, the population censuses, on the one hand include persons who, perhaps, should not be classed as immigrants and, on the other, are affected by underenumeration.

Table 1. *Population of Great Britain born abroad*

	New Common- wealth	Australia, New Zealand, Canada	Irish Republic[a]	Other immi- grants	All immi- grants	Total population of Great Britain
			(*Thousands*)			
Resident in 1951	256	93	533	695	1,577	48,854
1951–61						
Deaths[b]	(21)	(14)	(59)	(70)	(164)	
Immigration[c]	306	31	252	219	808	
Resident in 1961	541	110	726	844	2,222	51,284
1961–66						
Deaths[b]	(14)	(5)	(29)	(52)	(100)	
Immigration[c]	326	20	42	95	483	
Resident in 1966	853	125	739	887	2,603	52,304[d]
Immigration (annual averages)						
1951–61	31	3	25	22	81	
1961–66	65	4	8	19	96	
Annual growth rates			(*Percentages*)			
1951–61	*7.7*	*1.7*	*3.1*	*2.0*	*3.5*	*0.5*
1961–66	*9.5*	*2.6*	*0.3*	*1.0*	*3.2*	*0.4*
1951–66	*8.3*	*2.0*	*2.2*	*1.6*	*3.4*	*0.5*

SOURCES: *Census 1951, General Tables; Census 1961, Birthplace and Nationality Tables; Sample Census 1966, Summary Tables; Annual Abstract of Statistics, 1965*, No. 102; NIESR estimates.

[a] Includes all those born in Ireland unless Northern Ireland stated.
[b] Estimated from the death rates for England and Wales.
[c] Net of re-emigration.
[d] Sample census, probably deficient by 1–2 per cent.

The figures in table 1, derived from this source, include children born in the Commonwealth and colonies to British nationals. One group where the number of such children is large enough to affect significant basic characteristics of the immigrants comprises those born in India; a large number, estimated at about 80 thousand in 1966, of those born in India and resident in Great Britain are the white children of Indian army and civil service staff, or Anglo-Indians who left after the attainment of dominion status in 1947.[1] It would be wrong merely to pay lip service to the possible distortion which this factor can introduce. It should be constantly borne in mind when considering aggregates relating to Asian immigrants from the New Commonwealth, and no doubt it explains, for instance, some of the rather surprising features of their occupational distribution.[2] A comparable group consists of the sons and daughters born to British nationals in Commonwealth territories, being educated in Britain. They appear to be important, especially in the sub-division designated as other New Commonwealth. Finally, the other immigrants category in table 1 includes members of the United States forces in this country who, together with their families, number about 35 thousand.[3]

There appears to be a general tendency for immigrants, especially New Commonwealth immigrants living in crowded conditions, to be under-enumerated in population censuses, and particularly in sample censuses. In the 1961 Census, certain data were collected on a full census basis and other information from a 10 per cent sample. A comparison of the population estimates on the two bases reveals the large degree of under-enumeration, especially of the New Commonwealth population, in the sample census. It shows that New Commonwealth immigrants were 17 per cent underrepresented in the conurbations.[4] The degree of under-enumeration varied from 27 per cent for Pakistanis and 23 per cent for West Indians to 7 per cent for Indians. It is also known that there was some underenumeration in the full census, but it is impossible to quantify this. The 1961 data in table 1 relate to the full census result, but a major problem arises in the case of 1966: no full census is available, only 10 per cent sample census data. The question therefore arises: to what extent do the 1966 data understate the immigrant, and especially the New

[1] D. Eversley and F. Sukdeo, *The Dependants of the Coloured Commonwealth Population of England and Wales*, Oxford University Press, London, 1969, p. 10.
[2] Davison, *Black British*, p. 69.
[3] The data in table 1 include those who come to reside in Great Britain for a limited period only, but exclude transient visitors.
[4] See, especially, Eversley and Sukdeo, op. cit. p. 10 ; also P. Jenner and B. Cohen, *Commonwealth Immigrants and the 1961 Census (10% Sample)—Some Problems in Analysis*, unpublished paper. It should be noted that, in the conurbations where the bulk of coloured immigrants reside, the definition of New Commonwealth differs somewhat from that used throughout most of this study ; see chapter 4, p. 48.

Commonwealth, population? By combining the 1961 totals and data about migratory movements, to yield an alternative estimate for 1966, Eversley and Sukdeo calculated 11 per cent underestimation for Asians and West Indians in England and Wales: 29 per cent for Pakistanis, 11 per cent for West Indians and 5 per cent for Indians.[1] Underestimation of this order among coloured immigrants in 1966 would offset most of the overestimation of immigrants in table 1 due to the inclusion of basically non-immigrant groups but, because of the uncertainty which attaches to underenumeration in 1966, no adjustment has been made to the data.[2] However, the fact that such underenumeration certainly exists should not be forgotten and, throughout the study, reminders are issued whenever the factor is particularly important.

The structure of the immigrant population in 1966, in terms of Commonwealth and colonials, the Irish and other immigrants, is the culmination of trends which have persisted, although not necessarily at steady rates, over the previous fifteen years. The basic feature of these trends has been the rapid enlargement of the proportion of Commonwealth and colonial immigrants from about 22 per cent in 1951 to 29 per cent in 1961 and 38 per cent in 1966. Over the same period the Irish proportion declined from about 34 per cent in 1951 to 33 per cent in 1961 and 28 per cent in 1966; and similarly, the foreign share fell from 44 per cent to 38 per cent and to 34 per cent.

Table 1 shows that a rise in the proportion of immigrants from the New Commonwealth wholly accounted for the rise in the Commonwealth proportion. Immigrants born in these countries accounted for about 16 per cent of the total in 1951, a proportion that had risen to 24 per cent in 1961 and had more than doubled, to 33 per cent, by 1966. Over the same period, the proportion accounted for by immigrants from Australia, New Zealand and Canada declined a little, from about 6 to 5 per cent. It is because of this rapid rise in the proportion of immigrants from the New Commonwealth—a rise which, of course, is even more pronounced in terms of absolute numbers—and the special problems associated with it, that primary attention is paid in this study to this group of immigrants. We can start by considering the inflow of New Commonwealth migrants against a background of the trends in other immigrant flows.

Since children born in Britain to immigrants are excluded from the

---

[1] Op. cit. pp. 22–4. They believe that 'none of the official or unofficial data available in 1968 can be held to prove more serious underenumeration than we have allowed for in this report', (op. cit. p. 54). Certainly the absence of any allowance for deaths among these immigrants suggests that their estimated underenumeration is on the high rather than the low side.

[2] Also, to avoid a spurious impression of accuracy the 1966 data have not been adjusted for the 1–2 per cent underestimation that is known to apply to the total British population.

B

statistics given in table 1, changes in the immigrant population can arise only as a result of, on the one hand, new arrivals augmenting the number of immigrants and, on the other, mortality and the re-emigration of immigrants depleting their numbers. The method adopted in table 1 to obtain an impression of the flow of immigrants consists of adding an estimate of deaths among immigrants to the observed inter-censal difference in the immigration population, to yield an estimate for immigration less re-emigration.

That the number of immigrants in each group increased in each period reflects the fact that immigration exceeded deaths and re-emigration for all groups. Moreover, rates of immigration were such as to make the period under review one of rapid rise in the proportion and, a fortiori, in the number of immigrants in the total British population. Between 1951 and 1961, immigration less re-emigration was occurring at an annual rate of 81 thousand people, causing the immigrant population to rise by 3.5 per cent a year. And in the period 1961 to 1966, immigration less re-emigration was 96 thousand per annum, and the immigrant population continued to increase at a rate in excess of 3 per cent. These rises were much higher than the rate of increase of the total British population over this fifteen-year period—0.5 per cent per annum—with the result that immigrants formed a growing proportion of the population: 3.3 per cent in 1951, 4.3 per cent in 1961 and 5.0 per cent in 1966. Whilst some groups experienced sharp reductions in the *proportion* of the total immigrant population for which they accounted, in each case (and in each of the two sub-periods identified) their numbers increased. Moreover, except in the case of the Irish in the period 1961–6, their numbers rose faster than the total population.

Reflecting the shifts in the structural composition of the immigrant population which we have already noted, the most dramatic rise, of 8.3 per cent per annum over the period, was recorded by the New Commonwealth group. Their rate of increase accelerated from the not inconsiderable rate of 7.7 per cent per annum in the period 1951 to 1961, to 9.5 per cent between 1961 and 1966,[1] but this was not quite sufficient to offset the effect on the growth of the total immigrant population of the fall in the rate at which other immigrants, and especially the Irish, were coming to Britain.

The sharp decline in the rate of immigration from Ireland can be ascribed to the more rapid economic growth enjoyed by that country during the early 1960s. Since 1951 the rate of inflow of other immigrants has been relatively small: the major rise was the result of unsettled

[1] The largest increases were towards the end of the first period and early in the second period.

political conditions during and immediately after World War II and occurred prior to 1951. This deceleration of foreign arrivals continued throughout the period under examination—the annual average rate of increase being only 1 per cent per annum between 1961 and 1966 compared with 2 per cent between 1951 and 1961—but, in addition, there occurred a significant shift in the provenance of these immigrants. There has been a substantial net decrease in the Polish and Russian-born population,[1] alongside large increases of those born in Italy, Spain, Portugal, and the United States.

This new pattern mirrors a fundamental change in the factors prompting the migration of foreign-born people to the British Isles. The political factors, so strong prior to 1951, have largely yielded to economic forces:[2] the rise in immigrants—albeit short-term ones—from southern Europe is part and parcel of a European movement based on the economic advantages which employment in the northerly countries offers; and a large proportion of the increase in those born in the United States represents a reverse brain drain—professional and technical workers seeking to acquire or improve specific skills in this country.

An attempt must now be made to account for the most dynamic element in British immigration during these fifteen years: the sharp rise in the inflow of people born in the New Commonwealth which, because of its importance and the special problems it poses, is the central theme of this study. It is a surprise to discover that this migration is so new that comprehensive studies of international population movements completed little more than a decade or so ago make little or no reference to the migration of persons from developing to developed countries in general, and from the New Commonwealth to Britain in particular.[3] There is a need, therefore, to place this new migration in its proper historical perspective: to determine to which type of migration, when classified by cause, it properly belongs and why it occurred when it did.

The literature devoted to the principles of migratory movements has broadly distinguished three types: those caused by demographic, political and economic factors. In the final analysis, however, the apparent demographic content of international migration, the movement of large

---

[1] Many of those classed as Russian in 1951 were in fact likely to have been natives of the former Baltic States: Estonia, Latvia and Lithuania.

[2] With the exception of immigrants from Hungary.

[3] See, for example, chapter VI, 'Economic and Social Factors Affecting Migration' in *The Determinants and Consequences of Population Trends*, United Nations, New York, 1953 ; and B. Thomas, *International Migration and Economic Development : a Trend Report and Bibliography*, UNESCO, Paris, 1961.

To the extent that population movements between developed and developing countries attracted attention in the 1950s, it was directed to the need for providing the latter with skilled manpower.

numbers of people from densely populated to less populated countries, resolves itself into an economic explanation. People have not changed their country of residence, at least not on a significant scale, simply to acquire more breathing space. That the demographic explanation held sway at all can be attributed to the fact that the most important migratory movement in recent economic history occurred between the comparatively densely populated European continent and a sparsely populated North America. This movement was, in fact, economically motivated. European immigrants, many unemployed, were attracted by the availability of jobs in a land where living standards promised to be high. That they were not drawn by more living room *per se* is shown by the fact that, for the most part, they left rural backgrounds for jobs in urban communities. In so far as the promise of the higher living standards stemmed from a high ratio of (largely fertile) land to population in North America, this was an economic rather than a demographic cause. However, higher living standards are frequently a result of high capital intensities, and these are as likely to be found, if not more so, in densely populated areas.[1] The United Kingdom is more densely populated than Jamaica or Pakistan.

If the rather special, politically motivated, migrations are left aside, economic betterment is seen to be the basic cause of significant population shifts. Migrations have occurred 'because the resources used in conjunction with labour, together with the technological skill and other factors affecting the use of agents of production, gave promise of producing more income per worker in the countries of destination than in the countries of provenance'.[2] If this is so, there is a need to explain why migration from the developed countries of Europe is of such long standing and movements from poor to rich countries so novel. Relatively rich European countries have for decades lost significant numbers of their population, firstly, because the migrants moved to countries where living standards, if not already high, promised to be so and, secondly, because the decision to migrate is taken by individuals. Differences between the wage and salary structures of rich and poor countries may make it attractive for certain people—members of a colonial service for example—to move from the former to the latter. More important, impoverished unemployed workers in relatively wealthy European countries were in the past more than ready to move to the United States, where jobs were available.

[1] For a discussion of these questions see Thomas, op. cit.

[2] J. J. Spengler, 'Effects Produced in Receiving Countries by Pre-1939 Immigration', in B. Thomas (ed.), *The Economics of International Migration*, Proceedings of a Conference held by the International Economic Association, Macmillan, London, 1958, p. 38. For a similar statement, see also *The Determinants and Consequences of Population Trends*, p. 98.

The latter factor, the sheer availability of jobs as opposed to, say, higher wages, has no doubt been the most important cause of migration from the New Commonwealth to Britain. Few would deny that economic considerations of some kind are at the root of this movement. Davison discerned an 'unmistakable' negative relationship between the *per capita* national incomes of the various West Indian islands and the rate of emigration.[1] And, in a sample survey conducted in Jamaica in 1960, the reason given by emigrants for going to Britain was almost unanimously 'to seek employment'.[2] Surveys in India and Pakistan would very likely yield similar results.

Whilst economic, rather than political, factors have spurred the New Commonwealth migrants towards Britain,[3] the movement has drawn plenty of political problems in its train. Moreover, whilst political pressures in countries of the New Commonwealth may have done little to prompt these moves, political events in the receiving country do much to explain the *timing* of the flow of immigrants. Granted that significant income differences have existed for many decades between Great Britain and the countries of the New Commonwealth at all levels of the population, and given the absence of restrictions on migration, why did the movement not get under way until the 1950s? And why has this migratory flow 'peaked' at certain times?

An essentially political event, World War II, seems to have been partly responsible for triggering off migration from the New Commonwealth to Britain. Many of the large numbers of Indians and West Indians who came to Britain during the war as members of the armed Forces or as factory workers saw the opportunities for employment and economic advancement and stayed or subsequently returned. Moreover, migration from these countries was directed more surely to Britain by two other political factors. As citizens of the United Kingdom and Colonies, their entry to the United Kingdom was then unimpeded, whilst migration to other Commonwealth countries with high living standards was not. Many West Indians would have eagerly emigrated to Canada but for the restrictions which ruled out any large-scale movement in that direction, and Australia might have offered a similar attraction to Indians and Pakistanis but for the white Australia policy. Secondly, the natural outlet outside the Commonwealth for West Indians is the United States,

---

[1] He found none between population densities and migration. (Davison, *West Indian Migrants*, pp. 42–4.)

[2] Ibid. p. 36.

[3] Except perhaps in the case of some Indian and Pakistani immigrants who arrived in the late 1940s, for whom the unsettled conditions following partition afforded an inducement to move. It has been estimated that about 8 million people were displaced from Pakistan and 9 million from India.

but successive administrations applied hardening restrictions to the free movement of people from the Caribbean, culminating in the 1952 McCarran-Walter provisions. Had these not been imposed, the large-scale population movement from the West Indies to Britain might never have occurred.[1]

There is evidence that these political factors, especially the nature of immigration restrictions, have strongly influenced the timing of migration from the New Commonwealth to Britain, not only in the larger sense, but also from year to year. It is difficult to be certain about this, largely because, prior to the early 1960s and the statistical innovations resulting from the 1962 Commonwealth Immigrants Act, information about the annual movements of immigrants is inadequate. However, it seems fairly certain from the data which are available that in the 1950s the rate of immigration, and especially of immigration from the New Commonwealth, accelerated towards the end of the decade.[2]

Table 2 takes up the story for New Commonwealth immigrants from the 1961 Census benchmark, using official estimates for the period up to July 1962 when the Commonwealth Immigrants Act came into force and the improved statistics made their appearance. These data, and our knowledge of the broad trends in previous years, make it clear that there was a marked acceleration in migration from the New Commonwealth for a couple of years before the 1962 Commonwealth Immigrants Act, and some deceleration, especially in the case of Indians and Pakistanis, in the following six months. It is arguable, and indeed it is widely believed, that the migrants' anticipation of the restrictive policy, then being widely discussed in the United Kingdom, was the major force behind this spurt in the rate of immigration.[3] If so, the sequence

---

[1] See, for instance, Davison, *West Indian Migrants*, p. 1.

[2] Two sets of estimates are given below :

	Tropical Commonwealth[a]	*Thousands* West Indians[b]
1955	42.7	24.5
1956	46.8	26.4
1957	42.4	22.5
1958	29.9	16.5
1959	21.6	20.4
1960	57.7	52.8
1961	136.4	..
1962 (1st half)	94.9	..

[a] Davison, *Black British*, p. 3.
[b] Davison, *West Indian Migrants*, p. 5.

[3] See, for example, Davison, *West Indian Migrants*, p. 7 ; and *The Economist*, 17 February 1968, pp. 15–16.

was repeated early in 1968, when speculation about restrictions on the entry into Britain of Kenyan Asians produced a rush of immigrants and, in turn, the very curbs (the 1968 Commonwealth Immigrants Act) that the Asians were seeking to avoid.   Large numbers of Kenyan Asians were not subject to the immigration restrictions of the 1962 Act because, when given the option of Kenyan or British citizenship upon Kenya's independence, they had opted for the latter.

Table 2. *New Commonwealth immigration, 1961–6[a]*

	New Commonwealth	India & Pakistan	British Caribbean	*Thousands* Other New Commonwealth
1961 April–December	102.3	..	..	..
1962 January–June	94.9	..	..	..
July–December	27.7[b]	6.2[b]	8.4[b]	13.1[b]
1963	72.4	35.8	13.1	23.5
1964	70.9	26.7	18.3	25.9
1965	66.0	28.1	17.0	20.9
1966 January–March	9.0	..	..	..
Immigrant population 1966	853	316	270	267

SOURCES: *Commonwealth Immigrants Act, 1962: Control of Immigration Statistics, 1962–3; 1964; 1965; 1966* (Cmnd 2379; 2658; 2979; 3258); H.C. Deb. 1 and 5 July 1965; *Sample Census 1966, Summary Tables;* NIESR estimates.

[a] These immigration flows relate to the United Kingdom, but the number of New Commonwealth migrants who have entered Northern Ireland is thought to be very small.

[b] From July 1962, comprises holders of Ministry of Labour vouchers, dependants, students and persons coming for settlement not included elsewhere.

But, if political considerations have played a role in determining the timing of New Commonwealth immigration to this country, they have done so alongside those economic factors which are at the root of the movement.   In particular, the existence of full, or almost full, employment since World War II has provided the basic attraction previously missing.   Indeed some observers believe that the postwar 'pull' of jobs in this country was greater than the 'push' of unemployment and low living standards in New Commonwealth countries.[1]   As early as 1956 (and in the context of coloured immigration this was very early), Senior related the increase in Britain's coloured population directly to changes in the supply of labour.   He states that the unfavourable effects of emigration on the expanding war and postwar economy, together with a long-term decline in the British rate of natural increase, had combined

[1] Peach, *West Indian Migration to Britain*, pp. 1–44.

to produce a declining rate of growth in the labour force; and it was this growing shortage of labour which was filled in part by the large-scale immigration of coloured people.[1] The mechanism linking the British labour market with migrant flows was frequently no more complex than letters home from earlier migrants;[2] but there were some direct arrangements, for example the British transport authorities' recruitment in Barbados. Peach finds confirmation for a relationship between immigration from the West Indies and employment vacancies in the late 1950s, and he believes that, between the break associated with the 1962 Act and the 1965 voucher limitations, and within the framework of restraint, 'economic determinants (i.e. changes in numbers of vacancies) resumed their role of controlling numbers and trends'.[3]

Table 3.   *Composition of New Commonwealth immigration, 1962–6*

	All immigrants	Voucher holders	Dependants	Students	Thousands Other settlers
1962 July–December	27.7	4.2	8.2	11.2	4.1
1963	72.4	28.7	24.4	16.4	2.9
1964	70.9	13.9	35.8	18.0	3.2
1965	66.0	12.1	39.2	12.4	2.3
1966	63.5	5.2	44.1	12.4	1.8
Total	300.5	64.1	151.7	70.4	14.3

SOURCES: *Commonwealth Immigrants Act, 1962: Control of Immigration Statistics, 1962–3; 1964; 1965; 1966* (Cmnd 2379; 2658; 2979; 3258).

In the context of this report three related developments between the 1962 Act and 1966 merit attention: a strict application of the work voucher system, the 'teeth' of the 1962 Act, sharply reducing the number of male family heads migrating from the New Commonwealth; an increase in the number of dependants arriving; and a tendency for immigration from Europe to rise alongside the restrictive policy applied to the New Commonwealth. The first two developments are reflected in table 3. Between July 1962 and the end of 1966, about a fifth of New Commonwealth immigrants were voucher holders and a half were dependants. Yet the trends have been such that, in 1963, as much as 40 per cent were voucher holders and only 34 per cent dependants; a picture which by 1966 had changed radically to one of 8 per cent voucher holders and 69 per cent dependants. The sharp decline in the number

[1] C. Senior, 'Race Relations and Labour Supply in Great Britain', *Social Problems*, vol. 4, 1957, referred to in Wright, *The Coloured Worker in British Industry*, p. 41.
[2] Peach, *West Indian Migration to Britain*, p. 42.
[3] Ibid. p. 53.

of New Commonwealth immigrants admitted as voucher holders—the numbers had fallen to less than 5 thousand in 1967—resulted, initially, from the non-repetition of, apparently, rather 'liberal' treatment of Indians and Pakistanis in 1963 and, later, a conscious policy of few admissions by this route. In August 1965, it was decided that, henceforth, vouchers for Commonwealth immigrants would be limited to 8,500 per annum.[1] The steady rise in the number of New Commonwealth dependants entering the country—they are admitted without vouchers and reached 50 thousand in 1967—reflects the reunion of families that were divided by the large pre-1962 migration of male adults and, it is anticipated, will therefore prove to be a transient phenomenon.[2]

It seems likely that one effect of the restrictive immigration policy, even though muted by the free entry of dependants, has been to reduce immigration from the New Commonwealth and encourage compensatory rises in immigration from Europe. For while immigration from the New Commonwealth declined from the high levels recorded at the beginning of this decade to 72 thousand in 1963, 71 thousand in 1964, 66 thousand in 1965 and 64 thousand in 1966, immigration from Europe rose sharply from 11 thousand in 1963 to 19 thousand in 1964, 25 thousand in 1965 and 30 thousand in 1966. Significantly, an upward movement, to 67 thousand, of New Commonwealth immigration in 1967 was accompanied by a falling off, to 16 thousand, in immigration from Europe.[3]

Before considering some basic characteristics of the New Commonwealth immigrant population, a comparison of tables 1 and 2 yields interesting results. The principal difference between the immigration flows given for the period 1961–6 in table 1 and those in table 2 (other than the fact that the latter are available on an annual basis) is that the immigration flows in table 2 are gross flows, whilst the method used to derive those in table 1 means they are net of any re-emigration. A brief examination of the re-emigration element serves two purposes: it affords a check on the consistency of the two, quite independent, sources used in compiling tables 1 and 2—the population censuses and immigration data collected under the Commonwealth Immigrants Act—and more especially, on the degree of underenumeration in the 1966 Census; and it focuses attention on an aspect of the immigration problem which is currently attracting much attention, re-emigration.

---

[1] Home Office, *Immigration from the Commonwealth*, Cmnd 2739, H.M.S.O., London, 1965.
[2] Other interesting features are the relative importance of voucher holders in the Indian and Pakistani group, of dependants from the British Caribbean and of students among those from the other New Commonwealth.
[3] Home Office, *Statistics of Foreigners Entering and Leaving the United Kingdom*, various issues, H.M.S.O., London (annual).

An estimate for the re-emigration of New Commonwealth immigrants was then made from the immigration statistics. Briefly, the method employed was to deduct from the figures of total departures an estimate of those who were only temporarily in Britain, or who were not quitting the country permanently,[1] to give an estimate of the number of New Commonwealth residents in this country subsequently re-emigrating. This yielded a figure for the period July 1962 to December 1965 of 64 thousand, which needed to be grossed up to cover the full inter-censal period April 1961 to April 1966. Because of the much smaller size of the New Commonwealth population at the beginning of this period it was decided to base the adjustment on the relative population sizes at the beginning and end of the period.[2] The result is an estimated 83 thousand re-emigrants from among New Commonwealth residents in the period April 1961 to April 1966. Eversley and Sukdeo estimate, for the same five-year period, 46 thousand re-emigrants from among the Indians, Pakistanis and West Indians.[3] Adjusting this figure to extend its coverage to the whole New Commonwealth population[4] suggests total re-emigration of about 69 thousand, rather less than our estimate.

Deducting 83 thousand re-emigrants from the recorded 443 thousand immigrants (table 2), yields a net immigration figure of 360 thousand which, when added to the 1961 Census total, 541 thousand, and allowing for deaths, gives a 1966 New Commonwealth population of 887 thousand. This figure suggests that underenumeration in the 1966 Sample Census might be of the order of 4 per cent. However, other errors enter the discrepancy between the 1966 population estimated in this way and the sample census figure: errors in the estimated number of deaths in table 1, in the immigration estimates for the period April 1961 to July 1962, the identification of 'persons leaving for temporary absence abroad' with 'persons returning from temporary absence abroad', and errors introduced by the necessity for grossing up the figures for total embarkations and the embarkation of transients relating to the period July 1962 to December 1965 to cover the whole period April 1961 to April 1966.

If, however, we accept the results, they indicate that re-emigration

---

[1] Identified in the immigration statistics as visitors in transit, crews and, for want of a category of 'persons leaving for temporary absence abroad', the group 'persons returning from temporary absence abroad'. By calculating the flows over a period of about four years, it is hoped that the error introduced by this latter device is small.

[2] The overall effect was to gross up the 64 thousand by a factor of 1.33 compared with what would have been a pro-rata adjustment of 1.44.

[3] Eversley and Sukdeo, *The Dependants of the Coloured Commonwealth Population of England and Wales*, p. 24.

[4] A pro-rata correction was applied, though the presence of a large number of students in the other New Commonwealth group suggests that the adjustment should be more than proportionate to the relative sizes of the groups.

of New Commonwealth migrants from Britain was in the region of 16 thousand per annum compared with 14 thousand on the Eversley-Sukdeo reckoning. This represents an annual rate of re-emigration equivalent to 3 per cent of the 1961 New Commonwealth population and about 2 per cent of the numbers recorded in the 1966 Sample Census. Whilst almost certainly it is lower than that which characterises the European-born population of the British Isles, many of whom intentionally come here for a short period to work in hotels or domestic service,[1] it is by no means negligible in comparison with the anticipated expansion rates of the New Commonwealth population that are considered in the final section of this chapter.[2]

THE SEX COMPOSITION AND AGE DISTRIBUTION OF THE IMMIGRANT POPULATION

The sex ratio and age distribution of an immigrant group greatly influence its economic and social impacts on the total population. In particular, they have an almost overriding influence on the group's quantitative impact on the economy's labour force, the natural growth of the group, and the immigrants' health, educational and other demands on the social services. When considering such basic characteristics of an immigrant group it is important to be aware that at any one moment of time they can differ quite pronouncedly from the corresponding features of the indigenous population and they may change fairly dramatically over a relatively short period of time.

Table 4. *Sex ratios[a] of immigrants in Great Britain*

Percentages

	1961	1966
All immigrants	95	98
New Commonwealth	75	78
India and Pakistan	69	62
British Caribbean	80	94
Other	78	83
Total population	106	107

SOURCES: *Census 1961, Birthplace and Nationality Tables; Sample Census 1966, Summary Tables.*
[a] Females as percentages of males.

[1] It is reasonable to include short-term immigrants—those who stay for only a short time and are then replaced by others with similar characteristics and objectives—in the immigrant population because they have become a permanent feature of British life and there is a large number of them in the labour force at any one time.
[2] Eversley and Sukdeo comment : 'The outflow rate in this country of coloured immigrants is considered to be remarkably high.' (op. cit. p. 55.)

The greater number of females than of males in the total population is due to a lower mortality rate: there are over 50 per cent more women than men over 65 years old. The proportion of females in the immigrant population is appreciably lower and, in both 1961 and 1966, they constituted a little less than half the total number of immigrants. This 'deficiency' in the proportion of females in the immigrant population can be ascribed to the low ratio, 75 per cent in 1961 and 78 per cent in 1966, in the New Commonwealth community. The sex ratio for other immigrants, like that of the indigenous population, exceeds unity (100 per cent) partly for the same reason—lower female mortality—but also because many Irish and European immigrants are women in the 15 to 24 age group bent upon short-term employment in the service sectors.

The low ratio of females in the New Commonwealth group is due to the sharp acceleration in the number of New Commonwealth immigrants, coupled with the fact that the initial influx consisted to a disproportionate extent of males in the 25 to 44 age group. It is to be expected that, because of the more recent deceleration of this inflow resulting largely from the 1962 Commonwealth Immigrants Act, the proportion of females to males will rise, as the women dependants, not subject to restrictions, follow the men. Table 4 confirms that this has indeed happened in the case of immigrants from the British Caribbean, the other New Commonwealth and the whole New Commonwealth—the sex ratios having risen between 1961 and 1966 in all cases. The ratio for India and Pakistan, however, which in 1961 was the lowest at 69 per cent, declined further between 1961 and 1966 to 62 per cent. This may be due to the fact that Asians were accorded a large number of vouchers immediately after the 1962 Act;[1] it also reflects an amazingly low sex ratio, 24 per cent in 1966, for Pakistani immigrants. As the New Commonwealth population becomes more stabilised and earlier migrants enter the older age groups, the lower female mortality rates will also contribute to a rise in the female proportion.

When considering the age distribution of the immigrant population it is especially important to be precise about the group with which we are concerned: persons resident in Britain but born abroad, or the same people together with the children born to them in this country. The age distribution of the immigrant population, especially New Commonwealth immigrants, assumes quite a different shape according to which of these definitions is adopted. Since we are principally concerned with the impact of new immigrants in the period 1961–6, our primary interest lies in the former concept—immigrants excluding children born to them

[1] See above, p. 15.

here. If relatively few of these immigrants are children, then it is proper to take account of this factor and appreciate, for instance, that the economy is gaining workers in whom it has not been necessary to invest the resources—such as food, education and health services—that are required to nurture people from birth to the time they enter the labour force. Attention is paid first to the peculiarities of the age distribution of residents born abroad, which reflects this gain. However, since at some points we use information about the New Commonwealth community inclusive of British-born offspring, and because some immigrant problems, especially those related to colour, are closely connected with this population concept, the age distribution associated with it is also considered below. The implications of this conceptual choice are referred to in the following section.

Table 5. *Age distribution of immigrants, 1961 and 1966*

Percentages

	Age groups					Total
	0–14	15–24	25–44	45–64	65+	
All immigrants						
1961	11	15	44	22	8	100
1966	..	..	..	..	..	..
New Commonwealth						
1961	15	20	46	15	4	100
1966	18	18	47	14	3	100
India & Pakistan						
1961	9	17	44	22	8	100
1966	12	17	47	18	6	100
British Caribbean						
1961	8	23	59	9	1	100
1966	13	17	58	11	1	100
Other New Commonwealth						
1961	29	20	36	12	3	100
1966	32	19	36	10	3	100
Total British population						
1961	23	13	26	26	12	100
1966	23	15	25	25	12	100

SOURCES: *Census 1961, Birthplace and Nationality Tables; Sample Census 1966, Summary Tables* and *Commonwealth Immigrant Tables.*

Table 5, which excludes children born in Britain, reveals that, compared with the indigenous population, a relatively large number of New Commonwealth immigrants are to be found in the 25 to 44 age group, and few at either end of the age scale, up to 14 years and over 65 years. The large proportion in the 25 to 44 age group, almost half the total in 1966 compared with a quarter for the indigenous population, is simply attributable to the fact that people who undertake a change of residence, especially between countries, are usually of this age. As we shall see, it is a feature of the immigrant population that has a strong influence on its labour force participation rate. In sharp contrast, a mere 3 per cent of New Commonwealth immigrants, compared with 12 per cent of the indigenous population, were in the oldest group, over 65, in 1966. This has especially important implications for the New Commonwealth community's demands on the social services. The low proportion of New Commonwealth immigrants under 15 years of age, 18 per cent compared with 23 per cent for the whole population, reflects the exclusion at this juncture of children born to them in Great Britain.

Table 5 also shows that the overall age distribution for New Commonwealth immigrants results from quite marked disparities between the groups of which it is composed. On the one hand, there is the other New Commonwealth group with an age distribution which, whilst it conforms to the immigrant pattern in having a high proportion in the 25 to 44 age bracket and a very low proportion among the oldest, has as much as a third in the youngest age group—a figure which is not only much higher than the proportions recorded for Asians and West Indians, but appreciably greater even than the quarter of the indigenous population in this age bracket. This aberration is attributable to a large number of children sent back to the United Kingdom for educational purposes by British personnel in, especially, East Africa and the Far East. For their part, both the Asian and Caribbean groups exhibit immigrant age traits in rather extreme form. This is especially true of Caribbean immigrants. Only 13 per cent of them, compared with the national 23 per cent, are under 15; as many as 58 per cent, compared with the national 25 per cent—this is especially striking—are between 25 and 44; and a mere 1 per cent, compared with the national 12 per cent, are over 65 years old. Corresponding proportions for the Asian group are 12, 47 and 6 per cent.

Differences in mortality rates, which produce a higher proportion of older women than men, affect immigrants as well as the population as a whole. In the case of the total population 15 per cent of females compared with 10 per cent of males were over 65 years old in 1966; the corresponding proportions for New Commonwealth immigrants being 9 and 3 per cent. In both populations, but especially among the New Commonwealth immigrants, males are more numerous in the 25 to 44 age group: 52 per cent of Asian males were in this age bracket compared with only 38 per cent of females, and 61 per cent of Caribbean males compared with 55 per cent of the females. The cause of the contrast is, of course, a basic feature of an immigrant population: the preponderance of males in this age group among those who move.

Two other points should be noted about the age distribution of immigrants born in the New Commonwealth. First, the tendency for New Commonwealth immigrants to be concentrated in the 25 to 44 age group has helped to offset the relatively low numbers of indigenous residents in this bracket which stemmed from low British birth rates in the interwar period. Secondly, while the later arrival of dependants has helped to restore the male-female imbalance, it has also tended to raise the proportion of children towards the national average. The proportion of Asian immigrants under 15 years of age rose from 9 to 12 per cent between 1961 and 1966, the proportion of West Indians from 8 to 13 per cent, and the overall proportion of New Commonwealth immigrants from 15 to 18 per cent.[1] The proportionate enlargement in this group took place at the expense, especially, of the relative numbers in the adjoining, 15 to 24, age group.

It is possible to calculate, from population census data, age distributions which include children born to New Commonwealth immigrants in this country.[2] For 1961 this is possible only for New Commonwealth immigrants in the conurbations, who represented 61 per cent of the total in Great Britain. For 1966 it can be done at the national level. The relevant distributions are presented in table 6. Because of the likely distorting effect on the other New Commonwealth figures of children born to British personnel in East Africa and the Far East, and the lack of consistency in the definition of this group in 1961 and 1966, it has been omitted as a separate group from table 6.

As might be expected, there was little difference in 1961 between the national and conurbation age distributions, exclusive of British-born offspring, for either the Asians or the West Indians. In contrast, for both these immigrant groups the conurbation age distribution undergoes a remarkable transformation when British-born offspring are included. In the case of Indians and Pakistanis, the proportion under 15 years old rises from 10 to 32 per cent, showing that 76 per cent of their children were born here, and for the West Indians the increase is from 7 to 26 per cent, meaning that as many as 79 per cent of their children were born in Britain.

Of course, increases in the numbers in this lowest age group are accompanied by reductions in the proportions in all the other age groups, and it is instructive to compare the resulting distribution with that of the indigenous population, given in table 5. The inclusion of children born

---

[1] The percentage of other New Commonwealth in this age group also increased, from 29 to 32, but in this case it represented a further departure from the national average.

[2] Children born in this country in households where the head, or the spouse of the head, was born in the New Commonwealth. Implications of this definition and the method of obtaining the required age distributions are examined in the following section.

in Britain to New Commonwealth immigrants raises the fraction of Asians and West Indians who are under 15 to higher proportions than that for the population as a whole, 23 per cent—substantially so in the case of Indians and Pakistanis. In the 25 to 44 age bracket the differences between the total population and these two groups narrow, but still leave the latter with a substantial (and in the case of the British Caribbean, pronounced) excess; and the disparities that exist between the immigrant groups and the indigenous population in the higher age brackets widen still further.

Table 6. *Age distribution of New Commonwealth immigrants, including and excluding children born in Great Britain, 1961 and 1966*

Percentages

	1961			1966	
	National	Conurbations		National	
	Excl.*a*	Excl.*a*	Incl.*b*	Excl.*a*	Incl.*b*
New Commonwealth*c*					
0–14	15	11	30	18	36
15–24	20	20	17	18	14
25–44	46	52	40	47	36
45–64	15	14	11	14	11
65 & over	4	3	2	3	3
Total	100	100	100	100	100
India and Pakistan					
0–14	9	10	32	12	34
15–24	17	17	14	17	13
25–44	44	45	33	47	35
45–64	22	22	16	18	14
65 & over	8	6	5	6	4
Total	100	100	100	100	100
British Caribbean					
0–14	8	7	26	13	41
15–24	23	22	18	17	12
25–44	59	61	48	58	39
45–64	9	9	7	11	7
65 & over	1	1	1	1	1
Total	100	100	100	100	100

SOURCES: *Census 1961, Birthplace and Nationality Tables* and *Commonwealth Immigrants in the Conurbations; Sample Census 1966, Commonwealth Immigrant Tables.*

a Excluding children born in Great Britain.
b Including children born in Great Britain.
c National figures relate to all Commonwealth countries and colonies, other than Australia, Canada and New Zealand; conurbation figures relate to India, Pakistan, British Caribbean, Commonwealth countries in Africa, Cyprus and Malta.

The effect of the choice between definitions of the immigrant population on the age distribution is equally dramatic in 1966. In this year, however, the numbers of children born in this country are added to an appreciably larger total of immigrant children strictly defined, many of the latter having arrived among the inflow of dependants during the period 1961–6. The result is that the immigrant-indigenous contrast in the proportion of children becomes even sharper. In 1966, including children born in this country, 36 per cent of the New Commonwealth community compared with 23 per cent of the indigenous population were under 15 years old. The corresponding proportion for Asians was 34 per cent, and for West Indians as high as 41 per cent. Correspondingly, immigrant-indigenous differences in the proportions in the middle age group narrowed somewhat, whilst those in the older age groups became even more pronounced. Obviously, given the importance of the age distribution in the evaluation of so many economic and social implications of immigration, a great deal hinges on the immigrant concept to which attention is directed.

A PROJECTION OF THE NEW COMMONWEALTH POPULATION

A projection of the New Commonwealth population might almost be regarded as superfluous in a study where the primary concern is with the more immediate economic implications of migration to this country. However, the subject was thought worthy of attention on three grounds. First, certain forecasts of the future size of this group of immigrants that have received considerable currency are so ill-founded that it is desirable that they be challenged. Secondly, whilst the ensuing debate has drawn attention to the statistical difficulties and pitfalls implicit in population projections, remarkably little emphasis has been placed on the conceptual problems, of a definitional nature, that are posed by attempts to project the size of just one group in a country's total population. Thirdly, a very useful by-product of the projection is an estimate of the age structure of the New Commonwealth community at future dates—figures which are needed for evaluating their future demands on the social services.[1]

The conceptual difficulties referred to are associated with the definitional choice previously encountered: the suitability of defining the New Commonwealth population as the sum of those migrating here from the New Commonwealth, or as these immigrants plus their children born in this country. More precisely, the difficulties stem from the need to choose, in the context of population projections, the latter concept. For

---

[1] See chapter 6.

C

no one doubts that the concern which is raised relates to the future numbers of coloured people in this country.

A minor and a major conceptual difficulty are encountered, each derived from the nature of the census data which are used as a basis for these projections. As previously stated, the population censuses contain two series of New Commonwealth data, one relating simply to people born abroad, the other—and this is the relevant one in the present context —to all the people who were enumerated in households of which the head or the wife of the head was born in one of the specified New Commonwealth countries. The minor problem is inherent in the following figures. The 1966 Census shows that of the 425 thousand offspring in New Commonwealth immigrant households (defined as above), 316 thousand were born in Great Britain and 108 thousand abroad. Yet the tables dealing with members of the population born abroad show that there were as many as 156 thousand children under 15 years of age in this category.[1] The discrepancy merely reflects the fact that many children born in New Commonwealth countries are not members of New Commonwealth households but the offspring of British-born, current and former, colonial civil servants and the like. Thus the statistical procedure by which children in New Commonwealth households are substituted in the totals for children born in the New Commonwealth not only enlarges the concept of the New Commonwealth population to include members of New Commonwealth households born in this country, it also has the effect of eliminating from the total children born in the New Commonwealth who are not members of New Commonwealth households.[2] This procedure, used in the previous section to obtain distributions presented in table 6, yields a base year (1966) figure of 1,093 thousand for the New Commonwealth population.[3] Given that the excluded children are mainly white, the procedure, in the present context, results in an improvement in the statistics.

It can hardly be claimed that the major difficulty referred to above has a comparable beneficial effect. A usual method of making population projections, and the one adopted here, is to classify, separately for males and females, the base year population into age groups, and to apply

---

[1] The discrepancy is even larger than that suggested in the above figures, 156 thousand less 108 thousand, because some 28 thousand of the 425 thousand offspring in New Commonwealth households were over 15 years old. (General Register Office, *Sample Census 1966, Commonwealth Immigrant Tables*, H.M.S.O., London, 1969.)

[2] An alternative to the above procedure would be simply to add only the children of New Commonwealth households born in this country to the total born in New Commonwealth countries. Unfortunately a breakdown by age group is only available for all children in New Commonwealth households, wherever born, not for those born in this country, and the age composition is an important requirement for population projections.

[3] That is, 853 thousand plus 424·8 thousand less 156·4 thousand and 28·3 thousand.

mortality rates to these groups, and fertility rates to the female age groups.[1] An implication of this method, however, is that the population projections exclude children born to New Commonwealth males who marry outside the New Commonwealth group, even though such children are included in the base year totals from which the projections are made. Essentially, this inconsistency stems from the inherent difficulty (indeed impossibility) of measuring for future years a population concept which becomes increasingly nebulous as time goes by and the group becomes merged to a greater or lesser extent with the whole population. The dilemma can be posed in the following way: in 1986, the limit to which we have taken our projections, should there be included in the population which is to be labelled 'immigrant' those who had one, two, three or four grandparents who were born in New Commonwealth countries? In short, whilst an immigrant population defined as residents born abroad is unambiguous, one defined as residents born abroad together with children born to them in this country is not, since decisions must be made as to how children of one indigenous parent and one born abroad, or grandchildren of whom one or more grandparent was born abroad, should be classified. Whilst there is some inconsistency between the coverage of the base year population and the projections, the method employed is such that, for later years, those are included whose ancestry can be traced to the New Commonwealth community on the maternal side.

The mortality rates on which the projections have been based have been identified with those for the country as a whole. In any case these have relatively little effect on the size of the New Commonwealth population over the period in question. Much more hangs upon the choice of fertility rates and immigration assumptions. The fertility rates which have been applied are the average, by age group, of Jamaican and United Kingdom females.[2] The Jamaican rates, which tend to overstate

[1] The 1966 age distribution of New Commonwealth immigrants is available in the census with the following breakdown: 0–4 years old, 5–9, 10–14, 15–19, 20–24, 25–44, 45–59, 60–64, and 65 years and over. The more detailed breakdown required, especially in the 25–44 group, for population projections was estimated with the help of 1966 age groups projected from the 1961 Census figures.

[2] These fertility rates are:

Age group	Jamaican	Births per 1000 women United Kingdom
15–19	205	45
20–24	230	176
25–29	267	178
30–34	225	102
35–39	100	48

SOURCES: *Annual Abstract of Statistics, 1966*, No. 103; *Census 1961, Fertility Tables*.

the fertility rates among New Commonwealth females as a whole, are much higher than those for the indigenous population. There are, however, good reasons for expecting them to fall substantially, and therefore a lower rate, the average of the Jamaican and the United Kingdom rates, has been used. As the immigrants assume some of the *mores* of their new homeland, fertility rates will decline. 'Coloured Commonwealth immigrants in Britain have modified their marriage patterns, and . . . in some respects they are now more similar to those of the British. This should ultimately result in reduced fertility rates among immigrants in Britain.'[1] Not least important in this context is the fact that, as stressed at several points in this study, immigration from the New Commonwealth consists largely of a rural-urban movement, traditionally associated with a sharp fall in fertility rates.

Using these fertility rates, two projections, based on different immigration assumptions, were made. In the first, no immigration was postu-

Table 7. *A projection of the New Commonwealth immigrant population*

	Old immigrants^a and their children	Assumed New Commonwealth immigration M F	New immigrants and their children	Thousands Old and new immigrants
1966	1,093			1,093
1966–70				
Age 0–15		135		
Age 15–64		35 65		
1971	1,240		235	1,475
1971–75				
Age 0–15		85		
Age 15–64		35 45		
1976	1,383		455	1,838
1976–80				
Age 0–15		35		
Age 15–64		35 25		
1981	1,525		650	2,175
1981–85				
Age 0–15		35		
Age 15–64		35 25		
1986	1,696		881	2,577

SOURCE: NIESR estimates.
^a Those resident in Great Britain in 1966.

[1] Eversley and Sukdeo, *The Dependants of the Coloured Commonwealth Population of England and Wales*, p. 31.

lated for the period 1966 to 1986. For the second, it has been assumed that immigration will take place at the rates shown in table 7. These assumptions are based on several considerations. In the first two years of the first five-year period, 1966 and 1967, on average some 10 thousand immigrants (8 thousand males and 2 thousand females) arrived each year with work permits. At the same time a large number of dependent relatives, 45 thousand including 13 thousand women and 31 thousand children, were brought in each year. This inflow of dependent relatives will doubtless fall away, and we have based our assumption accordingly. Also, for the later periods it has been assumed that work permits (including those for Kenyan Asians who are included in these estimates) will be granted at the rate of 8 thousand a year. Eversley and Sukdeo, making estimates of the '*maximum* number of coloured Commonwealth immigrants who may be expected to arrive in this country', suggest a figure of about 50 thousand newcomers a year for the period 1966–75, compared with our 40 thousand. Adjusting their estimates to a twenty-year period up to 1985, suggests an average annual inflow of about 34 thousand compared with our 30 thousand.[1]

Our projections are presented separately for the two immigration assumptions in table 7. The table suggests that, had immigration been halted in 1966, the New Commonwealth population would rise to about 1.7 million by 1986, that is by 2.2 per cent per annum. At the rates of immigration we have postulated it would increase to about 2.6 million, that is by 4.4 per cent per annum.[2]

Two qualifications to these projections should be noted especially. They make no allowance for underenumeration in 1966 nor for the possible re-emigration of some members of the New Commonwealth population. Underenumeration was not taken into account because of the considerable degree of uncertainty about its likely size. It should be appreciated, however, that an adjustment for it would not raise the projected 1985 population pro rata.[3] Assuming, say, underenumeration of the order of 10 per cent in 1966, the projected 1985 numbers would be about

---

[1] Ibid. p. 2, tables 37, 42 and 43, and p. 47. Tables 42 and 43 together suggest that, at a maximum, about 300 thousand dependants of the 1966 New Commonwealth population might still not have arrived. This would indicate an arrival rate of 30 thousand per annum over a ten-year period, or 15 thousand per annum over a twenty-year period. Table 37 shows an annual average arrival rate of about 19 thousand for new voucher holders and their dependants.

[2] Projections made in Rose and Associates, *Colour and Citizenship*, on a much more sophisticated basis than ours suggest a rather smaller figure, 2.1 or 2.4 million for 1986 on lower and higher fertility assumptions. Their totals exclude certain Mediterranean migrants included in our estimate, but include an allowance for under-counting in the census, for offspring of coloured fathers and for illegitimacy.

[3] Also, the presence of some whites in the estimates will tend to offset the effects of underenumeration.

3 per cent greater than shown in table 7. In contrast, an allowance for re-emigration would greatly reduce the projections. Should re-emigration occur at the rate of 2 per cent per annum,[1] it would cut the projected rate of growth (of 'old' and 'new' immigrants) from 4.3 per cent to 2.3 per cent per annum, yielding a 1985 coloured population of the order of $1\frac{3}{4}$ million.

---

[1] See p. 16 above.

CHAPTER 3

THE QUANTITATIVE IMPACT ON THE LABOUR FORCE

This chapter will be concerned essentially with the quantitative impact of New Commonwealth immigrants on the labour force: a qualitative appraisal must await the examination of the geographical, occupational and industrial distribution of immigrant workers in chapter 4. In addition to the implications for the labour force of the sex composition of the immigrant groups and the immigrant population of working age (see the previous chapter), attention is also devoted here to the proportion of immigrants economically active and in work. The first section of the chapter considers these determinants of immigrant participation rates in 1961 and 1966, and the contribution which New Commonwealth immigration in this period made to the growth of the British labour force. In a second section, attention is paid to New Commonwealth unemployment rates, because of the special considerations, of measurement and interest, that attach to them.

IMMIGRANTS AND THE LABOUR FORCE

The data presented in this chapter concerning the determinants and size of the immigrant labour force, for the most part relate to immigrants born abroad, not to members of immigrant households.[1] There are two reasons for this. First, the qualitative breakdown of the immigrant labour force (its distribution between regions, industries and occupations) is available only for the former and there are obvious advantages in carrying out the quantitative and qualitative appraisals on the same statistical basis. Secondly, much interest centres on the interrelationship between new immigrants and the growth of the British labour force in the early 1960s and the former population concept is appropriate in this connection.

However the distinction between the two population concepts is by no means academic in this context. For although they differ little for either the number of immigrants over 15 years old or those economically active, there exists, as demonstrated in the previous chapter, a sharp distinction between the concepts in terms of the number of children and therefore in the number of dependants whom, on average, a New Commonwealth worker must support. The distinction is especially

---

[1] For the distinction between these two population concepts and its significance, see chapters 1 and 2.

relevant, therefore, when the *per capita* income of the New Commonwealth community is examined.[1] Here it suffices to indicate the general magnitude of the difference implied by the two population concepts in the context of labour force participation rates. Table 8 reveals that, in 1966, 82 per cent of New Commonwealth immigrants were of working age (over 15), 72 per cent of these were economically active and 96 per cent of the latter actually in employment. That is 57 per cent of the total New Commonwealth population had a job. Taking those in New Commonwealth households (1,093 thousand),[2] only 63 per cent were of working age which, in conjunction with rates of 72 per cent economically active and 96 per cent in work, means that on this basis the participation rate—the proportion of the population in work—was only 43 per cent. This rate is not very different from, indeed it is slightly below, that for the indigenous labour force—46 per cent. However, this similarity disguises two pronounced contrasts in the determinants of the participation rate: on this reckoning only 63 per cent of the New Commonwealth population were of working age compared with 77 per cent of the indigenous population; but 72 per cent of coloured adults were economically active compared with only 62 per cent of the British population.

However, although the number of immigrants born abroad is derived for 1961 from a full population census and for 1966 from a sample census, the immigrant labour force data—the numbers economically active and in employment, their industrial and occupational distributions—are available in both years only on a sample census basis. Whilst, therefore, the 1966 immigrant labour force data are automatically consistent with the immigrant population data for that year presented in chapter 2, this is not true of the 1961 immigrant labour force data and the discrepancies are by no means small. The procedure adopted in this chapter and the following one has been to 'key' the 1961 sample figures to the full 1961 Census totals, by applying to the latter the relevant factors (the proportions economically active and employed, and their distribution between industries and occupations) derived from the sample census.

The assumption implicit in this device, that the factors causing underenumeration in the sample census did not materially bias the proportional distribution of the various population characteristics, is open to some doubt,[3] but clearly it is preferable to make this adjustment rather than to use the uncorrected sample census figures. However, an attempt has been made, where necessary, to draw attention to areas where this

---

[1] See chapter 5.
[2] See chapter 2, p. 24.
[3] Jenner and Cohen, *Commonwealth Immigrants and the 1961 Census*, pp. 11 and 12.

assumption might be especially misleading.   The application of sample census factors for the whole New Commonwealth, India and Pakistan, and the British Caribbean to the full census data means that residuals obtained for the other New Commonwealth group are not identical with the figures that would be obtained by applying the sample census factors for this group to the other New Commonwealth total in the full census. For the sake of arithmetical consistency the residual figures have been used, and whilst the discrepancies are not unduly large,[1] this shortcoming should be borne in mind when the other New Commonwealth characteristics are under review.

Table 8 sets out, for each population group, each sex, and in each of the two years, three rates: the proportion of the group of working age (over 15 years old); the proportion of this number who are economically active (termed the activity rate); and the proportion of those economically active who are not out of work through illness or unemployment.   These three rates combine by multiplication to yield a labour force participation rate which reflects the proportion of each group in work.

Table 8 reveals that, apart from the 'all immigrants' group, the rate for which rose appreciably, labour force participation rates for males and females together remained very stable between 1961 and 1966.   The rates for the British labour force were 45/46[2] and for the New Commonwealth immigrants they were significantly higher, 56/57.   The participation rates for the three New Commonwealth groups ranged downwards from the very high West Indian rates, 70/67, to India and Pakistan, 59/60, and the other New Commonwealth, 38/42: the latter participation rate being slightly below that for the indigenous population.

[1] The differences are as follows:

	Proportion of working age	Activity rate	Employment rate	*Percentages* Participation rate
Males				
Residual	71	75	95	50
Sample Census	72	76	95	52
Females				
Residual	66	36	96	23
Sample Census	67	41	96	26
Males and females				
Residual	69	58	95	38
Sample Census	70	61	95	41

[2] In the following paragraphs, two rates presented in this way indicate the positions in 1961 and 1966 respectively.

Table 8. *Labour force participation rates, 1961 and 1966*

	Proportion of working age		Activity rates		In-employment rate		Percentages Labour force participation rate[a]	
	1961	1966	1961	1966	1961	1966	1961	1966
Males								
All immigrants	89	..	89	..	96	97	76	82
New Commonwealth	86	83	85	88	95	97	70	71
India and Pakistan	92	89	86	91	96	97	76	79
British Caribbean	93	88	93	94	94	96	82	80
Other[b]	71	70	75	78	95	96	50	53
Great Britain	76	75	86	84	97	97	63	61
Females								
All immigrants	89	..	44	..	97	96	38	45
New Commonwealth	83	80	47	51	95	95	37	38
India and Pakistan	91	86	39	37	97	95	34	31
British Caribbean	91	87	64	65	94	94	55	53
Other[b]	66	65	36	47	96	95	23	29
Great Britain	78	78	37	42	97	97	29	32
Males and females								
All immigrants	89	..	66	..	96	97	57	63
New Commonwealth	85	82	69	72	95	96	56	57
India and Pakistan	91	88	66	71	96	97	59	60
British Caribbean	92	88	81	80	94	95	70	67
Other[b]	69	68	58	64	95	96	38	42
Great Britain	77	77	61	62	97	97	45	46

SOURCES: *Census 1966, Occupation Tables, Industry Tables* and *Birthplace and Nationality Tables; Sample Census 1966, Summary Tables* and *Economic Activity Tables.*

[a] Excluding out of work through sickness and unemployment.

[b] Obtained as a residual.

Part of the explanation for the higher New Commonwealth participation rates lies in the fact that this community contains a larger proportion of males, with higher participation rates than females, than the indigenous population. But most of the explanation resides in the fact that, for both males and females, the New Commonwealth participation rates are higher than the indigenous rates. Indeed, the basic group pattern noted for males and females combined is repeated when males and females are considered separately. For males, the British rates were 63/61, the total New Commonwealth rates 70/71, the West Indian rates 82/80, the Asian rates 76/79, and the other New Commonwealth rates 50/53: the last being below the indigenous rates. For females the indigenous rates were 29/32, the New Commonwealth 37/38, the

West Indian 55/53, the Asian 34/31 and the other New Commonwealth 23/29—again below the British rates.

Whilst 'out of work' and, especially, unemployment rates have much intrinsic interest in the context of immigration and have therefore been accorded special attention in the following section, the in-employment rates are bunched between 94 and 97 and have very little impact on either the general level or the group patterns of participation rates. But certain systematic patterns which these rates suggest do nothing to explain the observed group pattern of participation rates, rather the contrary: they are lower (that is a higher proportion of the economically active are out of work) for the New Commonwealth than for Great Britain, and lower for the West Indies than for the rest of the New Commonwealth.

The principal determinants of the pattern of participation rates are the working age and activity rates. Table 8 shows that, for both males and females, these two rates tend to be higher for the New Commonwealth population than for the total British population.[1] It should be noted that, whilst the higher New Commonwealth working age rates, 86/83 for males compared with 76/75 for Great Britain and 83/80 for females compared with 78/78, stem directly from the population concept used,[2] this is not the case with the higher New Commonwealth activity rates, 85/88 for males compared with an indigenous value of 86/84, and 47/51 for females compared with 37/42.

There is little difference between the working age rates of Asians and West Indians, males or females, but the other New Commonwealth working age rates are very low, lower than the national rates.[3] The high proportion of children in this group no doubt reflects the choice of a British education for the offspring of United Kingdom nationals in, especially, the Far East. But whilst this helps to explain their very low participation rates it is by no means the only factor. More especially, the male activity rate for the other New Commonwealth, 75/78, is below those of both the total New Commonwealth and Great Britain, largely as a result of a high incidence of students—many of them African—in this group. The remaining feature of interest is the low activity rate, 39/37, recorded for Asian women, which by 1966 was below the indigenous rate, 37/42. The very sharp contrast between this rate and that for West Indian females, 64/65, reflects different group attitudes to the economic role of women: the relative passivity of Asiatic females in this respect compared with the tradition of female labour in the Caribbean.

[1] The only exception being the activity rate for New Commonwealth males which in 1961, at 85, was slightly below the indigenous rate, 86.

[2] See above, p. 30.

[3] Regardless of how these rates are measured; see p. 31n.

In order to assess the impact of these features of the New Commonwealth population on the British labour force, a useful distinction can be made between the 'static' and 'dynamic' effects. The former refers to the impact, in terms of numbers of workers, of the indigenous-immigrant differences in the relevant features—proportion of working age, activity and employment rates—*at any one moment of time*. By a 'dynamic' effect we mean the impact, again essentially in terms of numbers of workers, of New Commonwealth immigrants on *changes* in the indigenous labour force in the period 1961-6. This impact, which is the more important in the context of this study, takes into account the relative increases during the period in the indigenous and New Commonwealth populations as well as contrasts in the relevant characteristics (proportions of working age, activity and employment rates) and the changes they underwent between 1961 and 1966.

Table 9. *Labour force gains from immigrant population features, 1961*[a]

	Sex ratio	Proportion over 15	Activity rate	Out of work	*Thousands* Net effect
All immigrants					
Male	+ 57.4	+ 133.1	− 2.5	− 11.4	+ 176.6
Female	− 57.4	+ 131.4	+ 13.9	− 5.0	+ 82.9
Total	—	+ 264.5	+ 11.4	− 16.4	+ 259.5
New Commonwealth					
Male	+ 47.5	+ 19.1	− 11.7	− 5.6	+ 49.3
Female	− 47.5	+ 21.2	+ 35.4	− 2.5	+ 6.6
Total	—	+ 40.3	+ 23.7	− 8.1	+ 55.9
India and Pakistan					
Male	+ 21.6	+ 13.3	− 5.7	− 1.4	+ 27.8
Female	− 21.6	+ 14.9	+ 5.2	− 0.2	− 1.7
Total	—	+ 28.2	− 0.5	− 1.6	+ 26.1
British Caribbean					
Male	+ 12.8	+ 13.6	+ 2.7	− 3.3	+ 25.8
Female	− 12.8	+ 12.7	+ 18.8	− 2.1	+ 16.6
Total	—	+ 26.3	+ 21.5	− 5.4	+ 42.4
Other New Commonwealth[b]					
Male	+ 13.1	− 7.8	− 8.7	− 0.9	− 4.3
Female	− 13.1	− 6.4	+ 11.4	− 0.2	− 8.3
Total	—	− 14.2	+ 2.7	− 1.1	− 12.6

SOURCES: Tables 7 and 8.

[a] The differences between the actual figures relating to the specified immigrant groups and those which would have obtained had the groups in question been characterised by the same sex ratio, proportion of working age, activity and employment rates as the indigenous population.

[b] Obtained as a residual.

The static impact, for the base year of the period, 1961, is considered first.[1]   Table 9 shows, for 1961, the difference between the actual quantitative impact on the labour force of the immigrant population and its impact had it not differed in certain relevant features from the indigenous population; it also reveals the relative contributions of these immigrant characteristics to the impact on the labour force.[2]   Although there are substantially fewer females among the immigrants than there would be with the indigenous sex ratio, these women (apart from Asians) still make a larger contribution to the labour force than if they possessed *all* the characteristics, including lower proportions of working age and lower activity rates, of indigenous females.   Secondly, the major contribution of the West Indian community stands out.   Thirdly, whilst indigenous-immigrant differences in activity rates are, rather unexpectedly, not sufficient in the case of males to ensure a general and substantial positive contribution to the labour force,[3] those of females, apart from Asians, are.   Fourthly, taken together, unemployment and sickness among immigrants is such that they contribute less to the labour force than if they were characterised by the corresponding national rate, but the effect is not very large.   Finally, for all the groups except the other New Commonwealth, the labour force contribution is higher, indeed substantially higher, given their actual characteristics, than it would be if they had the characteristics of the indigenous population.

The participation rates in table 8 throw some light on the nature of the changes between 1961 and 1966 in the British labour force.   The overall rate for the indigenous population shows little change (45/46), but this masks sharply divergent moves in the rates for males and for females, changes which had an almost overwhelming importance for developments in the British labour force during this period.   The participation rate for males showed a decline from 63 to 61, and that for females a rise from 29 to 32; the movement in each case reflecting, essentially, changes in activity rates—down from 86 to 84 for males, and up from 37 to 42 for females.

A more or less unchanged New Commonwealth participation rate (56/57) masks some important offsetting developments during the period. In this instance, however, the counteracting developments relate not to movements in the male and female participation rates—the rates showed

---

[1] It can be argued that the appropriate concept of the immigrant population for consideration of the static impact on the labour force is that which embraces children born in this country.   The above analysis is conducted on the basis of the 'born abroad' concept to be consistent with the dynamic analysis, our primary concern.

[2] No impact is calculated for the effect of different age characteristics of those over 15 years old.

[3] This had altered somewhat by 1966.

little change in both cases—but to two of the component elements in participation rates.   There were significant falls, for both sexes and all three New Commonwealth immigrant groups, in the proportions of working age as a consequence of the later arrival of children left behind in the large migratory movements at the beginning of the decade. However, the negative impact on labour force participation rates which resulted was offset (indeed slightly more than offset) by a rise in the activity rates of both male and female New Commonwealth immigrants.[1]

The impact on the British labour force of the combination of New Commonwealth arrivals and of these developments in the period 1961-6 can be seen clearly in table 10.   The first feature to catch the eye is the much larger proportionate increase in the New Commonwealth population, 58 per cent, compared with the rise in the indigenous population of about 1½ per cent,[2] resulting in a New Commonwealth contribution of 31 per cent to the total rise in the British population.   Surprisingly, however, despite the size of this contribution and the higher (than indigenous) participation rates of the New Commonwealth, the contribution of the new immigrants to changes in both numbers economically active and the total employed is no greater than 22 per cent.   The surprise is all the greater given an actual fall in the number of economically active indigenous males, by 2.3 per cent or 369 thousand workers, over the period.

One development explains all these anomalies: the sharp rise in the activity rates of British women.   While the number of indigenous females in the population increased by only 1.3 per cent during the period, the number economically active rose sharply by about 13 per cent, equivalent to more than a million additional workers.   Had the participation rates of each population group and sex remained unchanged at their 1961 levels, the arrival between 1961 and 1966 of the 312 thousand New Commonwealth immigrants would have made a 36 per cent contribution to the growth of the British labour force, compared with its actual 22 per cent contribution.

---

[1] The only exception was the rate for Asian women.

[2] Table 10 also shows that, while the sizes of the three New Commonwealth groups and the two sexes increased roughly in step, there were significant differences in the group rates of increase for each sex.   In the case of males, the Asian rate of increase was the highest and the West Indian the lowest; in the case of females, the West Indian rate was the highest and the Asian the lowest.   This suggests that, despite similarities in the total flows, the immigration wave from Asia lagged behind that from the West Indies, with the result that the arrival of female West Indian dependants overlapped with the initial influx of male Asians.

Because of the importance in this period of New Commonwealth changes relative to indigenous changes, the latter have in this case been specifically computed in table 10 as total British changes less New Commonwealth changes.

Table 10. *New Commonwealth contributions to changes in the labour force, 1961–6*

	1961	1966			
	Residents	Residents	Aged 15 and over	Economically active	Employed
	(Thousands)		*(Indices, 1961 = 100)*		
Males					
New Commonwealth	308	155.4	150.8	156.2	158.8
India and Pakistan	117	166.2	161.6	171.7	173.7
British Caribbean	96	144.5	137.1	138.1	141.5
Other	95	153.0	151.8	158.0	159.7
Indigenous[a]	24,479	101.5	100.4	97.7	98.1
Great Britain	24,787	102.1	101.2	98.5	98.9
Females					
New Commonwealth	233	160.5	153.9	164.9	164.1
India and Pakistan	81	150.0	142.4	137.0	134.9
British Caribbean	77	171.1	162.3	165.0	165.3
Other	75	161.0	159.0	209.6	208.2
Indigenous[a]	26,264	101.3	100.8	113.3	112.7
Great Britain	26,497	101.8	101.3	113.9	113.3
Males and females					
New Commonwealth	541	157.6	152.1	158.7	160.3
India and Pakistan	198	159.6	153.8	163.5	164.5
British Caribbean	173	156.3	148.1	147.5	149.8
Other	170	156.5	154.8	171.3	172.3
Indigenous[a]	50,743	101.4	100.6	102.8	102.8
Great Britain	51,284	102.0	101.2	103.5	103.6

SOURCES: *Census 1961, Occupation Tables, Industry Tables* and *Birthplace and Nationality Tables; Sample Census 1966, Summary Tables* and *Economic Activity Tables.*

[a] Great Britain less New Commonwealth.

A final adjustment must be made to obtain a more complete assessment of the impact of New Commonwealth immigration on changes in the British labour force in this period.   It is a very important one.   Against the rise of 3.5 per cent in the numbers economically active (table 10), should be set a fall of about 1.5 per cent in the number of hours worked— the result of a decrease in weekly hours and improvements in annual holidays, both, apparently, on an unusually large scale in this period.[1] As a result, man-hours of employment increased by only 2 per cent, or about 0.4 per cent per annum.   In terms of numbers working 1961 hours, this represents an increase in the total economically active by 480 thousand (compared with the actual rise of 841 thousand) of which the new workers from the New Commonwealth (186 thousand) constitute as much as 39 per cent.   On this reckoning, and despite the rise in

[1] See Department of Economic Affairs, *The Task Ahead: Economic Assessment to 1972,* H.M.S.O., London, 1969, pp. 38–40.

indigenous female activity rates, the new immigrants made an even larger contribution to changes in British labour inputs than they did to the growth of the population. Allowance for underenumeration in 1966 would raise this contribution yet higher.

NEW COMMONWEALTH UNEMPLOYMENT RATES

The previous section revealed that out-of-employment rates in the different population groups do relatively little to shape their various participation rates. However, since the element in these rates which reflects unemployment pure and simple—as opposed to sickness—arouses much interest in the context of immigration, it is the subject of special attention in this section.

A finding of this study is that disadvantages which are frequently attributed to recent New Commonwealth immigration emerge upon deeper analysis as, essentially, alternative repercussions. The first instance of this now becomes apparent: *either* the New Commonwealth labour force endures an unemployment rate above that of indigenous workers and, to that extent, will inflict a burden on the social services,[1] *or* a recession will tend to produce proportionately more unemployment among indigenous workers, in which case racial tensions might arise. Both fears have been expressed.[2] Whatever the precise nature of the apprehensions associated with unemployment, it is obvious that an attempt to compare indigenous and New Commonwealth unemployment rates would contribute to a more informed discussion of the problem. In this section an attempt is made to meet this need by considering, with little success, the relative unemployment rates in 1961; with rather more success, changes in the relative rates up to 1966; and, more successfully still, the relative unemployment rates of the indigenous and New Commonwealth labour forces in 1966.

There are two basic sources for the derivation of unemployment rates: the Department of Employment and Productivity (in 1961, the Ministry of Labour) unemployment series; and the population censuses which, *inter alia*, collect information about members of the labour force 'out of employment'. The difficulty with the former source is that whilst, for some time, the numbers of adult unemployed New Commonwealth workers have been collected,[3] the Department possesses no labour force series for the New Commonwealth, so that this source alone does not yield a *rate* of New Commonwealth unemployment. In contrast,

---

[1] See also chapter 6.
[2] See Davison, *Black British*, p. 82.
[3] And very kindly have been made available to us.

a figure for economically active New Commonwealth residents can be obtained from the population censuses, but frequently, the same source fails to distinguish the numbers out of work because of sickness from the unemployed.

The national economic activity tables of the 1961 and 1966 population censuses do not make this distinction in the case of the total New Commonwealth labour force.[1] In 1961 the necessary distinction was made for the New Commonwealth labour force in the conurbations,[2] and yields for this group a percentage of 4.3 for the economically active out of work for reasons other than sickness. The corresponding rate for the total labour force of Great Britain was 1.6 per cent. It seems highly probable therefore that, at the time of the 1961 Census, the unemployment rate among New Commonwealth workers was higher than in the indigenous labour force. However, it would be most unwise to accept these rates as a faithful reflection of the different degrees of unemployment in the indigenous and New Commonwealth labour forces. Not only does the New Commonwealth rate fail to cover all the group's labour force, but also, those included work in the conurbations which, in terms of employment rates at least, are hardly typical of the whole country.[3]

The 1966 Census (at least in the publications available at the time of writing) does not give a figure for New Commonwealth workers out of employment for reasons other than sickness, on either a national or a conurbation basis. Therefore an attempt has been made to compare indigenous and immigrant unemployment rates in 1966 by means of a hybrid measure of the unemployment rate, taking as numerator the Department of Employment and Productivity's unemployment figures and as denominator the size of the labour force given in the 1966 Census.[4] The number of unemployed juvenile New Commonwealth workers is not recorded and therefore the corresponding group has also been excluded from the unemployed British labour force. Whilst it may be that coloured school leavers find rather more difficulty than indigenous youngsters in obtaining jobs, the relatively small number of young workers in the New Commonwealth labour force in 1966 may well mean

---

[1] Davison in *Black British*, p. 89, calculates from census data some group unemployment rates for twenty-eight London boroughs, but from his statements and the fact that he obtains a rate as high as 3.2 per cent for English males, it is not at all clear that he has eliminated the sick from the total out of work.

[2] This being a restricted definition of the New Commonwealth.

[3] As will be seen, the regional pattern of New Commonwealth unemployment rates differs sharply from that of the indigenous labour force (see p. 41, below).

[4] The New Commonwealth unemployment data are classified by country of birth and so (by excluding coloured workers born in this country, of which in any case there must be relatively few as yet) are consistent in this sense with the census labour force data.

D

that their exclusion from the comparison overstates the indigenous-immigrant difference in unemployment rates.

In 1966, 8 thousand New Commonwealth workers were unemployed on average, compared with a census (April 1966) figure of 504 thousand economically active.   This yields an unemployment rate of 1.63 (table 11).   The corresponding figures for the total British labour force were 341 thousand unemployed out of an economically active population of 25 million, giving an unemployment rate of 1.37 per cent.   This national rate is below that calculated and published by the Department of Employment and Productivity, 1.55.[1]   There are two reasons for this: the denominator of the latter relates only to employees, whilst that of the former, the economically active population, includes employers and self-employed; and, more important, the numerator of the official rate, but not ours, includes unemployed juveniles.

Table 11.   *New Commonwealth and indigenous unemployment rates, 1966*

Percentages

Region	New Commonwealth	Total labour force
London, South East and East Anglia	1.67	0.95
Midlands[a]	1.90	1.17
Yorkshire and Humberside[b]	1.32	1.07
South Western	1.12	1.46
North Western	1.48	1.33
Scotland	0.48	2.56
Northern	0.95	2.31
Wales	1.64	2.31
Great Britain	1.63	1.37
Males	1.67	1.72
Females	1.52	0.76

SOURCES: *Sample Census 1966, Economic Activity Tables;* Department of Employment and Productivity.

[a] Including East Midlands.
[b] Excluding East Midlands.

On the basis of these figures, the New Commonwealth unemployment rate is higher than that of the total labour force, but perhaps by not so much, a fifth, as is generally thought.   And whilst, as we shall see, the observed differential must be set against, and qualified with respect to,

[1] The average for February, May, August and November of 1966.

trends in unemployment rates, these calculations certainly lend no support whatsoever to impressionistic assessments that would place the New Commonwealth unemployment rate 'at least twice as high' as the indigenous rate.[1] That the New Commonwealth rate is at all above the indigenous rate would seem to be due, according to the results presented in table 11, to the sharp contrast in the unemployment rates for women workers: 1.52 for New Commonwealth women compared with 0.76 for all women in the British labour force. The rate for New Commonwealth men, 1.67, appears to have been marginally lower than for men in the indigenous labour force, 1.72.

A rather curious feature is that the regional patterns of New Commonwealth and indigenous unemployment rates shown in table 11 differ quite sharply. The rates for the total labour force reflect the well-known pattern: low rates, around 1 per cent, in London and the South East, Yorkshire and Humberside, and the Midlands; and high rates, above 2 per cent, in Scotland, the North and Wales. In contrast, the two highest New Commonwealth unemployment rates are registered in London and the South East, 1.67, and the Midlands, 1.90, and the two lowest, less than 1 per cent, in Scotland and the North. In short, there seems to be a tendency for New Commonwealth unemployment rates to be highest where the coloured population is concentrated,[2] and these regions are those where the unemployment rates for the total labour force are lowest; as a result New Commonwealth unemployment rates exceed total rates. New Commonwealth unemployment rates appear to be lowest where there are few immigrants and since, in general, these areas are usually the high unemployment regions, here they tend to be below the unemployment rates for the indigenous labour force, sometimes substantially so. A partial explanation of this may be that unemployed New Commonwealth workers prefer to stay within their main communities, usually low unemployment areas, unless they are attracted by specific vacancies in other, higher unemployment, regions.

It is possible to analyse, on the basis of unemployment rates calculated in the same way, the group pattern as well as the regional pattern of New Commonwealth rates. There is a sharp contrast in this respect: unemployment rates ranging from as little as 1.0 per cent for Asians to

---

[1] Wright's views in *The Coloured Worker in British Industry*, for instance, appear to have been unduly, and permanently, influenced by the very high unemployment rates which, by general recognition, characterised the coloured labour force at the turn of the decade. After reviewing (pp. 50–5) references to unemployment among coloured workers at this time, he concludes on p. 55, 'The general picture which emerges is that coloured unemployment rates are higher than white, and in all probability . . . at least twice as high if not higher.' Wright, it should be noted, was writing as late as 1968.

[2] See chapter 4.

2.2 per cent for West Indians. This picture confirms the impressions of other observers.[1] This basic group pattern was repeated for both men and women and, in the case of each group, the unemployment rate for men was greater than the rate for women.

It is important to consider the indigenous-immigrant unemployment difference observed for 1966 against the background of trends in unemployment rates. Unfortunately this is not easy to do. The Department of Employment and Productivity (then the Ministry of Labour) started collecting the current New Commonwealth immigrant unemployment series only at the beginning of 1963. Prior to that a series existed, but related rather vaguely to 'coloured immigrants' and does not appear to have been comprehensive.[2] And whilst a comprehensive quarterly New Commonwealth unemployment count has subsequently been taken (by country of origin), simply to relate changes in these figures to the series of total unemployment in the country could yield a misleading picture of developments, since the relative size of the indigenous and immigrant labour forces has been changing significantly.[3] Therefore, it was thought preferable to extrapolate backwards from 1966 the number of New Commonwealth economically active. Apart from the fact that, roughly in accordance with the gross immigration flows shown in table 2, only about half of the recorded 1961-6 rise in the economically active was assumed for the three-year period 1963-6, the extrapolation is a simple one; the rise throughout the period being evenly spread (in terms of absolute numbers) from the beginning of February 1963 to the end of April 1966.[4] In order to lengthen the period of comparison, the New Commonwealth labour force has also been extrapolated, on this same rough basis, up to 1968. The national rate of unemployment as a percentage of the total economically active has been retraced from 1966 by means of the official series of unemployment rates adjusted to exclude juveniles.[5] The results are shown in chart 1.

It will be appreciated from the qualifications already made, and from

---

[1] Davison, *Black British*, pp. 89 and 90; and Wright, *The Coloured Worker in British Industry*, pp. 69 and 70.

[2] As such, it was probably not consistent with figures of the economically active New Commonwealth population derived from the population census, which are restricted to people born abroad. Also, local employment exchanges reported a count of coloured people only if their number exceeded a hundred.

[3] An examination of immigrant-indigenous unemployment trends using the data in this way does not in fact produce a picture that is markedly different from our own. See, for instance, Butterworth, *Immigrants in West Yorkshire*, pp. 14–18.

[4] A more sophisticated extrapolation based on annual net immigration (immigration less re-emigration) and the age characteristics of new immigrants is impossible due to the absence of the necessary breakdowns in the immigration statistics.

[5] The implicit assumption in this procedure being that the numbers economically active have moved in proportion to the number of employees.

the extrapolation of the indigenous labour force which was necessary, that the changes which chart 1 portray should be interpreted with some care.   The year 1966 for which the major unemployment rate comparison is possible was, for the most part, a year of generally low unemployment. It would be dangerous to assume, therefore, that the relatively small difference observed in that year between the New Commonwealth and indigenous unemployment rates would be repeated at times when general unemployment was higher.

Chart 1.   *Unemployment rates of the New Commonwealth and total labour force*

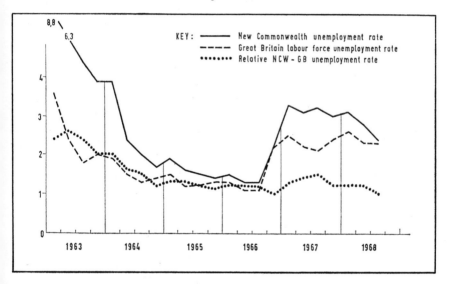

SOURCES: *Sample Census 1966, Economic Activity Tables;* Department of Employment and Productivity.

Note: The vertical scale represents both percentages for the New Commonwealth and Great Britain labour force unemployment rates, and the ratio between the New Commonwealth and Great Britain rates.

The chart shows that, at other times during the period 1963-8, the difference between the New Commonwealth and indigenous unemployment rates was rather more marked.   The explanation of the differences before and after 1966 is different.   The picture is to a large extent dominated by a sharp fall in the New Commonwealth unemployment rate from very high levels, apparently of over 8 per cent, at the beginning of 1963.   There seems to be no doubt that such high rates are quite untypical.

They reflect, essentially, the process of absorption into the economy of the large influx of New Commonwealth immigrants who arrived in the very early 1960s.[1]

After 1966 there was an essentially deflationary rise in the general level of unemployment. This was accompanied by an increase in the ratio of the New Commonwealth unemployment rate to the indigenous rate, suggesting that there may be some truth in the fear that New Commonwealth workers are more vulnerable to deflationary unemployment. Even in this situation, however, there seems to be no question of the indigenous-immigrant unemployment ratio rising to a value of 2.

In addition to possible discrimination, two factors might account for such vulnerability to deflationary unemployment. First, disproportionately large numbers of New Commonwealth workers may be employed in sectors that are prone to deflationary fluctuations. The following chapter of this study suggests that this is unlikely: the New Commonwealth labour force is not concentrated in only a few sectors and whilst, for instance, it has above-average concentrations in metals and engineering, not many are employed in construction and shipbuilding. A more likely explanation of their deflationary vulnerability is that, since many immigrants, even by 1967, had not been in the labour force for long, redundancy on the basis of 'last in first out' might affect them to a disproportionate extent. To the extent that this rather than any alternative explanation is correct, it is an effect which will weaken with time.

[1] A recovery from temporarily high unemployment rates can be seen from the following data which (disregarding changes in the coverage of the series, see p. 42 above) show changes in the proportion of 'coloured Commonwealth' unemployed to total unemployed:

	Males	Females
August 1960	2.4	3.0
November 1960	2.9	4.4
February 1961	3.2	5.0
May 1961	4.2	7.0
August 1961	3.9	6.3
November 1961	4.9	7.5
February 1962	6.7	7.8
May 1962	8.9	9.5
August 1962	6.9	7.5
November 1962	5.1	6.4
February 1963	3.9	5.5

SOURCE: Davison, *Black British*, pp. 83–7.
Note: The bars denote a break in the series.

In brief, the evidence suggests that when the general level of unemployment is low and the rate of new arrivals not unduly high there is probably no appreciable difference between New Commonwealth and indigenous unemployment rates.   However, a rise in general unemployment seems to produce a more significant difference: one which is such that proportionally more rather than less unemployment—the first of the alternative impacts referred to at the outset of this section—appears in the ranks of the coloured labour force.   Even then, the difference, judging from post-1966 experience, does not seem excessive, and the financial cost it implies in terms of social benefits is relatively small.[1]   To be set against this is the consideration that coloured immigrants bear, in these circumstances, an above-average amount of the economy's real burden of unemployment; a state of affairs which should improve naturally with time and as a result of a reduction in discrimination.

[1] See chapter 6.

CHAPTER 4

THE QUALITATIVE IMPACT
ON THE LABOUR FORCE

We now turn to what might be termed the qualitative impact of the immigrant population on the labour force. It needs to be stressed that qualitative is used not in the rather narrow way in which it is normally employed in this context, denoting the skills and abilities of a particular work force, but in a much broader sense which embraces the industrial and geographical distribution of immigrant workers as well as their occupational characteristics. As such, this section of the study is potentially one of the most important; for many are of the opinion that, on the one hand, the most important economic advantages of recent immigration will stem, if anywhere, from changes in the economy's structure that it facilitates and, on the other hand, that the social problems raised by immigration are largely attributable to the concentration of immigrants—in jobs, industries and areas—which such an impact requires.

In the context of this supposed structural economic impact, the industrial distribution of immigrant workers is rather more significant than their occupational characteristics or geographical location, for it is the impact on the output pattern of goods and services[1] which is of prime concern. Moreover, the industrial distribution of a labour force can to a large extent be regarded as the result, on one side, of a worker's occupational choice and, on the other, of his decision about where to live. This is not to say that the occupational and geographical distribution of immigrants holds no intrinsic interest. For instance, we consider at a later stage the impact on wage rises of the presence of a disproportionate number of immigrants in certain occupations and its implications.[2] And no one would question the importance, in the social context, of the geographical distribution of immigrants.

If we leave out of account those jobs, such as mining, where occupation and industry are virtually indistinguishable, few workers decide first that they wish to enter a particular industry and then look for occupations and locations which permit this; the points of decision for a worker

---

[1] I.e. the proportions of value added in the various sectors. There are, of course, other influences on this as well as additions to the labour force, e.g. inputs of capital and productivity changes.

[2] See chapter 9.

are essentially occupation and location, not industry.[1] Given a worker's locational and occupational decisions, other factors, such as sectoral vacancy rates, will then play their part in directing him to a specific industry. Therefore we examine first the regional and occupational distributions of the immigrant labour force together with certain factors which may have shaped them. The industrial distribution of the immigrant labour force is reviewed last.

Before examining the data some warnings must be sounded about the statistics, especially in connection with the occupational and industrial distributions of the labour force. These distributions were derived from the sample census and, in the case of 1961, have been applied to the labour force totals implied in the full census in accordance with the statistical procedure outlined in the previous chapter.[2] It was there noted that, whilst this stratagem circumvents some of the statistical pitfalls, it cannot avoid them all. Of particular relevance in the present context is the fear that the underenumeration of New Commonwealth immigrants is such that it is more pronounced in the case of immigrants in lower paid occupations and industries.[3]

Secondly, the 1961 Census data relating to the industrial and occupational distributions of the immigrant and indigenous labour forces have not been adjusted by means of the bias factors provided in the census reports.[4] There are two reasons for this: corresponding bias factors are not available for 1966; and, when using a hypothetical distribution obtained from the 1961 industry-occupation matrix for which no bias factors exist, it was felt to be more consistent to compare it with the actual, uncorrected distributions.[5] Where the number of immigrant workers is expressed as a percentage of the total labour force in a specific industry or occupation, the results would in any case be unaffected by corrections for bias since, at the national level at least, separate bias factors are not available for the immigrant labour force and both the New Commonwealth and indigenous distributions would need to be adjusted by the same small—typically less than 1 per cent—factors. Bias factors are available for the New Commonwealth labour force in the conurbations in 1961 and, because they differ from the indigenous bias factors in the conurbations and are large, occupational and indus-

---

[1] One exception was the movement, in the 1950s, to occupations and areas which afforded workers jobs in the high paid motor car industry.

[2] See above, pp. 30–1.

[3] Jenner and Cohen, *Commonwealth Immigrants and the 1961 Census*, p. 12.

[4] After the 1961 Census, the General Register Office did a check with some data which had been collected both in the full census and in the 10 per cent sample. As a result a bias was revealed and the G.R.O. calculated factors which could be applied to the sample data to correct for it.

[5] See appendix A.

trial distributions for the conurbations, where they are used, have been adjusted for bias.[1]

Another difference, one of coverage, exists between the 1961 national and conurbation data relating to New Commonwealth immigrants. The definition of this group of immigrants is more restricted for the conurbation statistics—covering only India, Pakistan, the British Caribbean, Commonwealth countries in Africa, Cyprus and Malta—than it is in the tables derived from the national census reports where the New Commonwealth embraces all Commonwealth countries, colonies and protectorates other than Australia, New Zealand and Canada. All of the discrepancy in coverage falls in the other New Commonwealth category; the definition of the Asian group (India and Pakistan) and of the British Caribbean is identical in both the national and conurbation tables, and they can be compared accordingly.

Some difficulties were also encountered when comparing the 1961 and 1966 geographical distributions of the indigenous and immigrant populations as a result of changes, in the interim, in regional definitions. Appropriate combinations of regions in both years circumvents some of the difficulties. Thus, the two former regions East and West Ridings and the North Midlands less Peterborough can now be equated with Yorkshire and Humberside and the East Midlands. And the former Eastern, London and South Eastern, and Southern plus Peterborough identify with East Anglia and the South East. Changes in the West Midland and Greater London conurbations meant that, respectively, they gained 1.3 per cent and lost 2.3 per cent of their populations—alterations that make an appreciable difference when changes in total population in the areas are being measured between 1961 and 1966, since the latter are small in relation to the totals. Accordingly, we have used the current definitions of the two conurbations in the case of both 1961 and 1966, a task facilitated by the method of presentation of the 1966 Sample Census results.[2] The same procedure could not be followed in the case of immigrants living in these two conurbations, but the consequent error in measuring changes between 1961 and 1966 is not very serious, given that the size of the change is large relative to the number of immigrants in these conurbations in 1961. The inconsistency in the treatment of immigrants and of the indigenous population of these two conurbations has much less serious implications for measuring changes between 1961 and 1966 than it would if unadjusted indigenous figures for 1961 had been compared with the 1966 totals.[3]

[1] See appendix B.
[2] See General Register Office, *Sample Census 1966, Summary Tables*, H.M.S.O., London, 1967, table 1.
[3] The same procedure was followed in the adjustment for Peterborough.

THE GEOGRAPHICAL DISTRIBUTION OF IMMIGRANTS

Not only may the geographical distribution of immigrants have an important bearing on their industrial distribution, but it is also very interesting in its own right. It has implications for economic and social questions apart from the pattern of industry: particularly its relationship to the geographical pattern of population development, regional unemployment rates and area population densities.

The basic information for an appraisal of the regional distribution of immigrants is contained in appendix table 1. Perhaps the first point to notice is that, while the geographical distributions of the total population and, even more, of the various immigrant groups changed between 1961 and 1966, these developments are not very large and are insignificant compared with the contrasts between the locational patterns of the indigenous and the immigrant populations. This means that, while at a later stage attention needs to be devoted to residential changes during the period, there is the advantage that at this stage the indigenous and immigrant locational patterns can be compared without a particular year, 1961 or 1966, having to be specified.[1]

Compared with the rest of the population, immigrants tend to be concentrated in the south eastern quadrant of Great Britain. More than half the immigrant population, compared with about a third of the total population, are to be found in the South Eastern region, the contrast being more pronounced in the former London and South Eastern area than in the southern or eastern parts of the region. The same proportion, about a tenth, of both the immigrant and total populations is in the West Midlands. The proportion of the immigrant population in the rest of the country, Scotland and the North, Wales and the South West, about a third, is very much below the proportion of the total population in these areas, rather more than a half.

The contrast between the immigrant and indigenous population distributions is repeated in the regional distribution of New Commonwealth immigrants, but in a more extreme form. That is, in regions where the proportion of all immigrants is higher than the proportion of the total population, the proportion of coloured immigrants resident there tends to be higher still, and vice versa. Thus 62/60 per cent of New Commonwealth immigrants were in the South Eastern region—a proportion not to be forgotten—compared with 56/57 per cent of all immigrants and 35 per cent of the total population. In the former London and South Eastern area the picture is even sharper, as the corresponding percentages for 1961, 51 per cent, 42 per cent and 22 per cent respec-

---

[1] Where two percentages are cited, the first refers to 1961, the second to 1966.

tively, show.   At the other end of the scale, only a little more than a quarter of the New Commonwealth immigrants were in Scotland, the North, Wales and the South West, compared with over a third of all immigrants and more than a half of the total population.   Between these two poles, the proportion of New Commonwealth immigrants in the West Midlands, at 12/13 per cent, was perceptibly higher than the proportions of all immigrants, about 10 per cent, and of the total population, about 9 per cent.

The three groups of New Commonwealth immigrants distinguished in this study also display significant divergencies in their locational patterns.   The West Indian group tends to accentuate the pattern noted for the New Commonwealth as a whole.   A higher than average New Commonwealth proportion—about 65 per cent and 16 per cent respectively—is to be found in the South East and the West Midlands, and something below the New Commonwealth average in the other regions— especially Scotland, the North and the South West.   In contrast, the Asians tend to have above the average New Commonwealth proportions in all regions except the South East, even though about half the Asians in Great Britain are to be found in this region.   The largest proportion in the South East, about two-thirds, is registered by the other New Commonwealth, reflecting to some extent the disproportionate number of students in their ranks, offset by relatively low proportions in Yorkshire, Humberside and the East Midlands, and also the West Midlands.

Before considering explanations or implications of this distribution, it is useful to examine the locational pattern of immigrants in another plane: the proportions of each group resident in urban areas, or more precisely in the country's six conurbations.   It is clear from appendix table 1 that, compared with the rest of the population, immigrants, and especially New Commonwealth immigrants, are very much town dwellers, and large town dwellers at that.[1]   While only a third of the total population reside in conurbations, about a half of all immigrants, three-fifths of New Commonwealth immigrants and more than three-quarters of the West Indians are to be found in these areas.   When account is taken of the fact that so many immigrants come from rural areas in their own countries, it is clear that, no matter in how many other respects recent migration to this country departs from traditional flows, it falls into the classical mould in that it is essentially a drift from country to town.   This factor has an important influence on the characteristics of these migrants: on their fertility rates, on the difficulties they experience in adjusting to a new way of life, and perhaps on their occupational distribution too.

The distribution of immigrants among the conurbations also displays

---

[1] A point emphasised by Peach, *West Indian Migration to Britain*, pp. 76–82.

interesting features. The picture is dominated by London. Whilst rather less than a half of all conurbation dwellers live in London, about 69 per cent of all urban immigrants and of New Commonwealth urban dwellers reside there. It is especially revealing that, whilst only 15 per cent of the total population dwelt in Greater London in 1966, the corresponding proportion for all immigrants was 36 per cent, for New Commonwealth immigrants 43 per cent and for Caribbean immigrants as high as 56 per cent.

Implications of the locational pattern can be more readily appreciated if the data are expressed in the form of concentration ratios: the percentage which immigrants comprise of the total population in each area. Unlike the distributions examined above, there are sharp differences between the 1961 and 1966 statistics, with appreciably higher concentration ratios for the latter year than for the former, as a result of the large increase in the New Commonwealth population over the period. The period witnessed a rise in all the area and group concentration ratios except for that of the West Indians in the Tyneside conurbation. The 1961 and 1966 New Commonwealth rankings are identical, except that the 1961 concentration ratio in the South Western region was greater than in Yorkshire, Humberside and the East Midlands, a situation that had been reversed by 1966.

Even where the concentration of immigrants was highest, in the South East, it failed to exceed a tenth of the population. The highest New Commonwealth concentration, found in the same region, was much lower, less than 3 per cent even in 1966, and represented almost identical concentrations of the three component groups. In the other high concentration region, the West Midlands, the observed ratio in 1966 was nearer 2 per cent, this time derived from rather different group concentrations—Asians 1.1 per cent, West Indians 0.8 per cent and the other New Commonwealth 0.3 per cent.

Given the immigrants' predilection for an urban environment, the conurbation concentration ratios tend to be higher than those in the regions, though not by very large margins. Taking all six conurbations together, 8.3 per cent of residents in 1966 were immigrants, compared with 5.0 per cent in the country at large; and 3.2 per cent of conurbation dwellers were New Commonwealth immigrants, compared with 1.6 per cent in the country as a whole. Even the two conurbations with the largest concentrations, Greater London and the West Midlands, did not have ratios above 5 per cent, their concentrations being respectively 4.8 and 3.6 per cent; whilst at the other end of the scale the ratios for the New Commonwealth in the Merseyside and Tyneside conurbations were under 1 per cent.

Even when allowance is made for underenumeration in 1966, total immigrant concentration ratios, let alone New Commonwealth concentration ratios, can hardly be considered large, either at the regional or the conurbation level. It is obvious, however, that the finer the area classification employed—borough, ward, street—the larger the immigrant concentration ratios that can be encountered.[1] More local New Commonwealth concentrations of some size are to be expected in those regions and conurbations where the overall concentrations are largest.

We are concerned with the economic impact of immigrants' location rather than with its social implications, and especially with discovering why New Commonwealth immigrants settled in certain areas, and the changes they made in the geographical pattern of the British population and labour force in the period 1961 to 1966.

Table 12.   *The regional pattern of immigrants and unemployment rates*

Percentages

| | Unemployment rates[a] | | | Concentration ratios | | | |
| | | | | All immigrants | | New Commonwealth | |
	1956	1961	1966	1961	1966	1961	1966
South Eastern	0.9	1.0	1.0	7.05	8.13	1.89	2.80
Yorkshire and Midlands	0.8	1.2	1.2	3.52	4.17	0.89	1.58
South Western	1.3	1.4	1.8	3.32	3.66	0.84	1.09
North Western	1.3	1.6	1.5	3.09	3.52	0.46	0.82
Scotland	2.4	3.2	2.9	2.31	2.40	0.35	0.44
Northern	1.5	2.5	2.6	1.37	1.50	0.31	0.42
Wales	2.0	2.6	2.9	1.96	2.00	0.30	0.38

SOURCES: Appendix table 1; *Statistics on Incomes, Prices, Employment and Production.*

[a] For total labour force.

Since most immigrants, and especially those from the New Commonwealth, came to Britain for work,[2] it is natural to compare their geographical distribution with the regional pattern of unemployment rates. The data for such a comparison are set out in table 12.   This underlines the stability over time of the regional pattern of unemployment rates, a pattern which recent research confirms is basically attributable to a persistent deficiency, in the high unemployment areas, of effective

[1] Information at such a narrowly defined level, say a ward or street, may not be available on a systematic and comprehensive basis. Impressionistic assessments suggest that 'the coloured population is in the minority in all but the tiniest sections of a very few towns'. (Burney, *Housing on Trial*, pp. 6 and 7.)

[2] See chapter 2, pp. 11 and 13–14.

demand.[1]   It also suggests a fairly strong negative association between the regional patterns of immigrant concentration ratios and unemployment rates: the proportion in the population of all immigrants, and of New Commonwealth immigrants, tends to be higher in regions with low unemployment rates and lower in regions with high unemployment rates. This is related to a feature noted in the previous chapter: the tendency for the regional patterns of total and New Commonwealth unemployment rates to be negatively associated.   Whilst New Commonwealth immigrants concentrate in regions where the general level of unemployment is low, their own unemployment rates in these areas tend to be higher than where there are few coloured immigrants.[2]

Even though the evidence points to the geographical pattern of job opportunities being a major determinant of the regional distribution of immigrants, it is clear that their arrival has done nothing to reduce the regional differentials in unemployment rates.   If anything these differentials were wider in 1966 than ten years earlier.

The relationship between unemployment and immigrant residential patterns has been noted by others.   Peach, for instance, has drawn attention to it and, using a rather finer regional classification than that in table 12, suggests that employment opportunities are a necessary but not sufficient condition for a high concentration of New Commonwealth immigrants.[3]   He sees in his data (relating, essentially, to developments up to 1961) a tendency for immigrants to go to regions of high labour demand—not those that are attracting, by means of domestic population shifts, the indigenous population (the East, the South and the South West), but to those (London, the South East and the Midlands) which have an outward migration of indigenous people or only a relatively small inward flow.   Looking first at the regional distribution, table 13, which displays the changes during the period 1961–6, gives little support to this thesis.   It is true that the South Western region which experienced the largest rise, 4 per cent, in the indigenous population, also had a below-average rise (36 per cent compared with a 57 per cent average) in New Commonwealth immigrants.   But, in contrast, the other regions with the largest indigenous population increase, Yorkshire and the Midlands with a rise of 2 per cent, also experienced increases in the New Commonwealth

[1] A. J. Brown et al. 'Regional Problems and Regional Policy', National Institute Economic Review, No. 46, November 1968.
[2] See chapter 3, p. 41
[3] West Indian Migration to Britain, pp. 62–72.   It seems to be the case, for instance, that the former Southern and Eastern regions, while having an unemployment rate comparable to that of the Midlands, have appreciably lower concentrations of New Commonwealth immigrants.   We have been obliged to employ in table 12 larger regional groupings both to obtain consistency with the Ministry of Labour's regions and to facilitate a comparison of 1961 and 1966 geographical distributions.

population of 79 and 84 per cent, which were among the largest.   Indeed, the location of new coloured immigrants does not appear to have had an unduly large impact on the geographical pattern of changes in the British population over the period 1961–6:[1] the rankings of changes in regional population sizes differ little for the indigenous and total populations.

Table 13.   *Changes in the regional distribution of immigrants, 1961 to 1966*

	1966			Change, 1961–6		
	Total popu-lation	New Common-wealth	Indi-genous[a]	Total popu-lation	New Common-wealth	Indi-genous[a]
	(Indices, 1961 = 100)			*(Thousands)*		
Regions						
South Eastern	102.5	152.0	101.6	+450	+174	+276
West Midlands	103.2	179.3	102.2	+152	+ 50	+102
Yorkshire, Humberside and East Midlands	102.6	184.3	102.5	+201	+ 41	+160
South Western	104.4	135.7	104.1	+149	+ 10	+139
North Western	100.7	180.0	100.4	+ 48	+ 24	+ 24
Scotland	99.8	125.9	99.7	− 11	+ 5	− 16
Northern	100.4	134.8	100.3	+ 12	+ 4	+ 8
Wales	100.7	126.5	100.7	+ 19	+ 2	+ 17
All regions	102.0	157.2	101.4	+1,020	+310	+710
Conurbations						
Greater London	95.9	151.4	94.2	−326	+125	−451
West Midlands	99.8	178.4	98.2	− 4	+ 37	− 41
West Yorkshire	100.3	214.7	99.2	+ 5	+ 19	− 14
S.E. Lancashire	99.0	201.3	98.4	− 24	+ 15	− 39
Merseyside	96.6	126.3	96.5	− 47	+ 2	− 49
Tyneside	97.3	133.8	97.2	− 23	+ 1	− 24
All conurbations	97.4	160.0	96.2	−419	+199	−618

SOURCE: Appendix table I.

[a] Total population less New Commonwealth.

However, taking a less aggregative view and concentrating on the conurbations, there is some validity in regarding New Commonwealth immigrants as, in a sense, a 'replacement' population.   This does not hinge primarily on the fact that, while numbers of indigenous residents increased in non-conurbation areas and declined in the conurbations, the numbers of coloured residents increased by more than a half in both types

[1] Though appreciably larger than on the changes in the occupational and industrial patterns; see below pp. 63 and 82.

of area. The significant feature is that the conurbations, where the indigenous population decreased, are the areas which have the highest share of the coloured population, both at a given moment of time and in terms of changes in the period 1961–6. The implication of this can best be seen in terms of the absolute changes given in table 13. Almost two-thirds of new coloured immigrants went to the conurbations and, whilst in other areas the indigenous population increased by 1,328 thousand and the New Commonwealth population by 111 thousand, within the conurbations there was a decline of 618 thousand in the indigenous inhabitants and a rise of 199 thousand in New Commonwealth inhabitants. Thus coloured immigrants replaced about a third of the indigenous inhabitants lost from the conurbations. There is other negative and more impressionistic evidence to support the conclusion that, up to now, New Commonwealth immigrants have not only been large town dwellers, but have also tended to settle in those cities that are losing their indigenous inhabitants: for example, there is an almost complete absence of New Commonwealth immigrants in the New Towns.[1]

What is the cause of this? Peach offers no special explanation but implies that it is bound up with the labour shortage in the older cities associated with the outward movement of the indigenous population, although logically this factor should have been taken into account in the observed relationship between unemployment and New Commonwealth residential patterns. We suggest that there is an important independent explanation: the availability, as a consequence of the outward movement of indigenous inhabitants, of otherwise scarce social capital, especially housing, poor in quality though it may be. The areas where coloured immigrants settle in these cities are often centrally situated and have been more precisely identified as those 'which are losing total population or showing net decreases of white population'; they are twilight areas 'of old, decaying private housing which often contain the only available accommodation for newcomers of limited means near the city centre'.[2] This is a theme, with important economic as well as social implications, developed in chapter 7.

It would be wrong to suppose that job availabilities and accommodation are the only important determinants of the location of New Commonwealth immigrants. As suggested in the quotation from Burney, the cost of housing may also be a factor. Another consideration is that, once residential concentrations of immigrants have been established, it is perhaps natural that, for social and cultural reasons, they should constitute points of attraction for later arrivals from the same countries of

[1] Burney, *Housing on Trial*, pp. 246–7.
[2] Peach, *West Indian Migration to Britain*, p. 89, and Burney, op. cit. p. 6.

E

origin. Asian immigrants in West Yorkshire have on occasion refused council houses 'in part because of a desire which is particularly strong among those not able to speak English to remain near those they know'.[1] Many among the more recent arrivals from the New Commonwealth are here as a result of specific contacts with friends or relations among the earlier immigrants. And it is not without significance that the most common method of finding employment has been through the personal effort of a relative and not by means of the employment exchange.[2]

THE OCCUPATIONAL DISTRIBUTION OF THE IMMIGRANT LABOUR FORCE

This section follows the pattern of the previous one. An attempt is made first to ascertain the occupational distribution of immigrants, and especially the degree to which they are found in some jobs in disproportionately large or small numbers; secondly, to suggest some reasons for their occupational choice. Appendix table 2 presents the percentage occupational distributions of the various immigrant groups and of the total labour force in 1961 and 1966. Twenty-seven occupations are distinguished in the table and, therefore, a shorthand statistic which summarises the differences between any two occupational distributions is indispensable. We have used for this purpose a simple variant of the mean deviation. For each occupation, the difference between the proportions of the two labour forces in question employed in that occupation has been taken; ignoring the signs of these differences, they are summed for all occupations and the mean deviation between the two distributions obtained by dividing this total by the number of units, in this case twenty-seven occupations.

Table 14.   *A comparison of immigrant and indigenous occupational distributions*

	Males		Females		Mean deviations Males and females	
	1961	1966	1961	1966	1961	1966
All immigrants	1.30	1.15	1.41	1.26	1.30	1.12
New Commonwealth	1.51	1.40	1.70	1.92	1.35	1.45
India and Pakistan	1.61	1.78	2.04	1.66	1.60	1.63
British Caribbean	2.35	2.41	2.66	2.60	2.14	2.12
Other	2.32	2.04	2.13	2.00	1.98	1.68

SOURCES: Appendix tables 2.1, 2.2, 2.3.

[1] Butterworth, *Immigrants in West Yorkshire*, p. 13.
[2] Davison, *Black British*, p. 77.

The results, given in table 14, reveal that the mean difference between the occupational distributions of New Commonwealth immigrants and the total British labour force was 1.35 per cent in 1961 and 1.45 per cent in 1966. However, unless they are set in some sort of perspective, such statistics have little meaning. One way of providing the necessary perspective is to compare the results with values of the mean deviation implied in certain hypothetical distributions. This is done for three such distributions in chart 2, in each of which the total labour force is assumed to be distributed equally between twenty occupations. In the first, where immigrants are assumed to be concentrated in one occupation, the mean deviation is as high as 9.5. In the second, where they are spread over ten occupations, it is 5.0. And in the third, where immigrants are present in each occupation, though to a varying extent, the mean deviation is 2.5 An identical occupational distribution of the total and immigrant labour forces would, of course, yield a mean deviation of zero.

Chart 2.   *Mean deviations between hypothetical occupational distributions*

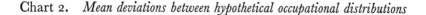

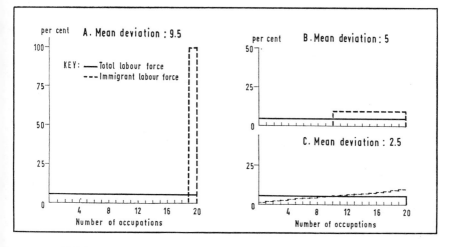

SOURCE: NIESR estimates.

A second method is to consider the observed values of the mean deviation between the immigrant and total labour forces alongside contrasts in occupational distributions in other planes. For instance, is the difference, as measured by the mean deviation, between the occupational distributions of the immigrant and total labour forces greater than the difference between the occupational distributions of male and female workers in the economy? The answer is no; the mean deviation for the latter being 3.27 in 1966. Alternatively, is the difference between the occupational distributions of the immigrant and total labour forces greater than the differences between the distributions of particular groups of immigrants? Again the answer is no: the mean difference between the occupational distributions of Asians and West Indians in 1966 was 1.87. However, the differences between immigrant and indigenous occupational distributions tend to be larger than the differences registered between the 1961 and 1966 occupational distributions of each group shown in table 15.

Table 15. *A comparison of 1961 and 1966 occupational distributions of the immigrant labour force*

| | | | Mean deviations |
	Males	Females	Males and females
All immigrants	0.50	0.24	0.40
New Commonwealth	0.80	0.62	0.69
India and Pakistan	1.44	0.56	1.29
British Caribbean	0.70	0.67	0.59
Other	0.53	0.45	0.48
Total labour force	0.30	0.26	0.31

SOURCE: NIESR estimates.

Table 14 suggests a few other generalisations. First, it would seem that indigenous-immigrant occupational differences tend to be more pronounced in the case of New Commonwealth females than in the case of males and the contrasts, such as they are, between the New Commonwealth and indigenous distributions cannot be ascribed exclusively to differences in the sex ratios of the labour forces, but also derive from contrasts in the indigenous-immigrant occupational differences of each sex. Secondly, indigenous-immigrant occupational differences would seem to be rather more pronounced in the case of the New Commonwealth labour force than in the case of all immigrants. Thirdly, within the New Commonwealth group, the occupational contrast is sharpest for the West Indian group and least pronounced for Asians.

As with the regional distribution of the immigrant population, it is useful to examine indigenous-New Commonwealth immigrant differences in occupational distributions in terms of concentration ratios—the proportion which immigrants comprise of each occupational labour force. These are shown in chart 3 where the 1966 patterns of New Commonwealth concentration ratios are ranked from the lowest to the highest.

Chart 3. *New Commonwealth occupational concentration ratios, 1966* 59

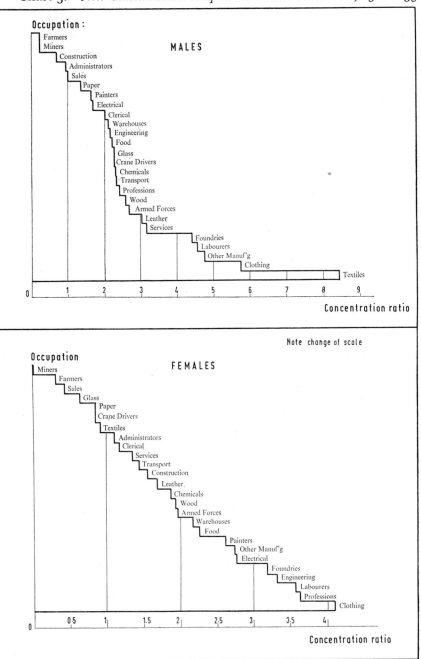

SOURCE: *Sample Census 1966, Commonwealth Immigrant Tables.*

Perhaps the most striking feature of the data presented in this fashion is that in none of these occupations can the New Commonwealth concentration be considered very large. Nowhere does it exceed 10 per cent even in 1966, and a concentration of more than 5 per cent is exceptional. However, care needs to be exercised when drawing conclusions of this sort from the observed concentration ratios. Underenumeration should not be forgotten. But more important is the consideration that a finer classification of occupations than that being used here would undoubtedly reveal specific jobs with higher concentrations. We pursue this matter below.

A second striking feature concerns the *pattern* of occupational concentrations rather than their size. Before considering the profiles of these ratios, it is useful to consider *a priori* the forms which they might assume. There is of course an infinite number of possibilities, but chart 4 portrays a few basic shapes, assuming twenty occupations each having the same total labour force and an average immigrant concentration ratio of 5 per cent. Chart 4A simply indicates an even occupational spread of the immigrant labour force. In this situation the structural impact of the immigrant labour force would, of course, be minimal, although it would not rule out a significant macro-economic impact. Chart 4B represents a situation in which the immigrant labour force is distributed evenly between the occupations except for one or two sectors where, perhaps because of restrictive labour practices or specialised labour requirements, no immigrants, or very few, are employed. Chart 4C portrays an extreme distribution in terms of structural impact: a situation in which the immigrant labour force is concentrated in two occupations. And chart 4D shows the occupational distribution of immigrants that lies between a zero structural impact (chart 4A) and an extreme structural effect (chart 4C).

The distribution of the New Commonwealth female concentration ratios broadly corresponds to the type depicted in chart 4D, a distribution which, whilst it implies some structural occupational effect, avoids an extreme one. Perhaps the best way of exposing the structural implications of such a distribution of concentration ratios is to point out that the bulk of coloured female workers do not appear to be playing a pronounced structural role in the British labour market in the sense that they are avoiding certain jobs and flocking to others. As many as twenty-one of the ratios, relating to occupations that included as much as 62 per cent of the female New Commonwealth labour force in 1966, were to be found in the relatively narrow range of $\frac{1}{2}$ to $3\frac{1}{2}$ per cent. The largest ratios were recorded for clothing workers, professional workers and labourers, all in the $3\frac{1}{2}$ to 4 per cent range; the lowest (neglecting mining)

Chart 4. *Hypothetical distribution of concentration ratios*

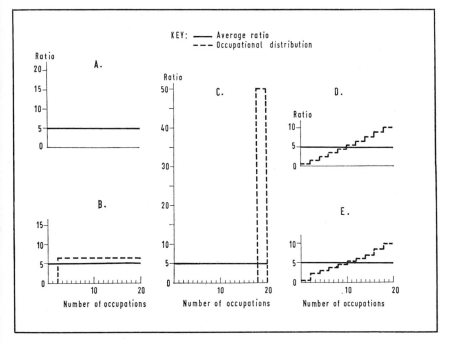

SOURCE: NIESR estimates.

for agricultural workers and sales workers, both less than ½ per cent.

Inspection of the distribution of the occupational concentration ratios of New Commonwealth males suggests that it corresponds to the hypothetical one presented in chart 4E.   That is, like chart 4D, it avoids both a zero and an extreme structural impact, but with a more pronounced upturn among the high concentration jobs and downturn among the low concentration occupations.[1]   Thus, there is an even stronger tendency than among females for the bulk of the labour force to be found in occupations with concentration ratios lying within a relatively narrow band.   As many as nineteen of the 1966 occupational concentration ratios, embracing as much as 87 per cent of economically active male New Commonwealth workers, lie between 1½ and 4¾ per cent.   Easily the highest ratio, 8.4 per cent, was recorded in the textile worker group, and second were clothing workers with a ratio of 5.7 per cent: ratios between 4 and 5 per cent were registered among other manufacturing workers, labourers and metal workers.   At the other end of the scale, low proportions, of less than 1.5

[1] The distribution of New Commonwealth female occupational concentration ratios also tended to be of this form in 1961.

per cent of male New Commonwealth workers, were recorded among agricultural workers, miners, construction workers,[1] administrators, sales workers, and paper and printing workers.

Considering these results—in conjunction with the mean deviations—it is difficult to avoid the conclusion that, over a wide range of economic activities, the bulk of the New Commonwealth labour force does not seem to have had a substantial structural effect in the sense that its members comprise disproportionately large or small proportions of the labour force.

Such a conclusion might need to be qualified in two respects. First, it could be argued that ratios calculated for a finer job classification would reveal much higher concentrations of New Commonwealth workers. This, as we shall see, is true; although even at a less aggregated level the number of jobs with higher concentrations is not really very large, neither are the concentrations so very much higher. But beyond this is the consideration that, unless the distribution of coloured workers between the jobs within these major categories is a very unusual one, it is highly unlikely that a large proportion of coloured workers will be in very high or very low concentration jobs. Secondly, it is possible that, despite the absence of pronounced differences between New Commonwealth and indigenous occupational distributions in 1961 and 1966, the major importance of new immigrant workers in the growth of the British labour force between these years could mean that, at the margin and in terms of changes during the period, the New Commonwealth labour force had a much more dynamic impact on developments in the occupational pattern of labour supplies.

Two conflicting possibilities have been suggested for the role of New Commonwealth immigrants in relation to changes in the occupational pattern of the British labour force. One is that coloured immigrants have done much to meet the demand for workers in those occupations where numbers are increasing most rapidly. The other is that, in a manner akin to their impact on the regional population pattern, they have served essentially as a 'replacement' labour force, entering those jobs where, because of unattractive conditions of employment or a fall in demand, the numbers of indigenous employees are decreasing.[2]

A cursory glance at the data might encourage one to believe in the 'replacement' effect. Leaving aside the armed Forces, in fifteen of the occupations the number of male indigenous workers[3] decreased and in all

---

[1] An occupation which, on the basis of all immigrant workers, has a high concentration ratio, thanks to the presence of large numbers of Irish.

[2] Some confusion between occupations and industries is evident in writings on this topic, e.g. Wright referring to other work in *The Coloured Worker in British Industry*, p. 41.

[3] Defined as the total labour force less New Commonwealth workers.

but one of these, agriculture, the number of male New Commonwealth workers increased; in eight occupations the number of indigenous female workers declined, and in all but two of these, mining, and paper and printing, more coloured women were employed.

However, looking at the data in this way, the 'expanding occupation' effect receives as much, if not more, support. In all ten occupations where indigenous workers increased in number, more New Commonwealth workers were also employed: and, in the seventeen occupations where the number of female indigenous workers increased, the number of female coloured workers also rose.

A rather different test confirms that neither explanation is much stronger than the other. Those occupations where numbers decreased between 1961 and 1966 afforded employment to 50 per cent of the males and 17 per cent of the females in the New Commonwealth labour force, compared with 49 per cent of indigenous male workers and 12 per cent of indigenous female workers.[1] This contrasts with the regional picture where high concentrations of coloured immigrants (both those who entered Britain before 1961 and those who came in between 1961 and 1966) were found in those areas, the conurbations, that had experienced a fall in the total population, thereby confirming an appreciable replacement effect.

Both explanations are in fact very inadequate, at least during this period. The only generalisation that can be made is that, while the indigenous labour force has risen in some occupations and fallen in others, the New Commonwealth labour force, both male and female, has risen in virtually every occupation.[2] The impact of these New Commonwealth workers has been to reduce the loss of workers in declining occupations and to augment the increase in expanding occupations. In the case of males, in only two occupations, agricultural workers and administrators, was the New Commonwealth employment index below that of the indigenous labour force; in the case of females there were only three such instances, agricultural and administrative workers again, together with paper and printing workers.

Thus New Commonwealth immigration in this period, while it had a sort of 'scale' effect—across-the-board additions to the occupational labour forces—had remarkably little impact on the pattern of occupational

[1] Still another way of looking at the data suggests the same conclusion: that neither explanation is superior to the other. In the case of neither males nor females are rises or falls in the size of the occupational labour force associated with a relatively large or small number of occasions where the increase in the New Commonwealth labour force is above or below average.

[2] Leaving aside the armed Forces, the exceptions are males in agricultural jobs and female crane drivers.

Chart 5. *Changes in the occupational pattern, 1961–6*

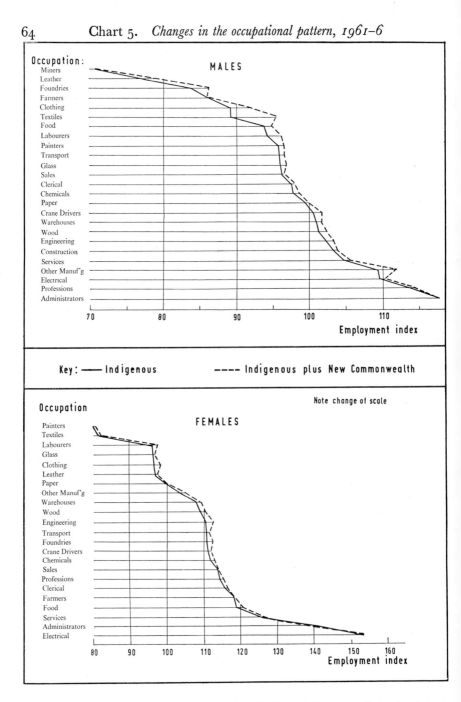

SOURCES: *Census 1961, Occupation Tables, Industry Tables* and *Commonwealth Immigrants in the Conurbations; Sample Census 1966, Economic Activity Tables* and *Commonwealth Immigrant Tables.*

labour force changes. This can be seen clearly from chart 5 in which, for males and females, the occupational employment indices inclusive and exclusive of New Commonwealth workers are compared.[1] The significance of these indices should not be underrated. We are dealing with a change in the British labour force to which, in terms of numbers of workers, the New Commonwealth immigrants contributed more than a fifth. That this contribution apparently had such a small impact on the occupational pattern of labour force changes is rather unexpected,[2] and must rank as one of the major conclusions of this study.

No single explanation of high or low concentrations of New Commonwealth workers in the occupations identified above suggests itself immediately. Even so, the data do encourage one or two generalisations. First and foremost, whilst the occupations with high immigrant concentration ratios and those with low ones are by no means identical for New Commonwealth males and females, quite a few of them recur to a surprising extent. Among the high concentration occupations, textile and clothing workers, labourers and other manufacturing workers seem to be of general importance. And miners, farmers and sales workers are found among the low concentration occupations for both men and women. This impression is to some extent reinforced by rank correlation coefficients calculated between the male and female occupational concentration ratios: $+0.65$ in 1961 (or $+0.69$ if textiles, where the switch from a female to a male labour force shows up rather dramatically in the male and female concentration ratios, are excluded), but, in 1966, $+0.49$ (or $+0.58$ if textiles are excluded). Secondly, the relative frequency of manufacturing sector jobs, textile and clothing, labouring, metal and other manufacturing occupations, is enough to qualify conventional ideas about immigrant occupations, which are often thought to be mainly in non-manufacturing sectors.

Thirdly, one or two special considerations, particular to individual occupations, spring to mind as possible explanations of relatively high concentrations of coloured workers: both textile and clothing jobs are widely regarded as low paid and, in addition, the recent large-scale adoption of shift work in the textile industry has created a demand for male workers which has been largely met by New Commonwealth immigrants, especially Asians; labouring jobs are not only relatively

---

[1] The armed Forces and 'inadequately described' groups are excluded from both diagrams and, also, construction workers and miners from that for females. Indigenous workers, it should be noted, are defined as all members of the labour force other than New Commonwealth workers.

[2] As can be seen, the New Commonwealth arrivals appear to have had a substantial structural effect on changes in the occupational pattern of the British labour force only in the case of male textile workers.

badly paid but also demand little skill—a feature thought to be charac-
teristic of New Commonwealth workers; and the arduousness and
unpleasantness of much foundry work may help to explain the relatively
high concentrations in these jobs of newcomers to the labour force. In the
case of the low concentration occupations, the urban location of most New
Commonwealth workers rules out agricultural and mining jobs, and
prejudice may explain their low concentrations among sales workers.

It is clear, however, that the examination of New Commonwealth
concentrations in occupations more finely classified would help to explain
their choice of jobs. It would, in addition, throw more light on the
absolute size of New Commonwealth concentrations in those jobs where
they bulk largest. New Commonwealth concentrations can be calculated
for a finer occupational classification in the case of workers in the conurbations in 1961.[1] Using these data, it proved possible to isolate twenty-
nine, rather finely prescribed, occupations, in which New Commonwealth
workers formed more than 3 per cent of the labour force in question,
compared with 2.1 per cent of all persons economically active in the conurbations.[2] These occupations accounted for 41 per cent of the economically active New Commonwealth workers in the conurbations—39 per
cent of the males and 49 per cent of the females—and since 73 per cent
of the economically active immigrants from the New Commonwealth
resided in the conurbations, 30 per cent of all New Commonwealth
workers in Great Britain in 1961 were covered.

Even when allowance is made for any underenumeration, it seems
highly unlikely that, in the two occupations where the concentrations
were largest, railway guards and foundry labourers, they constituted
more than a fifth of the labour forces in these jobs in 1961. Despite the
fact that these occupations were chosen for their high immigrant proportions, it is very improbable that the labour forces of many of them
contained more than 10 per cent of New Commonwealth workers in that
year. Of course, the more recent the year and the finer the job classification, the greater the chance of finding higher concentrations. The 1966
Sample Census reveals that male coloured workers comprised as much as
26 per cent of the winders and reelers (textiles) labour force, and in all
there were nine occupations with concentrations of over 10 per cent—a
level which New Commonwealth females failed to reach in any occupa-

---

[1] Subsequent to the research for this study the 1966 Sample Census yielded a fine occupational classification of New Commonwealth workers on a national basis (see below, p. 67 n.1).

[2] Not all occupations where New Commonwealth workers constituted more than 3 per
cent of the labour force are necessarily covered, but the most important, in terms of numbers
employed, are. The selection procedure comprised two stages: the identification of those
jobs in which more than 500 New Commonwealth immigrants were employed in the conurbations in 1961, and a screening of these by the 3 per cent criterion.

tion.[1] And if we look not at medical practitioners in 1961 but at hospital doctors in 1968, we discover that 18 per cent were born overseas,[2] many of them in the New Commonwealth.

However, the main purpose of this section is to consider possible explanations for relatively high concentrations of coloured workers in these jobs. It does not attempt to explain the complete occupational pattern of these workers which, in any case as we have seen, departs relatively little from the indigenous pattern, and is presumably shaped to a large extent by the factors determining the indigenous pattern. Nor does it attempt to show why, in some jobs, coloured workers constitute significantly less than average proportions of the labour force. It should be noted, however, that the high concentration occupations were basically the same for both 1961 and 1966.

It is perhaps natural to enquire first whether the employment situation in these jobs differed systematically from that in other occupations. An attempt was therefore made to compare with the average for all jobs, job availability, as measured by the ratios of vacancies to unemployment, in the high concentration occupations.[3] The vacancy-unemployment

[1] The 1966 Sample Census revealed the following twenty-six coloured male concentrations of 5 per cent or more: winders and reelers, 26 per cent; spinners, doublers and twisters, 22 per cent; foundry labourers, 18 per cent; fibre preparers, 13 per cent; hand and machine sewers, 13 per cent; tailors and dressmakers, 12 per cent; cooks, 11 per cent; bus conductors, 10 per cent; waiters, 10 per cent; textile workers n.e.c., 10 per cent; medical practitioners, 10 per cent; railway guards, 10 per cent; textile labourers, 9 per cent; rubber workers, 8 per cent; porters, 8 per cent; plastics workers, 8 per cent; engineering labourers, 8 per cent; kitchen hands, 8 per cent; deck ratings, 8 per cent; male nurses, 7 per cent; moulders and coremakers, 7 per cent; machine tool operators, 7 per cent; press workers, 6 per cent; weavers, 6 per cent; glass labourers, 6 per cent; and foundry metal workers, 5 per cent. In six occupations, female New Commonwealth workers formed more than 4 per cent of the female labour force: hospital orderlies, 7 per cent; nurses, 6 per cent; machine tool operators, 5 per cent; hand and machine sewers, 4 per cent; engineering labourers, 4 per cent; and tailors, 4 per cent. These occupations were identified from among those jobs in which more than a thousand New Commonwealth workers of the relevant sex were employed.

[2] Including 63 per cent of senior house officers, 51 per cent of registrars and 42 per cent of house officers (post-registration), see *Sunday Times*, 27 October 1968.

[3] It was possible to obtain information relating to vacancies and unemployment in seventeen of the selected male occupations and ten of the female occupations with an exact or reasonable degree of correspondence. The male occupations (with the corresponding census occupation title in brackets where different) are: moulders and coremakers, machine tool operators, miscellaneous engineering workers (press workers), carpenters and joiners, boot and shoe makers (leather workers), other textile workers (textile fibre preparers), bespoke tailoring workers (tailors), workers in food manufacture (bakers), rubber workers, plastics workers, railway workers (railway porters and guards), public service vehicle drivers and conductors (bus conductors), seamen, kitchen staff (cooks and kitchen hands), waiters, laundry and dry cleaning workers, labourers. The female occupations are: machine tool operators, miscellaneous engineering workers (press workers), boot and shoe makers (leather workers), bespoke tailoring workers (tailors), light clothing machinists (clothing sewers), plastics workers, public service vehicle drivers and conductors (bus conductors), kitchen staff (cooks and kitchen hands), waitresses, laundry and dry cleaning workers.

ratios for these occupations were compared with the male ratios of eighty-four other occupations and the female ratios of fifty-four other occupations. The results of the comparison, which was made for both 1961 and 1966,[1] are given in table 16.

Table 16.   *A comparison of employment situations in high concentration and other occupations, 1961 and 1966*

Vacancy-unemployment ratio	Males				Females			
	1961		1966		1961		1966	
	High concentration	Other	High concentration	Other	High concentration	Other	High concentration	Other
Up to 0.49	5	21	3	8	—	10	—	2
0.50 to 0.99	6	23	—	21	1	13	—	4
1.00 to 1.49	3	16	6	13	4	11	—	7
1.50 to 1.99	1	10	2	10	2	8	—	5
2.00 to 2.99	—	6	3	15	2	6	1	15
3.00 and over	2	8	3	17	1	6	9	21
Total	17	84	17	84	10	54	10	54
Mean ratio (unweighted)	*2.74*	*1.42*	*3.43*	*2.33*	*1.93*	*1.42*	*5.22*	*3.24*

SOURCE: *Statistics on Incomes, Prices, Employment and Production.*

There is some tendency, if not a very pronounced one, for New Commonwealth workers to form larger concentrations of labour in those occupations where the demand for labour is stronger. For males and females, both at the beginning and end of the period, the average vacancy-unemployment ratio is greater in the occupations with high New Commonwealth concentrations than in the others. However, this is by no means a clear cut effect in that the high concentration jobs coincide precisely with the high labour demand jobs, or even in the sense that the high concentration jobs are all to be found in the group of high labour demand jobs—a situation approached only by the female occupations in 1966. For males, in both years, there is much overlap between the vacancy-unemployment distributions of high concentration and other

[1] Department of Employment and Productivity, *Statistics on Incomes, Prices, Employment and Production*, various issues, H.M.S.O., London (quarterly). More precisely, the ratios for December 1961 and June 1962 were averaged for the earlier date, and those for June and December 1966 for the later year. This procedure was adopted to minimise seasonal influences on the occupational vacancy-unemployment pattern. Since data for June 1961 were not available on the same basis, those for June 1962 were substituted.

occupations. That is, there are many high vacancy-unemployment ratios in jobs where New Commonwealth concentration ratios are not large, and there are high New Commonwealth concentrations among jobs where the vacancy-unemployment ratio is below average. Indeed, in the case of males, the average vacancy-unemployment ratio is rather misleading. For in 1961, apart from two occupations, the ratios in the high concentration jobs were all towards the lower end of the scale. The two exceptions were railway workers and public service vehicle drivers and conductors, with huge ratios of 18.7 and 17.2 respectively.[1] Leaving these two jobs out of account, the average vacancy-unemployment ratio for the remaining fifteen high concentration jobs was only 0.7—much below that of other occupations. By 1966 the acute shortage of railway workers seems to have been much reduced (the vacancy-unemployment ratio having fallen to 2.9), but that for public service vehicle drivers and conductors had become even more pronounced, yielding an enormous vacancy-unemployment ratio of 31.6.[2] Leaving this occupation out of account, the vacancy-unemployment ratio for the remaining sixteen high concentration jobs was 1.7, once more below the average for other occupations.

An attempt to identify the skill levels of the specific occupations where New Commonwealth workers displayed highest concentrations, whilst bedevilled by the essential subjectiveness of the task, tends to confirm the view that, compared with the indigenous labour force, a relatively large number of coloured workers are to be found in less skilled occupations. The presence among high concentration occupations of as many as six specifically labelled 'labourer' as well as the lesser skilled service occupations—conductors, porters, waiters, kitchen hands and hospital orderlies—tends to confirm 'the tendency of immigrants to enter the lower reaches of the [occupational] pyramid.'[3]

At least one of the accepted explanations of this occupational impact is not valid in the case of the New Commonwealth workers in Britain, if indeed it ever is: 'Persons situated in the upper portions of the occupation pyramid of an emigrant-sending country are less likely to emigrate than those situated in the lower portions because they have relatively less to gain and more to lose by emigrating.'[4] The extent to which the British health service has gained from workers at the apex of the New Commonwealth occupational pyramid shows that they may well have much more

---

[1] The only other ratio reaching double figures in 1961 was that for miners (14.9), a job which, for locational reasons, attracts very few New Commonwealth workers.
[2] Again the only other double figure score, 19.7, was registered for miners.
[3] Spengler, 'Effects Produced in Receiving Countries by Pre-1939 Immigration', in *The Economics of International Migration*, p. 29.
[4] Ibid.

inducement and opportunity to migrate to Britain than less skilled workers.

Certainly, however, there is substance in the explanation which lies in the linguistic and educational shortcomings of New Commonwealth immigrants.[1] But whilst it is widely accepted that, because of inferior facilities, the general level of education attained by New Commonwealth immigrants is below that of the indigenous population, this is an impression which again proves difficult to substantiate. In Davison's view, 'the general level of education (of Jamaican migrants) is, inevitably, somewhat lower—perhaps considerably lower—than the comparable English school standards'.[2] 1961 Census data revealed that 80 per cent of males in the County of London finished their education prior to their sixteenth birthday, compared with 76 per cent of Jamaicans, 63 per cent of other Caribbean immigrants, 34 per cent of Pakistanis and a mere 24 per cent of Indians, but school-leaving age is an unreliable measure of educational standards in comparisons with countries where factors other than age may have a major effect on educational progress.

Perhaps the explanation which, in the present context, has the truest ring is: 'When a country of provenance is economically and technologically less advanced than a country of destination, the occupational structure of the migrants tends to be inferior to that obtaining in the immigrant-receiving country.'[3] In short, the jobs which migrants enter depend very much on those they have left—and these tend to be unskilled. The evidence suggests that this statement can be applied, at least, to West Indian immigrants. For large numbers of them were from the ranks of the chronically unemployed, in which event they are unlikely to possess any skills, or from unskilled occupations.[4] Such migrants would seem to be predestined, initially at least, for unskilled employment in the United Kingdom. A third major group which has swelled the ranks of migrants moving into unskilled occupations in Britain are those previously engaged in agricultural pursuits in the West Indies. The interesting feature of this, quite substantial, group of migrants is that there appears to be no record of any taking up agricultural employment in Britain.[5] If nothing else, the migration of West Indians to Britain falls into the traditional mould in that it represents, essentially, a shift from rural to urban activities and surrounds. Whatever the reason, after a careful consideration of the whole range of piecemeal evidence concerning coloured

---

[1] Ibid.

[2] *West Indian Migrants*, p. 19.

[3] Spengler, loc. cit. p. 29.

[4] Davison, *West Indian Migrants*, pp. 19–23.

[5] Davison draws attention to this, see *West Indian Migrants*, pp. 19–23, and *Black British*, pp. 67–75.

immigrants' industrial skills, Wright concludes that, 'West Indian immigrants are in general less skilled than native British workers,' and that, 'such evidence as there is indicates that Indian and Pakistani immigrants are, on the whole, less skilled than West Indian immigrants'.[1]

Whilst migration from the New Commonwealth might add proportionately more to the stock of unskilled than of skilled workers, it would be quite wrong to think of it as consisting wholly of unskilled labour. Two significant streams of skills from the New Commonwealth can be distinguished: additions to the medical, nursing and teaching professions; and, perhaps less widely appreciated, an inflow of migrants into certain skilled and semi-skilled manual occupations.

Each of these flows has its own special features. Professional workers come much more from Asia than the West Indies. This movement is perverse in the sense that the most needed international flow of skills is from industrialised to developing countries to aid the latter in their development quest; indeed, a decade or so ago, the possibility of a drain of skilled manpower from developing countries had barely been envisaged.[2] It is generally thought to consist of short-stay immigrants, and in so far as this is the case, the developing countries should gain in the long term from improvements in the skills of their migrants. However, it is not at all certain that this flow constitutes a supply of skills on which the British economy can rely permanently. There is some apprehension that a combination of new United States immigration laws and higher American salaries may deflect, away from Britain, foreign-born doctors—a group that currently constitutes an important proportion of all junior hospital doctors in this country.[3]

Concentrations of New Commonwealth workers in some skilled and semi-skilled manual occupations reflect to a considerable degree their possession of these skills prior to arrival in Britain. There is a repetition of certain occupations in both the lists of previous West Indian jobs drawn up by Davison and those derived from the British population census and presented above, especially carpenters, tailors and seamen.[4] The New Commonwealth contribution to the labour force in these jobs, lying as it does in the range between unskilled labourers and skilled workers, is often overlooked.

A question which automatically springs to mind in the context of the

---

[1] *The Coloured Workers in British Industry*, p. 40. It should be emphasised that Wright was not considering service workers. Also, in terms of the skill levels of the actual jobs taken by Asians and West Indians, there appears to be little difference between the two groups (ibid. pp. 83–4).

[2] See, for example, Thomas, *International Migration and Economic Development*, pp. 39 et seq.

[3] *The Economist*, 6 August 1968, p. 44.

[4] *West Indian Migrants*, p. 20.

F

occupational distribution of New Commonwealth workers is whether earnings in the jobs where they display above-average concentrations are below the average level. Important as the question is, it is one which it is almost impossible to answer other than impressionistically. The reason for this is the absence of earnings data on an appropriate occupational basis. The April and October surveys carried out by the Department of Employment and Productivity yield earnings only for industries, and such data are of little use for estimating immigrant earnings, since it may well be that the wages of New Commonwealth immigrants in a given industry are significantly below the industry average.[1] A series of special enquiries inaugurated by the Department yield some occupational earnings data but, as yet, these are limited to the engineering, metal, chemical and construction sectors. As this study was being completed, the results of a more comprehensive sample survey of earnings in September 1968 made an appearance.[2] The survey related to about 90 thousand workers, chosen by a sample of national insurance cards, for whom details were provided by employers. Although the results are available on an occupational basis, the job classification is unfortunately such that it is impossible to identify more than a handful of our census selected occupations.

Indeed, the only systematic information on occupational remuneration for which the necessary identification can be made, consists of the wage rates, not earnings, of manual workers prescribed in voluntary collective agreements or statutory wage regulation orders, collected by the Department of Employment and Productivity and presented in detail in *Time Rates of Wages and Hours of Work* and, in more summary fashion, in *Statistics on Incomes, Prices, Employment and Production.* Unfortunately these wage rate data are also unsuitable for a comparison of earnings in jobs where New Commonwealth workers form above-average concentrations with other occupations. Because of variations in the extent of wage 'drift' between jobs, the occupational pattern of basic wage rates cannot be accepted even as an approximate reflection of the pattern of occupational earnings.[3] Moreover, even if this difficulty could be avoided, problems would be posed in connection with the establishment of an 'average wage rate' for comparison with the rates in the chosen occupations.

We must reluctantly resort to an impressionistic assessment of the earnings characteristics of the high concentration occupations. The larger concentrations of New Commonwealth workers are to be found, for

---

[1] The inter-industry differences in the earnings of a given occupation are likely to be much smaller.

[2] Department of Employment and Productivity, *Employment and Productivity Gazette,* May 1969.

[3] They can, however, be used for other purposes, see chapter 9, pp. 152–4.

the most part, in occupations where earnings are low. In particular, it seems that a relatively large proportion of New Commonwealth workers are employed in unskilled occupations—jobs that are known to pay low wages. A sample survey of Jamaican immigrants revealed that, in 1962, Jamaican males were earning nearly 30 per cent less than the average for all male manual workers in Britain, and females some 20 per cent less than the average for all females. There is some evidence that this gap has narrowed since. By 1966 average earnings of all male manual workers were £20 a week. In the same year the average take-home pay of West Indians in a sample survey in Manchester[1] was £14 16s. a week; adjusting the 'take-home' concept to an average earnings basis would increase this to £16 10s. to £17 a week, or about 15 to 18 per cent below the average for Britain. Part of this difference would be accounted for by the fact that earnings in the North West are probably some 3.5 per cent below the average for England and Wales.

Wright repeats Senior's contention that 'the employment available to coloured workers was in the lower paid and "dead-end" jobs in industries where the value of output was low',[2] but broadens this to cover jobs that are 'dead-end' for any reason, in support of the replacement effect of coloured immigrants.[3] Even where New Commonwealth immigrants find themselves in a well paid occupation, they tend to be concentrated in the lower grades, receiving salaries below the average for the profession as a whole. It has already been pointed out that immigrant doctors form substantial proportions of junior and the less well paid categories of hospital doctors: while about 52 per cent of British-born hospital doctors are consultants, only 15 per cent of immigrant hospital doctors are in this group; in sharp contrast, 22 per cent of British-born but 67 per cent of immigrant hospital doctors are senior house officers or registrars.

THE INDUSTRIAL DISTRIBUTION OF THE IMMIGRANT LABOUR FORCE

When examining the occupational distribution of immigrants we were at some pains to show, by means of comparisons with actual and certain hypothetical distributions, that, taken all round, the New Commonwealth-indigenous differences are not really very large. At this stage we can, in addition, compare immigrant-indigenous differences in the industrial distribution of the labour force with the occupational differences. Such

---

[1] See below, chapter 5.
[2] C. Senior, 'Race Relations and Labor Supply in Great Britain', Paper for the American Sociological Society, Detroit, 1956, referred to in Wright, *The Coloured Worker in British Industry*, p. 47.
[3] See above, pp. 62–5.

a comparison is needed not merely to set the industrial differences in some sort of perspective, but also because of the intrinsic interest that attaches to the interrelationship between occupational and industrial distributions. The mean deviation has again been used to make the necessary comparisons between the distributions of the various labour forces set out in appendix table 3.

Table 17. *A comparison of the 1961 and 1966 industrial distributions of the immigrant labour force*

	Males	Females	*Mean deviations* Males and females
All immigrants	0.35	0.29	0.28
New Commonwealth	0.75	0.38	0.62
India and Pakistan	1.36	0.42	1.18
British Caribbean	0.54	0.57	0.46
Other	0.46	0.55	0.39
Total labour force	0.36	0.32	0.34

SOURCES: Appendix tables 3.1, 3.2, 3.3.

The comparison of the 1961 and 1966 industrial distributions, given in the form of mean deviations in table 17, reveals that the distributions for each of the three New Commonwealth groups were rather less stable over time than the occupational distributions of the indigenous labour force. For male workers, the least stable distribution was that for the Asians (the very large rise in this labour force being accompanied by a substantial shift in its distribution from services to metals and textiles); and among female New Commonwealth workers the least stable were the West Indians. Corresponding data presented in table 15 show that exactly the same statements can be made about the temporal stability of the occupational distributions. Indeed the extent to which the industrial and occupational distributions changed during the period was very similar, although the New Commonwealth industrial distributions appear to be rather more stable than the occupational distributions, and the indigenous industrial distributions tend to be less stable than the occupational distributions.

More to the heart of the matter is a consideration of the differences between the indigenous and immigrant industrial distributions. Examination of the relevant mean deviations for males, given in table 18, shows that, in 1961, differences between immigrant and indigenous industrial distributions were least marked for the Asian workers; the result was the same for both years in the occupational comparison. By 1966, however, there was little to choose, in terms of contrast with the indigenous industrial distribution, between the three New Commonwealth groups. The overall difference between the New Commonwealth and indigenous industrial distributions, 1.6 in 1961 and 1.8 in 1966, appears to be a little more pronounced than the occupational contrasts especially in the latter year (the occupational mean deviation values in 1961 and 1966 being 1.5 and 1.4), but can hardly be considered large alongside possible values, hypothetical and otherwise, cited in the section concerned with the occupational distributions.

Table 18. *A comparison of the industrial distributions of the indigenous and immigrant labour forces*

	Males		Females		*Mean deviations* Males and females	
	1961	1966	1961	1966	1961	1966
All immigrants	1.26	1.15	1.53	1.24	1.30	1.12
New Commonwealth	1.63	1.83	1.80	1.93	1.55	1.65
India and Pakistan	1.80	2.25	1.60	1.25	1.58	1.94
British Caribbean	2.07	2.14	2.84	2.75	2.19	2.22
Other	2.39	2.20	2.27	1.89	2.25	2.00

SOURCES: Appendix tables 3.1, 3.2, 3.3.

In both years, the smallest female industrial contrasts were registered for Asians and the largest for West Indians, again repeating the occupational picture. The size of the overall contrast—mean deviations between the female New Commonwealth and indigenous distributions of 1.8 in 1961 and 1.9 in 1966—was almost identical with the occupational contrast—1.7 in 1961 and 1.9 in 1966—although the industrial difference was rather sharper than the occupational difference in the case of West Indian women and closer to the indigenous distribution in the case of Asian women.

Thus, taking males and females together, there was a rather larger New Commonwealth-indigenous industrial difference (1.55 in 1961 and 1.65 in 1966) than occupational difference (1.35 in 1961 and 1.45 in 1966), but the distinction is not at all substantial and the absolute size of the industrial mean deviations, like the occupational deviations, cannot be considered large. Moreover, the general observations made in connection with the occupational distributions all apply in the context of the industrial distributions: that indigenous-immigrant differences appear to be more pronounced for New Commonwealth females than for males; that indigenous-immigrant differences are rather sharper in the case of the New Commonwealth labour force than for all immigrants; and that within the New Commonwealth group the West Indian differences are more clear cut than the Asian differences.

As with occupations therefore, it can hardly be claimed that the industrial distribution of immigrant workers is very different from that of the labour force as a whole. It is tempting to assume that this apparent absence of pronounced differences between the indigenous and New Commonwealth industrial distributions is merely a reflection of the degree of similarity, observed in the preceding section, in their occupational distributions. Such a supposition would, however, be very misleading. Many industries provide employment in a large variety of occupations, and it is possible for two groups of workers with identical occupational distributions to display very different industrial patterns; that is, to have very different occupation-industry matrices. That the industrial distributions of New Commonwealth and indigenous workers are fairly similar suggests not only that their occupational distributions must be akin—a fact verified in the previous section—but also that their occupation-industry matrices must be quite similar (see appendix A).

That differences between the occupation-industry matrices for immigrants and for the indigenous population do little to give rise to differences in their industrial distributions is as significant and surprising as the small size, and effect on industrial distribution differences, of the contrast between their occupational distributions. Little seems to be known about the nature and significance of occupation-industry matrices, but it is probable that two influences do most to cause variations between the matrices of any two groups in the labour force: differences in the geographical location of the two groups, and a combination of the industrial pattern of growth and the timing of their entry into the labour market. A claim that the occupation-industry matrices of the indigenous and New Commonwealth labour forces differ little is tantamount to saying that any differences in the location and time of entry to the labour force of these two groups have little effect on their industrial distribution. In fact it seems to be true that, despite significant contrasts (compared with the indigenous labour force) in both the location and time of entry to the labour force of New Commonwealth workers, neither factor has operated in such a way as to yield much of a deviation of their industrial distribution from that of the indigenous labour force.[1]

---

[1] For a demonstration that the contribution of the special features of New Commonwealth workers' locational pattern to differences in their industrial distribution is small, see appendix B. Confirmation that the timing of their entry into the labour force and the concurrent pattern of industrial expansion were of little more significance in shaping the industrial distribution of New Commonwealth workers must await the examination of changes in the industrial labour force pattern in the period 1961-6.

Chart 6. *New Commonwealth industrial concentration ratios, 1966*   77

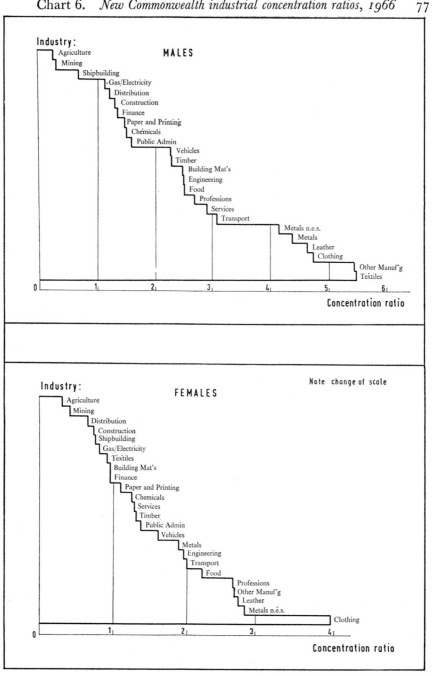

SOURCE: *Sample Census 1966, Economic Activity Tables* and *Commonwealth Immigrant Tables.*

The industrial distribution data can be presented and examined in the form of concentration ratios and these are shown in chart 6. Perhaps not surprisingly, in view of the fact that occupational differences play a significant role in determining what little contrast exists between the industrial distributions of the indigenous and New Commonwealth labour forces, the size and pattern of these differences broadly resemble those noted for the occupational divergencies. The profiles of the concentration ratios of male and female New Commonwealth workers are of the category displayed in chart 4D, both leaning towards the sub-type depicted in chart 4E. That is, the majority of New Commonwealth workers are employed in industries where the concentration ratios fall within a relatively narrow band around the average. In 1966, as many as 77 per cent of coloured male workers were employed in industries where the concentration ratios varied from $\frac{1}{2}$ per cent to a little over 3 per cent, and 89 per cent of coloured female workers were employed in sectors where the concentration ratios ranged between the same limits. New Commonwealth workers appear to have no more substantial impact on the industrial than on the occupational distribution of the labour force, in the sense that few of them are in industries where they form disproportionately large or small proportions of the work force.

In no industry in 1961 did New Commonwealth males or females form more than 3 per cent of the labour force. By 1966, concentrations had risen appreciably but, at this level at least, even then could hardly be considered large. In the case of males none exceeded $5\frac{1}{2}$ per cent, and in only six industries—textiles, other manufacturing, clothing, leather, metals, metals not elsewhere specified—was the ratio higher than 4 per cent. No New Commonwealth female ratio was greater than 4 per cent, and only in five industries—clothing, metals, leather, other manufacturing, professional services—did it exceed $2\frac{1}{2}$ per cent. Underenumeration means that in some industries these ratios understate the true concentrations.

A finer industrial classification reveals instances of appreciably larger New Commonwealth concentrations,[1] but even at this level, there were no concentrations larger than 7 per cent in 1961, and only four greater than 5 per cent. Indeed, it would seem that the higher industrial concentration ratios do not attain the values of the higher occupational ratios, a difference

[1] The method used to isolate these industries is the same as that used for selecting occupations employing relatively large numbers of New Commonwealth workers. On the basis of 1961 Census data, those industries were identified which gave employment to more than 500 of the New Commonwealth immigrants in the conurbations, and in which these workers constituted a relatively large proportion of the labour force, in this case $2\frac{1}{2}$ per cent or more. Applying these criteria twenty-four industries emerge, accounting for 39 per cent of all the New Commonwealth workers employed in the conurbations.

not apparent when industrial and occupational concentrations are considered at a more aggregated level. As many as ten concentration ratios
among the selected occupations were larger than the highest value, 6.6
in the dress, lingerie and underwear industry.[1] Again, 1966 Census data
reveal larger industrial concentrations of coloured workers, but only one,
of 11 per cent for coloured males in the woollen worsted trade, was
greater than 10 per cent, which contrasts with the appreciably more
numerous occupational concentrations found at this level.[2] Of course, a
still finer classification of activities—say by firm or establishment—would
reveal yet higher concentrations of New Commonwealth workers. The
medical services again illustrate the point: while 10 per cent of the
national hospital domestic staff were coloured in 1969, the proportion in
the London teaching hospitals was as high as 37 per cent.[3]

As in the case of the occupational distributions there is an association
between high male and high female concentration ratios, and between low
male and low female ratios. Other manufacturing, clothing, leather,
metals, transport and professional services are high ranking in both lists;
and to the low ranking agriculture and mining, can be added, for both
male and female New Commonwealth workers, shipbuilding, construction, the public utilities and distribution. A rank correlation coefficient
of +0.79 between the twenty-four male and female concentration ratios
confirms this relationship in a more general way; if textiles, which is at
the top of the New Commonwealth male list but eighteenth for females,
is left out of account, the coefficient is +0.91.[4]

A glance at the high and low ranking occupational ratios and the high
and low ranking industrial ratios confirms that occupational differences

---

[1] It is also significant that we were obliged to apply a criterion of 2½ per cent, not 3 per cent,
to obtain a list of high concentration industries comparable in size with the list of high
concentration occupations.

[2] Twenty-three trade concentration ratios for coloured males were higher than 4 per cent
(compare the 5 per cent cut-off applied to occupations) in 1966: woollen worsted, 11 per
cent; dresses, 10 per cent; man-made fibres, 9 per cent; iron castings, 9 per cent; women's
outwear, 8 per cent; rubber, 7 per cent; sea transport, 7 per cent; motor cycles, 7 per cent;
catering, 6 per cent; nuts and bolts, 6 per cent; plastics, 6 per cent; steel tubes, 6 per cent;
light metals, 6 per cent; copper and brass, 5 per cent; men's and boys' wear, 5 per cent;
weaving, 5 per cent; hairdressing, 5 per cent; accountancy, 5 per cent; road passenger
transport, 4 per cent; medical services, 4 per cent; metal industries n.e.s., 4 per cent; air
transport, 4 per cent; and railways, 4 per cent. Female workers in the New Commonwealth
community constituted more than 4 per cent of the female labour force in: women's outwear,
7 per cent; dresses, 7 per cent; medical services, 5 per cent; and railways, 5 per cent. These
proportions were derived after isolating those trades employing more than a thousand
coloured male or female workers.

[3] T. F. W. MacKeown, *Hospital Domestic Management Survey*, Hospital Domestic Administrators Association, London, 1968.

[4] A special explanation applies to this industry: the movement, in this period, to shift
working and the consequent swing away from women and in favour of male workers.

between indigenous and immigrant workers have played an important role in shaping those industrial differences that exist. Nevertheless it has been suggested that location, and perhaps the pattern of industrial growth at the time of the immigrants' arrival, also have roles to play in shaping these differences.

Within a given range of occupations, it is plausible that a group of workers will tend to be concentrated in those industries which were expanding when they entered the labour force. In fact, a comparison of the concentration ratios with labour force changes suggests that there is no such general effect in the case of New Commonwealth immigrants. We noted that the six industries with the highest male concentrations in 1966 were textiles, other manufacturing, clothing, leather, metals, and metals not elsewhere specified. Between 1961 and 1966 increases in the sizes of the indigenous labour forces in these industries were hardly bunched towards the upper end of the scale: ranking respectively sixteenth, third, tenth, nineteenth, twentieth and sixth from the largest increase, they were spread fairly evenly through the range of rises. Similarly, the six industries with the highest concentrations of New Commonwealth females (clothing, metals not elsewhere specified, leather, other manufacturing, professional services and food) experienced indigenous labour force rises twenty-second, sixteenth, twentieth, eleventh, fifth and twelfth from the highest respectively—again spread fairly evenly throughout the range.

By the same token—a wide variety of changes in the labour forces where coloured concentrations are high—there would seem to be little validity in the opposite thesis, the replacement effect: a tendency for New Commonwealth workers to replace indigenous workers in industries which, for some reason, the latter are quitting.[1] Peach, inspecting changes in the industrial pattern of the labour force in the period 1951 to 1961, thought he could discern such an effect.[2] Yet for neither males nor females does a comparison of the New Commonwealth and indigenous labour force indices suggest that there is a noticeable positive or negative relationship between the industrial patterns of immigrant and indigenous labour force changes. This impression is supported by the low values of the rank correlation coefficients: $+0.29$ for males and -0.15 for females.[3]

Changes in the industrial pattern of employment reinforce the conclusion reached in the discussion of occupational patterns: that in this

---

[1] See above, pp. 62–5.

[2] His industrial analysis led him to write: 'The conclusion seems clear that the majority of West Indians who were employed in England and Wales were in jobs which the white population was leaving or which could not attract sufficient white labour.' (*West Indian Migration to Britain*, p. 75.)

[3] The female correlation coefficient is obtained for the twenty-three industries, excluding shipbuilding where no coloured female employment was recorded in 1961.

Chart 7. *Changes in the industrial pattern, 1961–6* 81

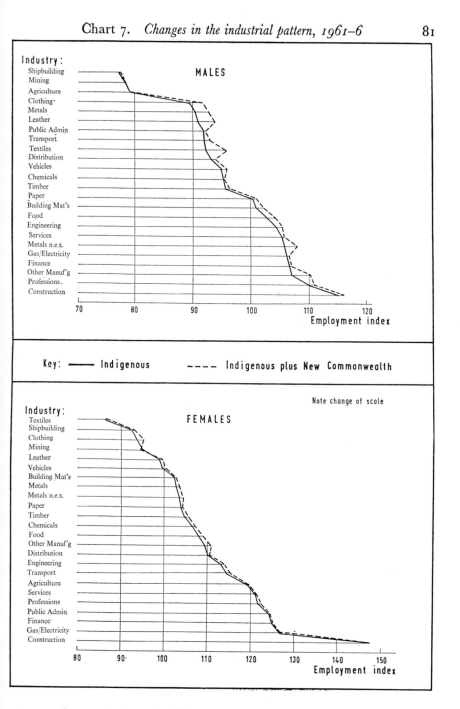

SOURCES: *Census 1961, Occupation Tables, Industry Tables* and *Commonwealth Immigrants in the Conurbations; Sample Census 1966, Economic Activity Tables* and *Commonwealth Immigrant Tables.*

period, New Commonwealth immigrants had essentially an across-the-board, scale effect on the British labour force, but did relatively little either to modify the existing occupational and industrial pattern or the manner in which it was changing. While in some industries the indigenous male and female labour forces increased and in others they fell, the New Commonwealth labour force registered a rise in virtually every activity, the exceptions being agriculture and shipbuilding for males, and mining for females. And in those industries where the indigenous labour force increased, the percentage rise in the New Commonwealth labour force was nearly always greater.[1]   Thus the impact of those immigrants was essentially, as in occupations, to reduce the loss of workers in industries where the labour force contracted and to augment the increase in expanding industries. This scale effect emerges very clearly in chart 7. Despite the large contribution which New Commonwealth workers made to the increase in the British labour force in the period 1961–6, its structural impact, even at the margin, was relatively small. The profile of industrial labour force changes inclusive of immigrant workers is represented broadly but simply by a horizontal displacement of the profile of the indigenous industrial labour force. Such structural impacts as can be discerned are rather more pronounced for males than for females and restricted to metals not elsewhere specified, textiles, clothing, metals and leather.

CONCLUSION

This has been a rather long and tortuous chapter, perhaps because its tendency to reveal only muted structural impacts prompted the authors to test the data at greater length in an attempt to unearth the effects which New Commonwealth immigrants are generally thought to have wrought on the occupational and industrial patterns of the British labour force. It is useful, therefore, to summarise its findings, and for this purpose the 1966 profiles of the regional, occupational and industrial concentration ratios have been standardised and are presented in chart 8.[2]

The profile of regional concentration ratios differs somewhat from those found for the occupational and industrial distributions. More than the others, it leans towards the type depicted in chart 4c, where most units

---

[1] An exception was construction, where the indigenous female labour force increased by 47 per cent and the New Commonwealth female labour force by 44 per cent. Also the male and female New Commonwealth labour forces in agriculture and mining respectively contracted rather more than their indigenous counterparts.

[2] Standardisation is achieved by expressing the concentration ratio of each unit as a proportion of the (unweighted) average ratio for the dimension—region, occupation, industry—in question. The profiles relate to male and female members of the New Commonwealth population and labour force.

Chart 8. *Profiles of standardised concentration ratios, 1966*

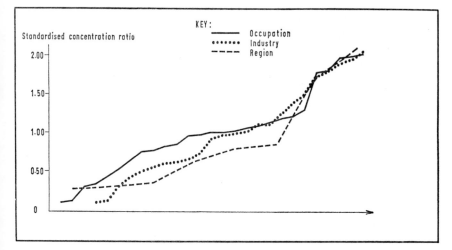

SOURCE: *Sample Census 1966, Economic Activity Tables* and *Commonwealth Immigrant Tables.*

contain only small proportions of immigrants, and one or two have relatively large concentrations. That is, it reflects a more extreme structural impact. Moreover, the difference as it is depicted tends to understate the true contrast between the regional distribution and the occupational and industrial distributions of New Commonwealth immigrants, since the former is measured for appreciably fewer units (ten regions) than the latter (twenty-seven occupations and twenty-four industries), and the finer the division the greater the frequency of regions, occupations or industries with high or low concentration ratios. The absence of economic concentrations as high as geographical concentrations may go far towards explaining 'the evidence that the level of social acceptance is higher in the works environment than in the community'.[1]

For the economist, major interest attaches to the industrial distribution of the New Commonwealth labour force, since it is the spread of coloured workers through the various industries which determines their impact on the output pattern of goods and services. It seems plausible that, in turn, their industrial distribution is largely determined by their occupational and regional distribution, and by the pattern of job opportunities existing when they arrived in Britain. In fact, however, the evidence examined in this chapter suggests that, in the period in question at least, none of the influences stemming from these three sources was such as to yield an industrial pattern for New Commonwealth workers that differed unduly

[1] Wright, *The Coloured Worker in British Industry*, p. 49.

from that of the indigenous labour force. On the basis of the standards applied, the occupational pattern of coloured workers was seen to be not markedly dissimilar from that of indigenous workers. Moreover, no general explanation was unearthed of the contrasts that do exist. Rather, certain immigrant-indigenous differences in skill levels, the earnings and vacancy characteristics of jobs and possibly employment discrimination,[1] all contributed in some degree to these, relatively small, differences.

However, differences between the regional distribution of New Commonwealth immigrants and the indigenous population are fairly pronounced. That no marked differences in the industrial distribution of coloured workers stem from this source is due to the fact that the industrial structure found in the areas where immigrants are concentrated (the conurbations) is not really very different from that found in the rest of the country; the difference between the industrial distributions of indigenous and New Commonwealth workers in the conurbations, relatively small as it is, tends to be larger than the differences, for both indigenous and immigrant workers, between the conurbation and other regional distributions.

The fact that newly arrived coloured immigrants contributed so much to the rise in the British labour force in the period 1961–6, also held out a promise of a significant impact on the development of the industrial pattern in this period. The evidence suggests that this was not fulfilled. Like the static effect, the more dynamic one proves to be rather flat. Newly arrived immigrant workers entered all activities, with the result that, in the sectors where the number of indigenous workers increased, the labour forces rose by even more thanks to the immigrants, and in sectors where the number of indigenous workers contracted, the labour forces declined by rather less as a result of the arrival of coloured workers.

The conclusion that immigrant workers are not highly concentrated in particular occupations or industries may come as a surprise, especially to people living in London who see a high concentration of coloured workers in transport. However, it would be very misleading to generalise from impressions of one industry to the situation as a whole. It is true that there is a high concentration of coloured workers in transport but it is not as high as people think, and it is only a small proportion of the total coloured people in employment. The rather negative economic conclusion may contain a very positive social implication. For it seems very likely that a policy for dispersing the location of the New Commonwealth community could be pursued without incurring economic costs in terms of a loss of a substantial structural impact on the pattern of industry. This chapter suggests that such a structural impact was never there to lose.

[1] As suggested by a degree of correlation between male and female concentration ratios.

CHAPTER 5

THE INCOME AND EXPENDITURE OF
NEW COMMONWEALTH IMMIGRANTS

There exists no set of national statistics which distinguishes between the income and expenditure of the indigenous population and of immigrants. This study, however, is fortunate in that its timing allows it to draw upon two surveys of New Commonwealth immigrants carried out during the course of 1966 and 1967 in Manchester and Birmingham. In both cases, some attempt was made to base the survey on a random sample of households in areas and streets where concentrations of the relevant ethnic groups were known to exist.[1] The coverage of the two surveys is shown in appendix table 4. The Birmingham survey, containing information relating to 920 New Commonwealth households, is appreciably larger than the Manchester survey from which information for only 199 households was usable in the present context:[2] indeed, in the case of the Manchester survey, the number of New Commonwealth households other than West Indian was so small that they have not been shown as a separate category. The composition of the 'New Commonwealth' differs sharply in these two surveys, four-fifths of the Manchester sample being West Indians and two-thirds of the Birmingham sample Asians.[3] This must be borne in mind when comparing the results of the two surveys, the most satisfactory direct comparison between them lying in the West Indian groups.

In this chapter, these surveys are used to try to discover whether the incomes and consumption of the indigenous population and New Commonwealth immigrants differ, and if so by how much. The first question which arises is the extent to which the incomes and expenditure of the households included in these surveys can be regarded as typical of all New Commonwealth immigrants. Several factors bear upon this: two of the most important being how representative the jobs are from which

[1] The Manchester survey was carried out by R. H. Ward, of the Department of Sociology, Manchester University, in conjunction with the National Institute of Economic and Social Research. A summary of the Birmingham survey, commissioned from R. Radburn by the Institute of Race Relations, 'Survey of Race Relations in Britain', was kindly made available by the Institute of Race Relations; it is analysed in some detail in Rose and Associates, Colour and Citizenship.
[2] The Manchester survey embraced ethnic groups other than the New Commonwealth, as well as thirty-nine 'mixed' New Commonwealth households, all of which are excluded from the tables in this chapter: in total it related to more than 400 households.
[3] Including the 'mixed' New Commonwealth households, two-thirds of the Manchester households were West Indian. Whilst the 199 Manchester households include some Africans, the Birmingham survey consisted entirely of West Indian, Indian and Pakistani households.

the earners in the samples draw their incomes; and differences between the sample households and the New Commonwealth population as a whole in certain basic household features—their composition in terms of children and adults, males and females, economically active and inactive.[1] These two factors are considered in turn.

First, it can be checked whether the occupational pattern, and by implication the average earnings, of the New Commonwealth immigrants in the two samples are more or less representative of the occupational structure of all New Commonwealth immigrants. The data from the two surveys were such that it was convenient to check this in terms of socio-economic characteristics, a classification based on employment status—for instance, self-employed, manager, foreman—as well as occupation. The distributions, survey and national, are presented in table 19.

Table 19. *Socio-economic distributions of New Commonwealth immigrants, 1966*

Percentages

	New Commonwealth			India and Pakistan		British Caribbean		
	A	B	C	A	C	A	B	C
Males								
Employers and managers	5	1	—	5	—	1	—	—
Professional workers	6	2	7	8	9	1	—	3
Non-manual workers	13	7	6	15	6	6	4	7
Personal service workers	4	1	5	2	3	1	—	7
Skilled manual workers	29	37	⎫			40	42	⎫
Semi-skilled manual workers	22	22	}80	65	80	26	23	}80
Unskilled manual workers	17	23	⎭			22	26	⎭
Other	5	7	2	5	2	3	5	3
Total	100	100	100	100	100	100	100	100
Females								
Employers and managers	2	—	..	..	..	1	—	..
Professional workers	1	—	..	..	..	—	—	..
Non-manual workers	42	21	..	..	..	31	20	..
Personal service workers	10	9	..	..	..	10	9	..
Skilled manual workers	8	6	..	..	..	9	7	..
Semi-skilled manual workers	28	54	..	..	..	39	56	..
Unskilled manual workers	6	9	..	..	..	8	7	..
Other	3	1	..	..	..	2	1	..
Total	100	100				100	100	

SOURCES: Manchester and Birmingham surveys ; *Sample Census 1966, Commonwealth Immigrant Tables.*

Notes:
A = National.
B = Manchester sample.
C = Birmingham sample, including 7 female heads of household.

[1] Another consideration is that earnings in the sampled areas may differ from the national level of earnings.

What this table does not reveal is the implications which any contrasts between the sex ratios of workers in the samples and in the New Commonwealth immigrant labour force as a whole might have for the comparison. The Manchester results are obtained from a labour force in which female workers are overrepresented, and the Birmingham results from a labour force in which they are underrepresented. Therefore, any Manchester based estimate of the national New Commonwealth income per head would tend to understate the actual level, and a Birmingham based estimate would overstate it. The usefulness of table 19 is also restricted by the fact that the summary of the Birmingham survey gives the socio-economic classification only for working heads of households, virtually all of whom are males, and no breakdown of manual workers into their various skill levels and therefore into the all-important earnings groups.

There is no evidence that average income per employed New Common-wealth worker in the Manchester survey, the best documented in this respect, would deviate greatly from the corresponding national level as a result of differences in socio-economic levels. In particular the socio-economic distribution of West Indian males in the sample is really quite close to the socio-economic distribution of all male West Indian workers in the country. National-sample differences are more pronounced for female West Indian workers, as there is a substantial overstatement of semi-skilled workers and understatement of non-manual workers. But only if the average earnings of these groups differ by an appreciable amount would there be important implications for the degree to which the estimates of income based on the Manchester survey are representative.

Because there is no distinction between the numbers in skilled and unskilled manual jobs, the relevant comparisons are much more difficult for the Birmingham data. In the case of the West Indian group, there is a broad similarity between the sample and the national socio-economic distribution with, respectively, 80 per cent and 88 per cent in manual jobs. There is a rather more pronounced difference between the Asian distributions: 80 per cent of the sample compared with 65 per cent of all Asians being manual workers, and only 6 per cent of the sample compared with 15 per cent in the conurbation distribution being in the non-manual category. In the absence of other information it is virtually impossible to establish, even in general terms, what the implications of these differences might be for the validity of an average earnings figure for Asians derived from the sample.

The second group of factors that strongly influence the degree to which the sample was representative is the composition of the household samples in terms of children and adults, males and females, economically active

G

and inactive. In table 20, some of these characteristics in the two surveys are set out and compared with the corresponding features of the national New Commonwealth immigrant population.

Table 20. *New Commonwealth household features in the Manchester and Birmingham surveys and at the national level, 1966*

	Adults: female/ male	Children/ total	Economically active[a]/adults			Dependency factor	Percentages Average house- hold size
			M	F	Total		
New Commonwealth							(*Persons*)
Manchester survey[b]	86	47	87	60	75	252	*3.19*
Birmingham survey[c]	48	37	..	..	72	223	*2.81*
National	74	36	86	48	70	224	*3.65*
India and Pakistan							
Birmingham survey	43	36	..	..	69	228	*2.61*
National	60	34	..	..	69	221	*2.73*
West Indies							
Manchester survey	107	48	89	64	76	253	*3.17*
Birmingham survey	60	39	..	..	76	216	*3.23*
National	92	41	93	62	77	221	*3.91*

SOURCES: Appendix table 4; *Sample Census 1966, Commonwealth Immigrant Tables.*

[a] More precisely, numbers employed.
[b] West Indies, India and Pakistan, Africa.
[c] West Indies, India and Pakistan.

Perhaps not surprisingly, in view of the restricted size and special locations of the surveys, and the difficulties inherent in attempting a random survey of households, the two samples reveal pronounced differences in some basic household characteristics, both between themselves and in comparison with the total New Commonwealth population. Even in the case of the West Indian group where the most valid direct comparison between the two surveys is possible, the differences can be large. The Manchester survey somewhat overstates the female-male ratio both for the New Commonwealth and for the West Indies: the Birmingham survey greatly understates it. Whilst the proportion of West Indian children in the Birmingham survey is close to the national level, in the Manchester survey it is rather high. However, in both surveys the proportion of West Indian adults economically active almost exactly coincides with the actual national figure. The ratio of the total population to the economically active yields the dependency ratio, which assumes an important role in the following paragraphs, and which is a little below the national rate in the Birmingham survey, but appreciably higher in the Manchester sample. The average household size in both surveys is significantly below the national average for the West Indian population. Including other coloured groups, the dependency ratio is virtually identical with the national New Commonwealth level in the Birmingham survey, but rather high in the Manchester sample. This is due to the fact that in the Birmingham survey both the child ratio and the activity rate are near the national New Commonwealth average, whilst in the Manchester sample the child ratio, though not the activity rate, is rather high. The female-male ratio is nearer the national New Commonwealth average in the Manchester survey than in the Birmingham survey.

Table 21. *Household and* per capita *incomes in the samples*

	Average household income		Shillings per week Income per head	
	Manchester survey	Birmingham survey	Manchester survey	Birmingham survey
New Commonwealth	352	420	110	149
India and Pakistan	..	410	..	157
West Indies	361	439	114	136

SOURCES: Manchester and Birmingham surveys.

The household has many attractions as a sampling unit, especially, for instance, when expenditure patterns are being compared. Taken alone, however, it has serious disadvantages when attempting to evaluate the living standards of a group. Income data derived from the Birmingham and Manchester surveys and presented as household averages in table 21 really tell us very little about the living standards of New Commonwealth immigrants. Such household averages cannot be accepted as indications of living standards even within the groups identified in these surveys, let alone of their national counterparts: they are strongly affected by the size of the households in the various groups, and by their composition in terms of children and adults, males and females, economically active and inactive. A more meaningful result might be obtained by calculating and comparing average household incomes for each type of household. This was unsuited to the data derived from these surveys, since the number of observations is too small. Another approach consists in calculating the *per capita* incomes of all the New Commonwealth immigrants covered by the survey. The results of this are also given in table 21. As reflections of the relative living standards of these groups at the national level, even these results can be misleading. For by proceeding from an examination of average household incomes to average income per head, an allowance has been made only for differences in the size of households. Household composition, and especially the dependency factors of the New Commonwealth groups identified in the surveys, may well differ appreciably from those obtaining for these groups at the national level.

Therefore an attempt has been made in table 22 to estimate incomes per head that are likely to be more accurate reflections of those applying to all New Commonwealth immigrants, by calculating the average income per economically active person in the sample groups, and adjusting this by means of the dependency factors that applied to these groups in 1966 at the national level.

Table 22. *Estimated incomes per head, New Commonwealth population, 1966*

	New Commonwealth	India and Pakistan	Shillings per week West Indies
Sample: economically active			
Manchester survey	278	..	289
Birmingham survey	333	358	293
National (inclusive)[a]			
Manchester survey	..	..	131
Birmingham survey	..	162	133
National (exclusive)[b]			
Manchester survey	..	..	194
Birmingham survey	..	214	197
Dependency factor (percentages)			
Inclusive[a]	..	*221*	*221*
Exclusive[b]	..	*167*	*149*

SOURCES: Tables 6 and 8; Manchester and Birmingham surveys.

[a] Including children born in Great Britain.
[b] Excluding children born in Great Britain.

Some comments are needed on this table. No adjustment has been made for the fact that the sex ratios of the groups in the surveys may differ from those for the corresponding national groups: the female-male ratio in the Manchester West Indian group is higher than the national ratio for West Indians, and the ratio in the Birmingham group lower. Secondly, no estimate has been made for all the New Commonwealth groups combined. To do this in the case of the Manchester survey, a national figure would have to have been derived by applying a national, all-New Commonwealth, dependency factor to what is largely a West Indian group; and in the case of the Birmingham survey, the same dependency factor would have to have been applied to a group that is mainly composed of Asians. The results of such procedures could be misleading. Thirdly, whilst the national dependency factor for the New Commonwealth population inclusive of children born in Great Britain is logically the correct one for modifying the Manchester and Birmingham survey data,[1] table 22 also contains estimates of income per head—derived by applying the appropriate dependency factors—for the New Commonwealth population strictly defined as persons born in the New Commonwealth because these statistics will be used in chapter 9.

We are left with estimated incomes for West Indians which are remarkably similar, 131s. per week based on the Manchester survey and 133s. per week based on the Birmingham survey. The Birmingham based estimates suggest an appreciably higher income for Asians, 162s., or, excluding children born in this country, 214s. But it should be remembered that, because of sex ratio peculiarities, the Manchester estimates may understate, and the Birmingham ones overstate, the true position.

Strictly speaking, the method employed to derive national estimates from the sample data is such that it should have been applied to, and would have yielded, figures for income from employment. Because a breakdown of total income into its major categories—employment income, rents, dividends, interest and social security benefits—was not available from the summary of the Birmingham survey, the analysis was based, in the case of both samples, on the total income. Since employment income constitutes about 85 per cent of total New Commonwealth income, the approximation involved should not materially affect the results.[2] However, significant errors would be introduced if all categories of income were not included in any indigenous income per head that was compared with the results presented in table 22. In the corresponding period, and on the corresponding basis—that is, inclusive of employment income, rents, dividends, interest and social security benefits, but less income taxes and national insurance contributions[3] the income per head of the United Kingdom population was 187s. per week.[4] On this

---

[1] Since the sampled households also included children born here to immigrants.

[2] See table 23: strictly, the relevant figures for *per capita* rents, childrens' allowances and old age pensions in the sample should be adjusted to national estimates by means of the corresponding rentier, child and old age factors in the New Commonwealth population.

[3] Employment income in the surveys related to take-home pay. Since the Birmingham survey extended into 1967, the indigenous figures represent an average of 1966 and 1967.

[4] Central Statistical Office, *National Income and Expenditure, 1968* and *Annual Abstract of Statistics, 1968*, no. 105, H.M.S.O., London, 1968.

reckoning, the estimates of income per head derived above for Asians and West Indians are about 13 and 30 per cent, respectively, below the indigenous level. A further refinement would have been not simply to take total numbers in the household, but to give some weighting, according to whether members of the household are adults, children of school age or very young children. A variety of coefficients is possible, but none would eliminate the difference between the United Kingdom population and that of the New Commonwealth although they would reduce it. A calculation of income per head, giving all children a weight of 50 per cent of adults, would still show the West Indian income about a quarter below the level of that of the indigenous population.

Table 23.   *Sources of income: indigenous and New Commonwealth*

	Employment income	Rents, dividends and interest	Social Security benefits	*Percentages* Total
Manchester survey				
New Commonwealth	85.9	8.1	6.0	100.0
West Indies	85.5	8.4	6.1	100.0
Indigenous	77.6	10.8	11.6	100.0

SOURCES: Manchester survey; *National Income and Expenditure, 1968.*

Table 23 gives a breakdown of income into its major categories for the New Commonwealth sample and the indigenous population. As the relevant detail was not available for the Birmingham survey, we must rely on the Manchester sample, which comprises mainly West Indians. To ensure comparability with the take-home pay concept used in the Manchester survey, indigenous employment income is net of national insurance contributions and income tax; the proportion for rents, dividends and interest is also derived from a figure net of tax.

The table suggests that the New Commonwealth community in the Manchester sample derives a higher percentage of its income from employment than does the indigenous population. If, as seems plausible, this is a general feature of the New Commonwealth population, it means that any disparity between the *employment* incomes per head of New Commonwealth and indigenous residents is less than the 13 to 30 per cent estimated above for the difference in total income per head. In contrast, the proportion of income provided by social security benefits is higher— indeed about twice as high—for the indigenous population than for the New Commonwealth group in the Manchester survey—a finding that anticipates to some extent the contents of the next chapter. Table 23 also suggests that the proportion of income contributed by rents, dividends and interest is rather larger in the case of the indigenous than the New Commonwealth population. A closer inspection of the Manchester survey reveals that the proportion of New Commonwealth incomes stemming from these sources would be even lower but for the fact that as much as 8 per cent of the West Indian group's income was derived from property.

There are two places in this study where a detailed expenditure pattern for New Commonwealth immigrants would have been useful: in chapter 7, where such information would facilitate an assessment of the degree to which differences in indigenous and immigrant expenditure patterns imply differences in industrial capital requirements; and in chapter 9, where it would have contributed to an estimate of indigenous-immigrant differences in import requirements. Unfortunately, given the limited scale of the immigrant surveys carried out in Manchester and Birmingham, it would be too much to expect them to yield expenditure information in sufficient detail for these purposes. Where, *inter alia*, they do play a very useful role, is in illuminating certain of the macro-economic characteristics of coloured immigrants with which this study is primarily concerned. In particular, both surveys yield information about the savings and remittances abroad of New Commonwealth immigrants. The results are presented in table 24, where the corresponding United Kingdom propensities to consume and save are given for comparison.

Table 24. *New Commonwealth expenditure and savings, 1966*

	Expenditure	Remittances[a]	Savings	Percentages Total income
New Commonwealth				
Manchester survey	84.1	7.9	8.0	100.0
Birmingham survey	80.7	7.6	11.7	100.0
India and Pakistan				
Birmingham survey	79.3	8.3	12.4	100.0
British Caribbean				
Manchester survey	84.6	7.5	7.9	100.0
Birmingham survey	83.5	6.2	10.3	100.0
United Kingdom	92.0	—	8.0[b]	100.0

SOURCES: Manchester and Birmingham surveys; *National Income and Expenditure, 1968.*

[a] To country of origin.
[b] Includes a relatively small figure, about 0.4 per cent of total income, for remittances abroad.

The degree of reliability that can be attached to these results is, if anything, less than applies to the income magnitudes examined in the earlier parts of this chapter. Differences in household composition between the survey groups and the total New Commonwealth population again mean that the patterns depicted in table 24 may not accurately reflect the national immigrant characteristics but, unlike the preceding income analysis, available information does not allow any corresponding adjustment to be made to the surveys' expenditure-savings results. However, the absence of any alarming dissimilarities in the observations relating to the West Indian groups in the two surveys encourages some faith in the results.

On the basis of the information presented in this table, it appears that the propensity to consume of New Commonwealth households, at about 80 to 85 per cent, is appreciably below the indigenous rate of 92 per cent. The table also suggests that the proportions of New Commonwealth income saved and retained in this country, of the order of 8 to 12 per cent, may not be so very unlike the indigenous savings proportion, 8 per cent. The balance comprises New Commonwealth immigrants' remittances to their country of origin which, if the evidence in the table is to be believed, were running at a rate of almost 8 per cent of income.

Specific questions were posed in the Manchester survey about mortgage and rent payments by immigrants. Although this area of expenditure is not of special concern in the context of this study, unusual interest has been shown in it, and a summary of the results seems in order. In the Manchester survey, 9.2 per cent of New Commonwealth income was taken by rents and 5.3 per cent by mortgage payments. The corresponding income proportions, 7.1 and 5.1 per cent, spent on these items by the 3,274 British households covered by the 1966 *Family Expenditure Survey*, were rather lower, especially the former.[1] The higher rent proportion among immigrants partly reflects a higher percentage of New Commonwealth households that rent accommodation—67 per cent compared with 49 per cent in the national sample. But it also reflects the fact that these households pay, on average, rents 15 per cent higher than those paid by the renting households in the national sample. In contrast the average mortgage payment of the New Commonwealth households was about 25 per cent below the commitment of house owners in the national sample.

Unfortunately the information available on incomes did not allow us to make any assessment of immigrant income tax payments per head

---

[1] Ministry of Labour, *Family Expenditure Survey, Report for 1966*, H.M.S.O., London, 1967. In both the Manchester and national surveys, the rent and mortgage proportions include figures for the appropriate rates; rates paid by house buyers in the Manchester survey amounted to 1.5 per cent of income and in the national household sample to 1.3 per cent.

compared with those of the indigenous population. We have already concluded that there is some evidence that average income per employed New Commonwealth worker is lower than the national level, but we also know that the labour force participation rates are higher for the New Commonwealth than for the indigenous population, so total household income from earnings alone for New Commonwealth households may well not deviate much from the national average. If this were the only factor it would imply similar national insurance payments and income tax payments per head. But we also know that the dependency factor is higher for the New Commonwealth households and this would lead to greater income tax allowances and in consequence smaller payments. It is also known that there has been some tax evasion by immigrants and this has been estimated at £5 to £7 million in 1966/7 by the Board of Inland Revenue;[1] but now that this has been identified, an attempt will presumably be made to stop it. Whilst it is not practicable to estimate the relative contributions of immigrants in the form of national insurance contributions and income tax payments, it seems unlikely that, if New Commonwealth immigrants do pay less, the difference would more than outweigh their smaller share of the social services.

---

[1] There is, of course, also some tax evasion by the indigenous population.

96

CHAPTER 6

IMMIGRANTS AND THE SOCIAL SERVICES

It is frequently suggested that, because immigrants have a higher birth-rate, because a higher proportion of immigrant women have their babies in hospital, and because immigrants are more prone than others to certain diseases, their demands on the social services are exceptionally large. This chapter addresses itself to this question, of the current costs of social expenditure; social capital requirements are considered in chapter 7. It attempts to quantify the aggregate demands made by New Commonwealth families, including children born in this country, on the social services and local authority housing, and compares the average current expenditure per immigrant with that of the average member of the population as a whole. The main conclusion is that, largely because of their age structure, immigrant families make smaller demands on the social services than other families; and this is likely to hold true for some time to come.

We examine in turn expenditure on health, education, national insurance benefits and housing subsidies. The base year for the comparison is 1961, but estimates have been made for 1966—and also for 1981 to see how far the conclusions might change in the future. The average national cost of the health and welfare services by different age groups, and for education, are calculated for England and Wales. The assumption is then made that any difference in average costs in Scotland would not be large enough to alter the national averages. For national insurance and housing, data for Great Britain are used.

HEALTH AND WELFARE

Probably about a quarter of the expenditure on health and welfare services in England and Wales goes on the old (aged 65 and over), although they form only about an eighth of the total population.[1] Average health and welfare expenditure in 1961/2 was about £14 a head for those aged under 65 and £39 for those aged over 65. In addition the cost of maternity care was about a further £2 per head of the total population. However, some adjustments have to be made to these figures of average expenditure for each age group before they can be applied to the immigrant population since, for a number of services, the

---

[1] See Deborah Paige and Kit Jones, *Health and Welfare Services in Britain in 1975,* Cambridge University Press, 1966, pp. 9–10.

demands of immigrants appear to be rather different from those of the population as a whole.

Table 25. *The cost of the health and welfare services in England and Wales by age group, 1961/2*

	Age groups			£ millions Total
	0–14	15–64	65+	
Maternity services	..	..	..	72.9[a]
General practitioner services (other than maternities)	16.7	47.3	12.0	76.0
Dental	9.6	42.6	4.3	56.5
Pharmaceutical	18.7	52.9	13.4	85.0
Opthalmic	1.0	11.1	3.2	15.3
General hospitals	43.0	177.0	110.0	330.0
Mental illness	0.8	46.1	27.2	74.1
Mental subnormality	4.4	25.0	1.0	30.4
Local authority health services (excluding maternity and mental)	22.5	16.2	21.8	60.5
Welfare homes	—	3.2	23.2	26.4
Welfare foods	25.0	—	—	25.0
Total cost	141.7	421.4	216.1	852.1
Population (millions)	*10.6*	*30.0*	*5.5*	*46.1*
Cost per head (£s)	13.4	14.0	39.3	18.5

SOURCES: *Report of the Ministry of Health for the year 1962: the Health and Welfare Services,* Cmnd 2062; *Census 1961; Annual Abstract of Statistics, 1964,* No. 101; Office of Health Economics, *The Cost of Medical Care;* K. Jones, 'Immigrants and the Social Services', *National Institute Economic Review,* No. 41, August 1967.

[a] Not allocated by age group.

There is some reason to believe that a much higher proportion of immigrant births than of other births take place in hospital.[1] Hospital births are more costly in terms of government expenditure than births which occur at home. We have assumed that 85 per cent of immigrant births took place in hospital in 1961 compared with only 63 per cent for the total population; and we have assumed a 25 per cent difference in cost. We also have to allow for the different ratio of births to population in the two groups.[2]

Secondly, an allowance has to be made for a higher incidence of tuberculosis among immigrants. The notification rate for tuberculosis

[1] See, for example, *Immigration from the Commonwealth,* Cmnd 2739; and K. Schwarz, 'Public Health Aspects of Migration' in G. E. Wolstenholme and M. O'Connor (eds.) *Immigration: Medical and Social Aspects,* Churchill, London, 1966.

[2] It is most appropriate to relate the cost of maternity care to the population as a whole as it does not necessarily vary in the same ratio as either the 0–14 or the 15–64 age group.

among immigrants is considerably higher than the notification rate for the population as a whole, where it is about 0.5 per thousand. The average rate for New Commonwealth immigrants in the conurbations was 3.3 per thousand in 1961.[1] But, when considering the relative costs of the disease, allowance must be made for the fact that, in 1961, well over 300 thousand cases in England and Wales attended chest clinics for treatment or supervision—roughly 7 per thousand of the population. The chest clinics are the responsibility of the local authority health services. Their cost is not listed separately and is very difficult to sort out, but it could not be much more than about £3 million per annum in 1961/2. Part of the cost of the health visitors is also attributable to tuberculosis, and general practitioners' treatment together with drugs might add another £1 million. However, the main cost falls on the hospital services where, in 1961, 45 thousand in-patients were treated for chest diseases (mainly tuberculosis) at an average cost of about £290 per patient.

The total cost of tuberculosis to the community in England and Wales in 1961 was probably about £18 million or £0.4 per head of the total population. It is impossible to be precise about the cost of treating immigrants for tuberculosis. For one thing, although there are estimates of the notification rate, there are no estimates of the total numbers being treated for the disease; we therefore, rather arbitrarily, take four years' notifications as equal to the number of immigrants being treated for tuberculosis. Secondly, we do not know how many immigrants are treated in hospitals; we therefore assume that the same proportion of immigrants with the disease as of the population as a whole are treated in this way. The cost per head of the New Commonwealth immigrant population then works out at £1.0 (£1.2 per head of the immigrant population born abroad) compared with £0.4 for the population as a whole. The incidence of venereal disease is also much higher for immigrants, although there is some evidence that this is now falling.

Another difference in the health requirements of immigrants and the total population shows up in the proportion of immigrants over 65 who are in hospitals or old people's homes. On census night 1961, 4 per cent of the total population over 65 were in hospitals, institutions or old people's homes, compared with 3.5 per cent of the immigrant population over 65. Moreover, of those immigrants over 65 in institutions, a relatively small proportion were in general hospitals, which are more costly.

An adjustment has also been made for the cost of mental subnormality, since it is unlikely that subnormal people would be migrating, and

[1] V. H. Springett, 'Tuberculosis among immigrants in Great Britain' in *Bulletin of the International Union against Tuberculosis, 1965*, vol. 36, p. 122.

therefore there can be hardly any immigrants between the ages of 15 and 64 in institutions for the mentally subnormal. On census night in 1961 there were no children born to members of the New Commonwealth community in hospitals for the mentally ill or mentally subnormal. Most of the children born here to immigrants were still under school age in 1961, and consequently any mentally subnormal children were still at home, although possibly receiving treatment in training centres. So, for the children of immigrants, the cost of subnormality is possibly about half the national average.

These are probably the main known ways in which the typical immigrant's demand on the health and welfare services differ from the average. There may be other differences; possibly a smaller proportion of immigrants in each age group go into mental hospitals. But the evidence for this is a little tenuous;[1] and it may be offset by a higher incidence of minor psychiatric disorders.[2]

These various adjustments to the figures lead to the conclusion that the average cost of health and welfare services in 1961 was relatively high for immigrants in the 15–64 age group because of the higher incidence of tuberculosis and venereal disease. It was relatively low for immigrants aged over 65 because a smaller proportion of them were in institutions. In addition, the cost of maternity care per head of the immigrant population was more than twice that of the total population because of a larger number of births per head of the population and a higher proportion of hospital births.

The next step is to weight these two sets of figures, of cost per head in the different age groups, by the age distribution of the total population and the immigrant population respectively. In 1961, a rather higher proportion of the immigrant than of the total population was aged under 15 (30 per cent as against 23 per cent); but those over 65 comprised only 2 per cent of the immigrants, compared with 12 per cent of the total population. Because of this, in spite of the higher cost per head for the 15–64 age group, the average cost of health and welfare services per head for all ages comes out somewhat less for the immigrant population than for the total population.

Between 1961 and 1966 a large number of immigrants of working age came into the country. The proportion of immigrants in the country aged 65 and over hardly changed. But the proportion aged 0–14 rose to 36 per cent. The incidence of venereal disease declined. The net result

[1] Census data are not particularly helpful, since no distinction was made between hospital patients and staff on census night, and a fairly high proportion of the staff in mental hospitals are immigrants.

[2] See A. Kiev, 'Psychiatric illness among West Indians in London', *Race*, vol. V, no. 3, January 1964, pp. 48–54.

Table 26.   *Cost per head of health and welfare services for the home population[a] and the New Commonwealth population[b]*

£s, 1961 prices

	Age groups			Maternity care[c]	Total
	0–14	15–64	65+		
1961					
Average cost, home population	13.4	14.0	39.3	1.6	18.5
Adjustments for immigrants					
Maternity care				+2.2	
Mentally subnormal	−0.2	−0.8	—		−0.3
Tuberculosis and venereal disease	—	+1.2	—		
Fewer aged in institutions	—	—	−7.9		
Average cost, New Commonwealth					
immigrants	13.2	14.4	31.4	3.8	18.2
Population distributions (%)					
Total, home (46.1 million)	*23.1*	*65.0*	*11.9*		*100.0*
New Commonwealth (716,000)	*29.8*	*67.9*	*2.3*		*100.0*
1966					
Average cost, home population	13.4	14.0	39.3	1.9[d]	18.6
Adjustments for immigrants	—	+0.2	−7.9	+2.0[d]	−0.3
Average cost, New Commonwealth					
immigrants	13.4	14.2	31.4	3.9[d]	18.3
Population distributions (%)					
Total, home (48.1 million)	*23.1*	*64.6*	*12.3*		*100.0*
New Commonwealth (1,093,000)	*36.2*	*61.2*	*2.6*		*100.0*
1981					
Average cost, home population	13.4	14.0	39.3	1.9[d]	19.1
Adjustments for immigrants					
Assumption A[e]	—	+0.4	—	+0.3[d]	−1.9
Assumption B[f]	—	+0.4	—	+0.5[d]	−2.0
Average cost, New Commonwealth					
immigrants					
Assumption A[e]	13.4	14.4	39.3	2.2[d]	17.2
Assumption B[f]	13.4	14.4	39.3	2.4[d]	17.1
Population distributions (%)					
Total, home (53.3 million)	*26.5*	*60.1*	*13.4*		*100.0*
New Commonwealth					
Assumption A[e] (1,525,000)	*32.7*	*63.6*	*3.7*		*100.0*
Assumption B[f] (2,175,000)	*35.2*	*62.2*	*2.6*		*100.0*

SOURCES: Table 25 and NIESR estimates.   For a more detailed background to these calculations see 'Immigrants and the Social Services', *National Institute Economic Review*, No. 41, August 1967.

[a] For England and Wales.
[b] Including children born here.
[c] Excluded from costs allocated to age groups.
[d] Adjusted for number of births and proportion in hospital.
[e] Assuming no immigration 1966–81.
[f] Assuming immigration 1966–81 at the rates shown in table 7.

of these factors is that in 1966 the average cost per head of health and welfare services for all immigrants was still less than the national average.

In spite of special factors, immigrants' demands on the health and welfare services have been lower than the national average because the inflow has hitherto consisted largely of relatively young men and women of working age. It seems likely that this effect will be a fairly long-lasting one. In table 26, two calculations are made of the relative cost of health and welfare services for immigrants and others in 1981. The first calculation assumes no further net immigration from the New Commonwealth: in other words, it examines the consequences of the ageing of the present immigrant population.[1] By 1981, on the assumption of no further net immigration the number of births would probably be falling, for by then a relatively high proportion of immigrant women would be aged 40–50. However, the proportion of immigrants aged over 65 would still be very small.[2] Incidence rates for tuberculosis and venereal disease will probably have fallen to something nearer the national average. We have no information about the incidence of tuberculosis among immigrants after 1961, but in view of declared government policy to prevent tuberculosis being brought into the country, and assuming some improvement in housing conditions, we have estimated that by 1981 expenditure per head for immigrants will have fallen to twice that of the home population instead of three times as in 1961 and 1966. The result of all these assumptions is that, in 1981, the average immigrant's demands on the health and welfare services would still be lower than the national average.

The assumption of 'no further net immigration' is made in order to analyse the demand on the social services of the immigrants who have already arrived. A more realistic assumption is to assume that net immigration from the New Commonwealth continues. This second assumption[3] would increase the number of births and the proportion of the immigrant population aged 0–14, but reduce the proportion over 65, and so further reduce slightly the average cost of the health and welfare services per immigrant. But the effect is very small.

EDUCATION

Reasonably good estimates can be made of the number of children at

---

[1] See chapter 2, pp. 23–8. Appropriate adjustments are made for the assumptions about the proportions of births in hospital; the proportion of those aged 65 and over in institutions; and the proportion of mentally handicapped children.

[2] The calculation assumes that immigrants stay in this country for life, and do not return to their country of birth to retire.

[3] Details of which are given in chapter 2, pp. 23–8.

school who belong to the immigrant population, and these are used in table 27 to make a comparison of the costs of schooling per head of population on the same lines as the comparison of the costs of health and welfare services.   This comparison is restricted to school expenditure, because there is not enough information about the number of young immigrants who are receiving higher education.   In any case, the cost of schooling, together with the allied cost of teacher training, accounts for well over four-fifths of total current public expenditure on education.

Table 27.   *Public expenditure on education and child care[a]*

	Schools		Extra cost of special teaching	Child care	Total cost	Cost per head of population
	Primary[b]	Secondary[c]				
			(£ millions)			(£)
1961/2						
Total population	240.0	305.0	0.5	26.0	571.0	*12.4*
Immigrants	4.4	4.1	0.5	0.6	9.6	*13.4*
1966						
Total population	254.0	301.0	1.0	28.0	584.0	*12.1*
Immigrants	8.4	7.5	1.0	1.2	18.1	*16.6*
1981						
Total population	329.0	456.0	1.0	34.0	820.0	*15.4*
A. Immigrants[d]	11.9	22.4	1.0	1.9	37.2	*24.4*
B. Immigrants[d]	17.9	31.9	1.5	2.7	54.0	*24.8*

SOURCES: *Statistics of Education, 1962;* NIESR estimates (see text).

[a] At 1961 prices.
[b] Cost per pupil £58.
[c] Cost per pupil £104, including direct-grant pupils' fees and grants.
[d] Assumptions as in table 26.

In 1961, the proportion of children of school age in the immigrant population was slightly lower than for the rest of the population.   If this was the only consideration, the average cost of education in 1961 would also have been slightly lower for the immigrant than for the total population.

However, some special adjustments are needed to the estimates of the cost of education for immigrant children.   First, there is some additional expenditure incurred in teaching English; this can be put at about £1 million a year in 1966;[1] so we have allowed £0.5 million in 1961, when the

[1] Based on information supplied by the Home Office.   This would be £1.5 million at current prices.

number of immigrant schoolchildren was only about half the number in 1966. Secondly, immigrant families make more use of child care facilities than the average population—and child care is here included with the educational estimates. In table 27 an estimate is made of these additional costs which assumes twice as many children are in care per head of the immigrant population as of the total population. They bring the average cost of education per head of population to 7 per cent higher for immigrant families in 1961. By 1966, the average cost per head was probably about 37 per cent higher for immigrant families.

Moreover, disparity of educational costs is likely to grow. By 1981, whether we assume continued immigration or not, the proportion of children of school age in the immigrant population is likely to be a good deal higher than that in the total population. It seems reasonable to make some continuing allowance for additional education costs, and for a continued more intensive use by immigrants of provision for child care. The calculation suggests the cost of education in 1981 might be about £24 to £25 per head (1961 prices) for the immigrant population, as against £15.5 per head for the population as a whole.

For further and higher education it is virtually impossible to make the kind of comparison which is appropriate to this particular study. The figures required are those for the children of settled immigrant families— and it is impossible in the published statistics to distinguish them from the large number of students who come from Africa or Asia for a few years and then return. The cost of the education of these visiting students is quite a separate policy question, which we do not attempt to cover in this study.

NATIONAL INSURANCE BENEFITS

The same method was used for national insurance and assistance benefits as for expenditure on health and welfare services. First, the total sum spent was split between the three age groups—the young, those over 65, and those of working age. Then some adjustments were made to allow for New Commonwealth families' special circumstances. Finally, the calculations were carried forward to 1981 on two assumptions—one with continuing immigration and one without. The results are shown in table 28. In 1961/2 nearly 60 per cent of total national insurance and assistance benefits went to the old, and by 1965 the proportion was even greater. Benefits totalled some £13 to £14 per head for those under 65, but £130 per head for those of pensionable age. Since there are so few old people in New Commonwealth families, this is bound to make the average payment per immigrant a good deal lower than the average for the whole population.

H

Table 28.   *Cost of national insurance and assistance benefits[a] in Great Britain by age group, 1961/2*

	Age groups			£ millions Total
	0–14	15–64	65+	
Retirement pensions	—	78	706	784
Widows and guardians	10	71	—	81
Industrial injuries	2	56	—	58
Sickness	12	137	6	155
Unemployment	5	31	—	36
National assistance	—	89	82	171
Family allowances	130	4	—	134
Total	159	466	794	1,419
Population (*millions*)	*11.9*	*33.4*	*6.1*	*51.4*
Cost per head of total population (£s)	13.4	14.0	130.2	27.6

SOURCES: *Report of the Ministry of Pensions and National Insurance for the year 1962*, Cmnd 2069; information provided by the Ministry of Social Security.

[a] Excluding maternity benefits, war pensions and administration.

There are special adjustments to be made for the circumstances of coloured families, but this serves to modify only slightly the effects of the very different age structure. First, when immigrants have families the average family size tends to be relatively large, so that the cost of family allowances is relatively high. Secondly, at least in 1961, the unemployment rate among immigrants was well above that of the total population.[1] Thirdly, because of their age structure, there were fewer widows under the age of 60 and fewer women between 60 and 64 receiving retirement pensions. These adjustments are shown in table 29.

In 1966 and 1981, the only adjustments that we have made are for family allowances, for widows and for women between 60 and 64. New Commonwealth unemployment rates had already come down roughly to the national average by 1966.[2] It is true that a slight 'unemployment gap' re-emerged in 1967, but this was a year in which unemployment generally was high and rising, and for the future it is reasonable to assume that such years will be the exception rather than the rule.

These adjustments are all fairly minor. The main point of the comparison is that benefits are some ten times as great for the old as for the rest of the population; and that the New Commonwealth community has, and will continue to have for many years, very few old people. So, for the

[1] See chapter 3, pp. 38–45.
[2] See chapter 3, pp. 40–1.

whole immigrant population the average benefit per head in 1961 was only some 60 per cent of that for the total population, falling to 56 per cent in 1966. In 1981 it would be some 62 per cent on the assumption of no further net immigration; but, assuming immigration continues, the average benefit per immigrant would then still be only 56 per cent of that for the total population.

Table 29. *Cost per head of national insurance and assistance for the home population and the New Commonwealth population*[a]

| | Age groups | | | £s, 1961 prices |
	0–14	15–64	65+	Total
1961				
Cost per head of total population	13.4	14.0	130.2	27.6
Adjustments for immigrant population				
Family allowances	+ 0.1	—	—	
Unemployment	—	+ 1.9	—	
Widows and retirement pensions for women				
aged 60–64	—	− 3.5	—	
All adjustments	+ 0.1	− 1.6	—	
Cost per head of New Commonwealth immigrants	13.5	12.4	130.2	15.4
1966				
Cost per head of total population	14.0	14.0	130.2	28.3
Adjustments for immigrant population				
Family allowances[b]	+ 1.2	—	—	
Widows and retirement pensions for women				
aged 60–64	—	− 2.0	—	
All adjustments	+ 1.2	− 2.0	—	
Cost per head of New Commonwealth immigrants	15.2	12.0	130.2	16.2
1981				
Cost per head of total population	13.7	14.0	130.2	29.5
A. Adjustments for immigrant population[c]				
Family allowances[b]	+ 1.7	—	—	
Retirement pensions for women aged 60–64	—	− 0.9	—	
Cost per head of New Commonwealth immigrants	15.4	13.1	130.2	18.2
B. Adjustments for immigrant population[c]				
Family allowances	+ 1.8	—	—	
Retirement pensions for women aged 60–64	—	− 1.5	—	
Cost per head of New Commonwealth immigrants	15.5	12.5	130.2	16.6

SOURCES: Table 28; NIESR estimates.

[a] For Great Britain with 1961/2 rates of benefit.

[b] Assumes that the mean family size in 1966 and 1981 is about 15 per cent greater for the immigrant population than for the total population.

[c] Assumptions as in table 26.

HOUSING SUBSIDIES

Lastly we add in the net cost of housing subsidies to the public authorities—the current cost of subsidising the rents of those in local authority houses. The subsidies do not take account of the benefit to local authority tenants from past inflation, so that probably less than a third of the difference between economic rents and actual rents paid is accounted for by the direct subsidy. In this sense therefore the figures in table 30 underestimate the benefit to occupants of local authority housing.[1]

Table 30 shows that, in 1961, less than 6 per cent of New Commonwealth households were in accommodation rented from local authorities compared with nearly a quarter of all households, and that the gap had not narrowed very much even by 1966. For 1981 we have assumed a substantial rise in the proportion of immigrant households in local authority dwellings, but by this time it seems likely that nearly half of all households will be in local authority dwellings, so that there will still be a large difference between the two groups. These estimates are necessarily

Table 30. *Public expenditure on housing in Great Britain, 1961–81[a]*

	Households in local authority dwellings	Total public expenditure on housing	Expenditure per local authority household	Average expenditure per head
	(%)	(£mn)	(£)	(£)
1961				
All households	23.0	128.0	33	2.5
Immigrant households	5.5	0.3	33	0.5
1966				
All households	27.6	164.0	34	3.0
Immigrant households	9.3	1.0	34	0.9
1981				
All households	45.0	344.0	40	5.9
Immigrant households				
A[b]	25.0	4.6	40	2.8
B[b]	20.0	5.2	40	2.2

SOURCES: *Census 1961, Housing Tables* and *Commonwealth Immigrants in the Conurbations; Sample Census 1966, Housing Tables;* NIESR estimates.

[a] 1961 prices.

[b] Assumptions as in table 26.

[1] The original capital cost of older local authority houses is substantially below their present market value and this enables authorities to fix rents well below current annual costs less subsidy. See D. C. Paige, 'Housing', in W. Beckerman and Associates, *The British Economy in 1975*, Cambridge University Press, 1965, pp. 366–403.

arbitrary,[1] but it seems probable that immigrants will continue to occupy older, privately rented accommodation as long as it exists and will have a low priority on local authority lists.

TOTAL REQUIREMENTS

The various comparisons are brought together in table 31. The cost per New Commonwealth immigrant of health and welfare services was below that of the population as a whole in 1961 and 1966 and seems likely to stay below it up to 1981. The cost per immigrant of education and child care, on the other hand, was already above average in 1961, and by 1981 might be 60 per cent higher than the average for the whole population. There is a very big difference in favour of the New Commonwealth population, which seems likely to continue, in the cost of national insurance. There is also a marked difference in housing, but the figures are much smaller. Taking all social security current expenditure and benefits together, the average immigrant received about 80 per cent as much as the average member of the indigenous population in 1961, and the figure seems likely to be 85 to 90 per cent by 1981.

Table 31. *Cost per head of social services, 1961–81*

£s, 1961 prices

	Health and welfare	Education and child care	National insurance and benefits	Housing subsidies	Total
1961					
Total population	18.5	12.4	27.6	2.5	61.0
Immigrant population	18.2	13.4	15.4	0.5	47.5
1966					
Total population	18.6	12.1	28.3	3.0	62.0
Immigrant population	18.3	16.6	16.2	0.9	52.0
1981					
Total population	19.1	15.4	29.5	5.9	69.9
Immigrant population					
A[a]	17.2	24.4	18.2	2.8	62.6
B[a]	17.1	24.8	16.6	2.2	60.7

SOURCES: Tables 26, 27, 29 and 30.
[a] Assumptions as in table 26.

The calculations for 1981 use 1961 figures of costs. This might give

[1] A largely notional adjustment for converting subsidies of later years to 1961 values also contributes to this degree of arbitrariness.

the wrong aggregate answer if there were very wide disparities in the movements of costs per head in the four groups of services between 1961 and 1981; if, for example, the cost per head of education rose very much faster than the cost per head of national insurance and assistance. However, there have been no such substantial disparities in the movements of costs in the last ten years; between 1955 and 1965 the cost per person roughly doubled in each of the three main groups.[1] The most reasonable assumption for the future is that they will continue to move up together. The cost of housing subsidies rose rather less, but as this is the smallest item it would not affect the totals much.

The New Commonwealth community has so far made fewer demands on the social services than the population as a whole because of its age structure. This has more than outweighed the additional social service costs incurred because of their special health and educational requirements and, our projections suggest, will continue to do so for some years. In time the age composition of New Commonwealth immigrants will presumably become fairly normal and their special requirements will disappear, so the once-for-all gain will disappear, but there is no reason to suppose that the immigrant population will ever have a disproportionately large number of old people.

The desire to make current cost estimates for coloured immigrants' future use of the social services meant that we were obliged to use projections of the New Commonwealth population, and these include children born in this country. On this basis, the immigrant-indigenous cost differences shown in this chapter will be less than the differences in the current social service requirements for newly arrived New Commonwealth immigrants only (that is, excluding children born to them in Britain). Parallel calculations for this group would need to exclude the cost of births to the coloured community, there would be appreciably fewer schoolchildren to take into account, and smaller family sizes would yield even smaller proportions of households living in local authority housing. Moreover, there would be no significant change in the immigrant-indigenous contrast in the old age proportion. Differences in the above elements would more than counteract higher costs per head in the new immigrant groups due to higher incidences of tuberculosis and venereal disease.

---

[1] Taking 1955=100, the cost per person in 1965 of health and welfare was 199, of education 231, and of national insurance and assistance 228.

CHAPTER 7

THE CAPITAL REQUIREMENTS OF IMMIGRANTS

Two aspects of immigrant capital requirements receive special attention in this paper. They have been selected because, in each case, they are topics which have attracted special interest and yet they constitute problems on which the available information allows us to say something constructive. They are, first, the relative living standards of the immigrant and indigenous populations that are associated with or permitted by certain kinds of capital, and the related question of whether the demands of new immigrants on these forms of capital have adversely affected the living standards of the indigenous population; and secondly, the extent if any, to which the capital requirements of immigrants have had an inflationary impact on the economy.

The first question centres around social capital requirements—immigrant and indigenous needs for such resources as houses, hospitals and schools. The services stemming from social capital (some current costs of which have been considered in the previous chapter) have an important direct impact on both absolute and relative living standards of the various groups in the community. In contrast, the total capital requirements of immigrants, including industrial as well as social capital, are relevant in the context of the second question—potential inflationary repercussions. There is a rather less obvious, but most significant, relationship between the two questions. To the extent that the social capital requirements of new immigrants are met by the appropriation of part of the capital stock hitherto yielding services for the indigenous population any, possibly inflationary, expenditure on new capital for immigrants is avoided. In short, adverse effects on indigenous living standards and inflationary impacts are to a considerable extent alternative possibilities.

The social capital requirements per head measured in this chapter relate to the 'household' definition of New Commonwealth immigrants, not to the 'place of birth' concept because of the nature of the available data. The implications of using these results in conjunction with the inflow of new immigrants is referred to at the end of the chapter.

At the end of 1966 the gross value, at 1958 replacement cost, of the United Kingdom's total stock of social capital was about £47 thousand million.[1] The bulk of these assets, £32 thousand million, or 68 per cent

---

[1] This figure includes a few industrial assets, namely agricultural buildings and vehicles and the assets of the textile industry (*National Income and Expenditure, 1968*, table 66).

of the total, consisted of dwellings. The inclusion in the following analysis of hospitals and schools[1] means that it covers about 80 to 90 per cent of all social capital.[2] More than half the country's capital is in the form of 'industrial' or 'productive' capital, the gross value of which, at the end of 1966, was £61 thousand million (at 1958 replacement cost) or 57 per cent of the total. Since in principle we deal with all productive capital requirements, the chapter as a whole embraces more than 90 per cent of the total capital stock. The social capital needs of immigrants, their requirements in terms of housing, hospitals and schools, are considered first.

SOCIAL CAPITAL REQUIREMENTS

The term 'housing requirements' is perhaps not very apt with its normative connotation in an area where conditions for both immigrants and the indigenous population are still far from ideal, when our primary concern is essentially with *actual* housing conditions and the usage of housing capital. The housing conditions of immigrants are notoriously bad and there can be little question that, whatever the desirable standards that should be sought on their behalf in the long term, their actual current housing conditions are, in general, inferior to those of the indigenous population and the value of housing capital used by immigrants correspondingly lower. Whilst it is not possible to measure these housing conditions and the corresponding capital usages with any precision, the disparity between immigrant and indigenous standards can be demonstrated quite easily in a general way.

The number of persons per room is a general indicator of relative housing conditions. The ratio of dwellings to households might be considered as an alternative indicator, but it is not as good since not all multiple occupation is unsatisfactory: 'bed-sitter' arrangements provide suitable accommodation for certain groups of people, and should perhaps be regarded as an explanation of differences in living densities. In contrast—and although the measure is not without faults—'in an extensive analysis of housing conditions in the British conurbations in 1961, firm proof was established of the overriding validity of persons per room as the most useful single diagnostic of housing conditions'.[3]

In 1961 the number of New Commonwealth immigrants[4] per room in the conurbations was 1.01 compared with only 0.68 for the indigenous

---

[1] But not universities and private schools.

[2] The main items excluded are roads, sewerage facilities, universities and private schools.

[3] Chapter 12, 'Housing', in Rose and Associates, *Colour and Citizenship*, commenting on unpublished research papers of the British Universities Census Tracts Committee, E. Gittus *et al.*

[4] That is, persons in New Commonwealth households.

population. However, this probably understated the densities in the country as a whole. In 1966 the New Commonwealth housing density in the country at large, 0.81, and that of the indigenous population, 0.57, show that the coloured population lives at densities about 40 per cent higher than those of the indigenous population, in other words their housing requirement is 29 per cent below the average. The higher New Commonwealth housing density in part reflects larger family size and, in part, their residence in smaller dwellings.[1]

Although the use of persons per room is the best measure of housing conditions and housing capital usage, it takes little or no account of the availability of household facilities such as bathrooms and water closets which are not counted as rooms in the census. Table 32, which reproduces some pertinent information, shows that in certain respects— especially the percentage of households without baths—the disparity between the housing conditions of New Commonwealth immigrants and the indigenous population may not be as marked as is suggested by data relating to persons per room.[2]

Table 32. *Availability of household facilities, 1966*

Percentages

	London conurbation	West Midland conurbation
Households sharing bath		
New Commonwealth	50.9	26.0
Indigenous	11.8	3.1
Households without bath		
New Commonwealth	14.1	31.4
Indigenous	14.8	14.1
Households sharing W.C.		
New Commonwealth	53.2	39.4
Indigenous	15.1	5.6

SOURCE: Rose and Associates, *Colour and Citizenship*, table 12.7, p. 131.

To be set against this is the widely held view that, especially in the case of coloured immigrants, population census data understate the degree of overcrowding on account of an instinctive fear of answering official enquiries.[3] It is impossible to be precise about the net effect of these two opposing factors on the observed room density as a measure

[1] 'Housing', loc. cit.

[2] In some areas New Commonwealth immigrants fare relatively well in respect of access to a bath because of their concentration in large Victorian houses. This contrasts with the relative importance, for the indigenous population, of small bath-less terraced houses.

[3] See, for instance, Ministry of Housing and Local Government, *The Report of the Committee on Housing in Greater London* (the 'Milner-Holland Report'), Cmnd 2605, H.M.S.O., London, 1965, p. 193.

of housing conditions and usage, but it seems unlikely that they would greatly disturb the broad picture revealed above.

Table 33. *Housing densities by New Commonwealth groups, 1961 and 1966*

	New Common- wealth	India and Pakistan	British Caribbean	Other New Common- wealth	*Percentages* Indigenous
1961: conurbations*a*					
Persons per room					
Over 1½	24.6	11.2	40.1	20.6	3.9
1 to 1½	14.1	12.9	13.3	17.6	8.4
½ to 1	53.4	61.9	43.3	56.4	64.9
Less than ½	7.9	14.0	3.3	5.4	22.8
Total	100.0	100.0	100.0	100.0	100.0
Households (*thousands*)	*101.4*	*39.2*	*39.5*	*22.8*	*5,490.5*
1966: conurbations					
Persons per room					
Over 1½	17.0	11.4	23.9	13.8	2.0
1 to 1½	15.4	13.0	19.1	13.0	4.9
½ to 1	58.0	61.0	51.3	63.7	60.5
Less than ½	9.6	14.6	5.7	9.5	32.6
Total	100.0	100.0	100.0	100.0	100.0
Households (*thousands*)	*202.5*	*64.9*	*80.4*	*57.2*	*5,443.2*
1966: national					
Persons per room					
Over 1½	12.3	7.4	20.9	9.6	1.6
1 to 1½	12.9	10.3	18.3	10.3	4.9
½ to 1	59.2	60.8	53.0	64.2	59.5
Less than ½	15.6	21.5	7.8	15.9	34.0
Total	100.0	100.0	100.0	100.0	100.0
Households (*thousands*)	*325.7*	*131.6*	*103.6*	*90.5*	*16,961.0*

SOURCES: *Census 1961, Commonwealth Immigrants in the Conurbations,* table B.3 and *Housing Tables,* table 11 ; *Sample Census 1966, Summary Tables* and *Commonwealth Immigrant Tables.*

a Restricted New Commonwealth definition in 1961.

The contrast in the housing densities of the New Commonwealth and indigenous populations is echoed in the data presented in table 33. Whilst in 1966 12 per cent of New Commonwealth households lived at densities of more than 1½ persons per room, the corresponding proportion for indigenous households was less than 2 per cent. At the other end of the scale, while only 16 per cent of the immigrant households enjoyed housing standards of less than half a person per room, a third of indigenous households did so. There are also some arresting differences in the housing densities of the various New Commonwealth groups. In 1966, 21 per cent of West Indian households, 10 per cent of the other New Commonwealth and 7 per cent of Asian households, lived at densities of more than 1½ persons per room; and only 8 per cent of the West Indians enjoyed densities of less than half a person per room, compared with 16 per cent of the other New Commonwealth group and 21 per cent of the Asians. This same group pattern was repeated in the conurbations in both 1961 and 1966.

Many factors have contributed to the high housing densities and, correspondingly, to the low housing capital usage of the New Commonwealth immigrants. Not least is their location. The conurbations in general, and especially London and the West Midland conurbation, contain disproportionately large numbers of New Commonwealth immigrants,[1] and it is in these areas that the housing shortage is most acute. The official view is that the main reason for the unsatisfactory living conditions of many coloured immigrants has been their settlement in urban areas. In such a situation, discrimination alone can do much to force immigrants into the poorest housing and, whilst this is a factor which, in principle at least, is now removed by the Race Relations Act, it is certainly one which hitherto has played an important role.

Relatively low income per head is hardly a factor calculated to yield better than average accommodation for New Commonwealth immigrants. Yet there is evidence that, in an effort to overcome their disadvantages in the housing market, many immigrants purchase old property at inappropriately high prices and then find themselves burdened with oppressive mortgage payments.[2] In order to meet these payments they find it necessary to sublet to their countrymen, or take in lodgers from among them, in conditions which give rise to much of the observed overcrowding.

That many of these immigrants are newcomers to the scene exacerbates their plight in the housing market. Their lack of residential qualifications is to their disadvantage in their ranking on the local authority housing lists. But, probably as important, they may suffer because, with few family and other long-standing ties in the area, they fail to hear of the more attractive rentings that come on the market. As a result, they are squeezed into that part of the market, privately rented accommodation, which the indigenous population does most to avoid.

[1] See chapter 4, pp. 49–56.
[2] See, for instance, Burney, *Housing on Trial*, p. 43. However, it would appear from chapter 5 that, even in relation to the *per capita* incomes of the New Commonwealth community, the degree of oppression in their mortgage payments may have been somewhat exaggerated.

The reason why the three New Commonwealth groups should take up the positions they occupy in the scale of housing standards—in descending order, Asians, other New Commonwealth and West Indians—is not very clear.   One factor in the relatively high position of Indians and Pakistanis is the inclusion of white expatriates.   And the large number of single students, usually with at least one room to themselves, among other New Commonwealth immigrants explains some of the disparity between this group and the badly-off West Indians.

There was a definite improvement between 1961 and 1966 in the housing conditions of both the New Commonwealth and indigenous populations.   But the data suggest that, both in absolute and relative terms, the improvement might have been rather more marked for the indigenous population than for the New Commonwealth community: the average indigenous density falling from 0.68 to 0.57 per room and the average New Commonwealth density in the conurbations from 1.01 to 0.93 per room.   Table 33 reveals that the percentage of households living at densities of more than $1\frac{1}{2}$ persons per room fell from 3.9 to 2.0 for the indigenous population in the conurbations and from 24.6 to 17.0 for New Commonwealth immigrants in the conurbations; percentages enjoying densities of less than half a person per room rose from 22.8 to 32.6 and from 7.9 to 9.6 respectively.[1]   This conclusion is confirmed by a rather more elaborate measure of changes in housing standards that takes account of criteria other than persons per room.[2]   But, whilst the broad pattern of housing conditions among the three groups of New Commonwealth immigrants did not change in this period, there are indications that the disparities narrowed, and in particular that, while the housing densities of Indians and Pakistanis changed little, those of the West Indians may have improved rather dramatically.   The proportions of Asian households in the conurbations living at densities of more than $1\frac{1}{2}$ persons per room were 11.2 and 11.4 per cent in 1961 and 1966 respectively.   For the other New Commonwealth they were 20.6 and 13.8 per cent and, for West Indians, 40.1 and 23.9 per cent.

Far from immigration being accompanied by a decline in the housing standards of the indigenous population, there was an improvement between 1961 and 1966.   There was a rise of 15 per cent in the total stock of housing (from £28 thousand million in 1961 to £32 thousand million in 1966, at 1958 replacement cost), and a larger rise in absolute terms in capital formation, possibly inflationary in character.   It could be argued that, if there had been no New Commonwealth immigration, some

---

[1] It is not thought that changes in the coverage of 'New Commonwealth' (for the conurbations between 1961 and 1966) will materially vitiate these comparisons.

[2] 'Housing', in Rose and Associates, *Colour and Citizenship*.

potentially inflationary new investment would have been avoided or, alternatively,[1] the housing standards of the indigenous population would have risen even more than they did.

These questions are faced more squarely in chapters 8 and 9, but any attempt to answer them must be made against the background provided by changes, during this period, in the group and area patterns of housing. The most relevant development in the housing market was the settlement of New Commonwealth immigrants in the older housing stock, near urban centres, vacated by indigenous residents or earlier immigrant groups as they moved to more modern housing in the suburbs.[2] If no New Commonwealth immigrants had appeared to occupy this old housing stock, one of two things would have happened: either the indigenous population would have remained in these old houses, or it could have behaved as it did and left. In the former case, movement to the suburbs and the demand for new housing would have been substantially lower, consequently indigenous residents would not have enjoyed such a large improvement in their housing standards, but there would have been less, potentially inflationary, investment in housing. In the latter, the old housing stock would have been scrapped, and an additional demand created for new houses. Doubtless, in the absence of immigration, the actual reaction of the indigenous population would have taken a middle course, implying rather less new housing demand than in fact appeared—and, paradoxically, a smaller all round improvement in housing conditions than that which actually occurred—but a higher rate of slum clearance. There are reasons, however, for supposing that the second of the two alternatives would have been the more important, and that most of the movement from slums to suburbs would have occurred in any case.

First, in a number of areas where there are large proportions of immigrants, the size of the total population has declined. This largely reflects a desire on the part of the indigenous community to improve their housing standards, an urge which would probably not have been much less strong in the absence of immigration.

Secondly, the improvement of the housing standards of the whole population, rather than just matching with extra houses marginal increases in the size of the population, has been for many years an object of government policy. All postwar governments have accepted some responsibility for overcoming the housing shortage, but by and large without specifying any particular target date for achieving this objective.

---

[1] See above, p. 109.
[2] For the wide variety of evidence in support of this generalisation see, for instance, Burney, *Housing on Trial;* Rex and Moore, *Race, Community and Conflict;* 'Housing', loc. cit. and Butterworth, *Immigrants in West Yorkshire.*

There is no evidence, however, that in setting their targets the governments of the day were particularly influenced by the number of new households expected to be formed, with or without account being taken of immigration. In the first eight years after the war, official policy was to build as many new houses as possible with the resources available. At various times the programme was reduced because of balance of payments difficulties. In 1951 the Conservatives came into power with a promise to build 300 thousand houses a year in Britain and this they achieved by 1953. But in the mid-1950s the government took steps to keep building down to 300 thousand houses a year and within this total to bring about a shift from public to private housebuilding. Local authorities were forced to borrow on the open market and were told to improve their finances by raising rents. As a result, the number of houses built by local authorities declined sharply between 1953 and 1959, and remained at a low level until 1964 when it started to rise again. The policy to limit housebuilding was confined to the public sector; the private sector, building almost entirely for owner-occupation, was allowed to expand in line with people's ability to buy. This situation changed after 1964 when local authority housebuilding was encouraged in an attempt to meet another political target of 500 thousand houses a year. But subsequently this target was abandoned. In the past, therefore, the level of immigration and its effect on the size of the population and new household formation can have had little influence on the size of the housing programme, which has been largely determined by political considerations or by limited resources.

It is hard to imagine that, in the absence of New Commonwealth immigration between 1961 and 1966, indigenous housing standards would have risen much more than in fact they did, or that the rate of new housebuilding would have altered very much. If anything, the result would probably have been a rather smaller improvement in indigenous housing standards and a little less investment in new houses, principally because the savings which immigrants have used to buy houses, frequently at prices above the market value, would no longer have been available to smooth the movement of indigenous residents to the suburbs.[1]

On the other hand, less immigration would have allowed a much higher rate of slum clearance near city centres. Evidence abounds of the deferred demolition of housing to meet New Commonwealth needs: local councils 'buy up slum houses well in advance of planned clearance, patch them up . . . and use them as a temporary addition to their own housing stock'—a tactic well suited to the larger Victorian buildings where many

---

[1] See, for instance, Burney, *Housing on Trial*, p. 43.

coloured immigrants are found.[1] And, 'A survey of Pakistani-owned houses in Halifax . . . found that over half the houses were due for slum clearance within the next six years.'[2] The Milner-Holland Committee received evidence that the rate of slum clearance in Greater London was restricted by shortage of technical staff, by the slow procedure of compulsory purchase and, in particular, by the difficulty in rehousing the overspill which is inevitable when densely packed areas are redeveloped. The Committee's report drew attention to the fact that a great deal of the unsatisfactory property nearing the end of its useful life finds its way into the hands of immigrants, who arrange their house purchases among themselves by pooling arrangements.

This, really, is where the arrival of New Commonwealth immigrants has cost implications in this field. Government housing policy has been directed towards slum clearance partly to improve housing standards by means of resettlement in better accommodation and partly to liberate space which, being near town centres, it is thought could be made to serve the economy more fruitfully. This policy has been substantially retarded by the arrival of new immigrants. The worst housing problems of the former boroughs of Stepney, Poplar and Bethnal Green are concentrated at their western end, 'right next door' to the City of London, in an area where commercial sites are worth £250 thousand per acre.[3] The capital costs of the new arrivals in terms of old, unwanted, bricks and mortar may well have been minimal; but in terms of land usage, an opportunity-cost which seems to have been generally overlooked, it may well have been substantial.

Official presentation of capital stock statistics makes it impossible to determine the proportion of total capital requirements per head of population represented by public health capital needs, or the extent to which changes in the latter, rather than an enlargement of the capital stock to match population increases, account for new capital formation in this sector. In the official statistics, hospitals are included in the 'other industries' group—statistically a rag-bag category embracing such diverse assets as those of the textile industry, universities, private schools and agricultural buildings and vehicles.[4] Nevertheless, a rough impression of the relative importance of the capital embodied in hospitals can be obtained from gross capital formation data. Gross capital formation in the local health and welfare services during the five years 1962 to 1966 constituted 14 per cent of total gross formation of social capital other than

---

[1] Ibid. p. 65.
[2] Butterworth, *Immigrants in West Yorkshire*, p. 35.
[3] Burney, op. cit. pp. 79 and 101.
[4] *National Income and Expenditure, 1968*, table 66.

dwellings. And two-thirds of this represented investment by the central government, the bulk of it, about three-quarters, consisting of investment in buildings, mainly hospitals.

Whilst precise data relating to the relative use of hospitals by the indigenous and immigrant populations do not exist,[1] some approximate estimates can be made. The figure for the average number of patients per night is a good measure of hospital usage since it takes account of both the rate of hospitalisation in the population and the average length of stay. If we assume that the rates contained in table 34 are applicable to the corresponding age groups in the New Commonwealth population then, given their 1966 age distribution, the usage rate for the New Commonwealth is about two-thirds of the indigenous rate.[2]

Table 34. *Hospital usage in England and Wales, 1961*

	Population	Average no. of patients per night			Rate per thousand population
		General hospitals	Mental hospitals	Total	
	(*Millions*)	(*Thousands*)			
Age group					
0–14	10.6	23.0	1.5	24.5	2.31
15–64	30.0	80.0	85.3	165.3	5.51
65+	5.5	93.0	50.3	143.3	26.10
Total	46.1	196.0	137.1	333.1	7.23

SOURCE: *National Institute Economic Review*, no. 41, August 1967, p. 37.

After making allowance for the relatively large number of New Commonwealth women who have their children in hospital,[3] usage is still a fifth below that of the indigenous population.

There are two other factors which would tend to make the hospital usage per head of the New Commonwealth population differ from that of the indigenous population. Both of them are difficult to quantify though quite clearly they work in opposite directions. On the one hand, the higher rate of tuberculosis among immigrants tends to raise their hospital usage and, on the other, their lower incidence of hospitalised mental patients tends to reduce it.

---

[1] The population census enumerates those in hospitals but, most unfortunately, fails to distinguish between patients and staff.

[2] We have also assumed that the 1961 rates for England and Wales are valid for Great Britain in 1966.

[3] See chapter 6.

As far as capital expenditure of local health and welfare authorities is concerned, all but 16 per cent of the total planned for the period 1965–76 is to go on services for the aged and handicapped and the mental health services; this is expected to be the pattern in the future.[1] All of these are for the benefit of groups which are underrepresented among immigrants.

Capital stock statistics preclude any definitive statement about the relative importance of increases in the hospital stock and enlargements of this stock to meet population increases as explanations of the hospital building that has occurred. However, the major need in this sector is for replacement capital rather than for any net expansion in the hospital stock. The demand for hospital beds for many types of illness has been falling and will continue to do so. But, as in housing and perhaps even more so, there is an urgent need to replace hospitals that should have been pulled down long ago. Therefore, the 1962 Hospital Plan for England and Wales is largely a replacement plan and, whilst the net increase in the number of beds in general hospitals was planned to be 19 thousand by 1975, it was envisaged that the total number of new beds would be as high as 81 thousand. In fact, later revisions to this plan make it clear that, although the original plan assumed that it would not be possible to replace more than 30 per cent of existing hospitals by 1975, even this expectation could not possibly have been fulfilled.

This might imply that hospital needs arising from a larger population could only have been met by keeping open more of the old hospitals which it is the intention of the various plans to pull down. At first sight there would therefore seem to be a close analogy with the impact of new immigrants on the housing market in the sense that the economic cost of the new immigrants is not the usage of dilapidated structures but, essentially, occupation of the ground on which these buildings stand that would otherwise have been devoted to alternative uses. However, other evidence suggests that the failure to carry out plans to close old and small hospitals is not related to population developments, but to local pressures to retain facilities in cottage hospitals nearby.

Official capital stock figures for the educational sector, like those for the health service, have not been published separately: universities and private schools are bracketed with textiles, hospitals, and agricultural buildings and vehicles; other educational capital, mainly the state schools, is included with sewage facilities and prisons. In the absence of capital stock data, a rough estimate of the importance of schools in total social capital can again be obtained from series of gross capital formation. Capital formation in education other than universities and private

---

[1] Ministry of Health, *Health and Welfare. The Development of Community Care*, Cmnd 3022, H.M.S.O., London, 1966.

schools, during the period 1962 to 1966, represented 27 per cent of total investment in social capital excluding dwellings. Local authorities undertook 89 per cent of this investment and 86 per cent of it consisted of new buildings.

The main determinant of a community's school requirements is the proportion of children of school age in the population. The use of the 'household' concept in this chapter, including as it does New Commonwealth children born in Britain, therefore has a major influence on the results, the implications of which are referred to below. In the case of such a recently arrived and rapidly increasing group as the New Commonwealth immigrants, the proportion of children is likely to be rather volatile because of such special features as the age distribution, the rate of family reunion and changing fertility rates in the New Commonwealth community. The evidence suggests that, between 1961 and 1966, the proportion of children in the New Commonwealth population increased appreciably,[1] and in 1966 the proportion of school age, 18.7 per cent, was much higher than the corresponding proportion in the indigenous population, 13.7 per cent. The disparity implies New Commonwealth school place requirements per head of population some 36 per cent above those of the indigenous population.

This result needs to be qualified in two ways. First, to the extent that New Commonwealth children attend the smaller, older schools in urban areas where the teacher shortage is most pronounced, the average size of their classes will tend to be above the national size and their usage of classrooms per head below the national average. Secondly however, the necessity of forming some relatively small classes of immigrant children for English lessons would work in the opposite direction, raising somewhat the building requirements per head of immigrant school children.[2]

The impact of recent immigration on the population's school facilties would appear to be very similar to that on housing. In the years immediately following World War II, the provision of new places seems to have matched fairly closely the rise in the school population, but since 1955 the number of new places provided has exceeded the increase in the number of children. To a considerable extent this is due to an attempt to raise educational standards by reducing the size of classes. It also reflects a basic structural shift: the movement of large numbers of the population from old urban areas to new towns and housing estates. However, by no means all old schools in bad condition have been closed

[1] In 1961 it was slightly below that of the indigenous population.
[2] Although the bulk of the government grants for special local government services directed towards immigrant needs are used for educational purposes, most is intended for additional current expenditure, essentially extra staff, rather than for new capital projects.

and replaced by new facilities: the *School Building Survey*[1] revealed that only 18 per cent of pupils in the London metropolitan region were in places provided since 1945 and the percentage for all England and Wales was 24. It is in areas such as the London metropolitan region that much of the New Commonwealth population is to be found and, indeed, there seems little doubt that large numbers of New Commonwealth children attend dilapidated schools in old urban areas; schools which, ideally, should have been abandoned and replaced. In five of the twenty local authority areas with the largest proportion of immigrants the number of children in schools actually fell between 1961 and 1965, and in four others the increase was negligible. In other words, immigrant children were being educated in schools for which demand from the indigenous population was falling.

The implications for school capital available to the indigenous population are virtually identical with those for housing. In the absence of immigration there would have been two possibilities. First, it might be argued that, but for the growth in the immigrant population, large numbers of people would not have left the urban areas and much of the new, potentially inflationary, school building that occurred elsewhere would not have been necessary. But, by the same token, their children would have continued to be educated in run-down schools and would have forgone the educational improvements embodied in the modern buildings. The second, and more likely, possibility is that the suburban movement from towns would have occurred irrespective of the rate of immigration, being accompanied by both potentially inflationary capital expenditure and educational improvements. The difference would have been that, with fewer New Commonwealth arrivals, more old schools would have been closed in towns and cities.

In a very real sense, therefore, the alleged phenomenon of 'one white child in a class of coloured children' in certain urban areas should be seen as a measure of the extent to which the indigenous population rather than the immigrants have benefited from the higher educational standards implied in new school buildings. The real cost of the new immigration again largely resolves itself into the retarding of the rate of demolition, and a failure to release urban land for alternative uses.

PRODUCTIVE CAPITAL REQUIREMENTS

The analysis of the productive capital[2] requirements of New Common-

---

[1] H.M.S.O., London, 1965, for Department of Education and Science.

[2] The capital stock of the agricultural sector, the industrial sector—mining, manufacturing, construction and public utilities—and many services—transport, communications, distribution and financial services. Altogether, the productive sector so defined contained 57 per cent of the country's gross capital stock (at 1958 replacement cost) in 1966.

wealth immigrants is not as straightforward as that of their social capital needs.   There is a fairly close relationship between social needs and social capital.   But in the case of productive capital, such an identification is impossible, due to the intrusion into the relationship, as a separate element, of the product or service.[1] In short, two basic relationships are involved, the consumption per head of goods and services, and the capital-output ratio : these are considered in turn.

Chapter 5 indicated that the income per head of members of New Commonwealth households is less than that of the indigenous population, and that the proportion of income saved—representing resources generated by the New Commonwealth labour force but made available for contributions to an increase in the capital stock—is higher than the average for the total population.   With the New Commonwealth community's income per head some 13 to 30 per cent below the average, and its propensity to save of the order of, say, 12 to 16 per cent compared with the indigenous rate of 8 per cent, the group's consumption per head should be about 17 to 36 per cent below the average, corresponding to the lower and upper values of these estimates.

However, the results of chapter 5 suggest that, if coloured children born in this country are left out of account—that is, if the estimates are intended to reflect more closely the consumption characteristics of new arrivals—there may be very little immigrant-indigenous difference. Combining estimates of New Commonwealth incomes per head that range from 104 to 114 per cent of the indigenous level with the observed immigrant and indigenous propensities to save, suggests that, on this basis, consumption per head of New Commonwealth immigrants would range from 95 to 109 per cent of the indigenous level.   Because the major use of the results of this chapter is their combination, in the context of an assessment of inflationary impacts, with the inflow of new immigrants, we shall adopt this latter range.   Or rather, since the New Commonwealth savings proportions given above are perhaps underestimates[2]—they were calculated on the assumption that as much as half the remittances abroad would return in the form of export demand for British goods implying additional capital requirements on this account—we shall assume that personal consumption per head of goods and services is identical for new immigrants and members of the indigenous population.

Some of the immigrants' consumption will, of course, be directed to imports, but no deduction has been made for this, on the rough assumption that its effect will be offset by the industrial capital needed to meet the additional exports required to maintain the balance of payments position.

---

[1] Though this assertion is rather less true of capital in the service sectors than in industry.
[2] See pp. 93-4 above.

Also, since personal consumption of goods and services from the productive sector accounts for about nine-tenths of total personal consumption (excluding imports), we assume that their identity in the consumption sectors applies also to the productive sector.

Little more than half of the total output of the productive sector goes to meet private consumption. The rest is destined for exports (about a fifth), capital formation (about a fifth) and government consumption (about a tenth).[1] Immigrant induced exports have already been taken into account and there are good reasons for believing that much of the other uses of productive output was unresponsive to population changes during the period in question. Although about two-thirds of this capital formation flow is responsive, in that it is channelled to the productive sector partly to meet the immigrants' needs, most of this is designed to raise living standards as opposed to matching increases in the size of the population. The rest is largely destined for social capital changes which, as we have suggested, have not yet been very responsive to immigration. Many current government purchases from the productive sector are for defence purposes, the size of which have hardly been geared to recent changes in the size of the British population. Nevertheless, in order to err on the side of a high estimate for New Commonwealth industrial capital requirements, we have based the total productive output requirements on the comparison of consumption per head and, as a rough approximation, assumed them to be identical for indigenous and immigrant members of the population.

A consideration of the capital-output ratio associated with new immigrants must take account of two possibilities. First, the pattern of New Commonwealth demand for output of the productive sector may differ from the national pattern in such a way that it is directed more towards capital intensive products. Unfortunately, as we do not know the detailed expenditure pattern of coloured immigrants it is impossible to say whether, and if so by how much and in what direction, it differs from the expenditure pattern of the total population.[2] However, it might be argued that, if incomes and consumption per head in New Commonwealth households are relatively low, a larger proportion of New Commonwealth income is likely to be devoted to the basic necessities—food, clothing, heating and lighting.[3] The sectoral capital-output coefficients presented in table 35 suggest that, if this is the case, it might be a factor tending to raise their relative industrial capital needs per head. For whilst the capital-output ratio in the food industries, 2.7, is a little below

[1] See the Summary Input-Output Transactions Matrix, 1963, in *National Income and Expenditure, 1968.*
[2] See chapter 5.
[3] And housing too, but that has been dealt with separately.

the average coefficient, 3.1; that of the public utilities, 13.5, is far above it. However, it is difficult to be at all certain of this effect. The food sector identified in table 35 includes the drink and tobacco industries, which are hardly producers of basic necessities. And a capital-output ratio could not be identified for the clothing industry. Because of the high degree of uncertainty about the nature of the adjustment that should be made for this factor, none has been carried out.

Table 35.   *Capital-output ratios in the productive sector, 1966*

£ thousand millions, 1958 prices

	Net output	Gross capital stock	Capital-output ratio
Agriculture	1.1	0.8^a	0.72
Mining and quarrying	0.6	1.6	2.59
Manufacturing	9.5	22.8^b	2.40
Food, drink and tobacco	1.0	2.7	2.71
Chemicals	1.0	4.0	3.83
Metals and engineering	4.7	11.9	2.51
Other manufacturing	2.7	4.2^b	1.55
Construction	1.6	1.3	0.79
Gas, electricity and water	0.8	10.7	13.48
Transport and communications	2.1	12.4	5.88
Distribution and other services	3.9	11.8	3.04
Total	19.7	61.4^{ab}	3.12

SOURCE: *National Income and Expenditure 1968*, tables 11, 15 and 66; *Annual Abstract of Statistics, 1968*, no. 105, table 152.

^{a} Excluding agricultural buildings and vehicles.
^{b} Excluding textiles.

Secondly, the capital-output ratio of additions to output tends to be appreciably higher than the average ratio. In the United Kingdom, production techniques changed during the period in such a way that the more modern plants for producing most products required more capital per unit of output than older ones. Thus, the capital-output ratio associated with the additional output produced in the period 1961–6 to meet the demands of higher incomes, and the needs of a larger indigenous population and more immigrants, is above the average which existed in this period. To be more precise, the incremental industrial capital-output ratio of the period was 3.61, or about 15 per cent higher than the average ratio, 3.12 in 1966.[1]   On this reckoning therefore, given the assumed identity in output requirements per head, the industrial capital require-

[1] See table 37, p. 147.

ments per head of new coloured immigrants would be about 15 per cent above those of indigenous members of the population.

In the case of social capital, it was concluded that the capital needs of the new immigrants had been largely met not by extra capital formation, but by a postponement of scrappings. There is no evidence that this is equally valid for productive capital. Industrialists shape their investment plans according to expected market developments, which in turn are strongly influenced by both anticipated growth in income per head and enlargements to the population, and there is no reason to suppose that they ignored the market enlargement attributable to the arrival of new immigrants. It should be emphasised that we have made no allowance for the possible existence of excess capacity and any effect it may have in delaying investment. This question is deferred to the following chapter.

TOTAL IMMIGRANT CAPITAL REQUIREMENTS

Apart from the inherent interest of these results, they are used in chapters 8 and 9 for a consideration of the growth and inflationary impacts of New Commonwealth immigration in the period 1961–6. For the evaluation of the possible inflationary impact especially, it is useful to draw together some of the quantitative results obtained. In the case of social capital, let us assume that, as suggested above, the housing requirements per head of coloured immigrants are 29 per cent less than for the indigenous population, their hospital requirements 21 per cent less and their school requirements 36 per cent higher. Taken together, and allowing for the relative sizes of the different forms of capital, these imply that total social capital requirements of New Commonwealth immigrants are 19 per cent below those of the indigenous population.[1] If this is combined with the industrial capital requirement, which was estimated to be about 15 per cent above the indigenous level, overall immigrant capital requirements per head would appear to be almost identical with the indigenous requirements.

These capital requirements are used later in connection with the inflationary impact of new immigrants and, accordingly, an attempt has been made to ensure that the results do not underestimate the capital requirements of this group. That is, productive capital requirements have been based on the incomes per head of immigrants born abroad rather than on the 'household' immigrant concept, since the former yields a higher capital requirement than the latter. The use of the household definition for school requirements will overstate the capital requirements

[1] The above average was derived with the assistance of the Central Statistical Office.

of new arrivals—since the much smaller proportion of children in this group means that their school requirements are significantly below those of the New Commonwealth 'household' population already in the country—and it is legitimate to use the same concept for housing requirements since it is unlikely that newly arrived immigrants will live in less crowded conditions than those already here.

It would be wrong to imply that, unlike their industrial capital needs, the social capital requirements of the new immigrants have yet been fully met: in the social field, capital formation required by New Commonwealth immigrants who entered the country between 1961 and 1966 is largely still to come. In particular, as time passes the coloured community will be looking for housing standards comparable to those of the indigenous population and, no doubt, the authorities will wish to accelerate slum clearance. Eventually, as the country catches up with its backlog of housing requirements, the rate of increase in the stock will inevitably decline and then population growth, whether by natural increase or immigration, will play a relatively more important role in determining the extent of capital formation in housing.

Finally, attention must be drawn to one aspect of immigrant capital needs which is very easily overlooked when, as here, concern is directed primarily to the living standard and inflationary impacts of these requirements. To be concerned with these effects is to be interested, essentially, in the shorter-term aspects. Introduction of the time dimension into the calculus of immigrant capital requirements, by a consideration not only of usage at a given moment but also of the number of years for which it applies, reveals other implications, the presence of which must be recognised in any broad assessment of the economic impact of immigration. More precisely, in any immigrant group, and New Commonwealth migrants in the first half of the 1960s were no exception, persons predominate for whom, in their formative years, the recipient country has been spared social capital investment. But whilst, therefore, the man-years of social capital which the recipient country will need to provide for an immigrant is, on average, appreciably below the figure required by a member of the indigenous population, the age distribution of immigrants is such that most of them will contribute almost as many years to the labour force, and about as much to the stock of capital, as does an indigenous worker.

CHAPTER 8

IMMIGRATION AND GROWTH

Unless the economy is prone to extremely perverse effects, clearly immigration, by adding to the country's labour resources, will increase total output. What is less certain, however, is whether or not immigration tends to raise or lower output per head and thereby general living standards in the host country. It is to the latter question, in the context of New Commonwealth immigration in the period 1961–6, that attention is turned in this chapter.

That this question remains a matter of debate and dispute is not due, in any large part, to the absence of those data measurements which economic theory suggests are necessary for evaluating the impact of immigration on the country's output per head. The preceding chapters of this study show that we can assess with a reasonable degree of accuracy such basic characteristics as the immigrants' contribution, both quantitative and qualitative, to the labour force, and their capital requirements. Rather does the difficulty stem from the absence of an accepted body of theory into which the relevant data can be fed to yield a measurement of the precise growth impact.[1] An effort has been made in this chapter to indicate the range of possible impacts of New Commonwealth immigration on output changes suggested by different approaches to the problem. An attempt has also been made, at a later stage, to attach to these possibilities, in a rough and ready fashion, degrees of probability which appear most likely to the authors on the basis of the nature of the immigration and the general characteristics of the British economy in this period, and also on the inherent plausibility of the different views.

As befits a situation in which the basic change is an enlargement of the population, much of the discussion centres on the role of labour in economic growth, although impacts which are transferred via changes in the stock of capital, and more especially via changes in the capital-labour ratio, are not neglected. For examining the theoretical possibilities, the most convenient framework was found to be one in which growth impacts of immigration are first considered in essentially 'static' conditions, followed by a more 'dynamic' and, in many respects, more realistic

---

[1] This uncertainty is well appreciated, of course, by economists not only in a general way, but also within the special context of gauging the growth impact of immigration. 'Much popular discussion of the economic impact of immigration is vitiated by the absence of clear theoretical concepts.' (Thomas, *International Migration and Economic Development*, p. 29.)

evaluation.[1]

OUTPUT IMPACTS IN STATIC CONDITIONS

The term 'static' is used here in a special sense to denote not only the absence in the production function of any exogenously determined, time related, 'technological change', or other 'progress' element, but also any economies of scale.   In these conditions aggregate output in the economy can change only as a result of changes in the inputs of labour and capital of more or less given quality, a condition that can be represented by the familiar Cobb-Douglas production function in the form:

$$X = aL^m C^{1-m}$$

where X represents aggregate output; L, units of labour; C, units of capital; and a and m are constants.

Chart 9.   *The impact of immigration on output*

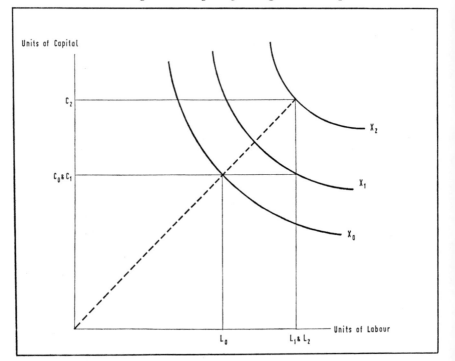

<hr />

[1] This method of exposition was found much more convenient than, for instance, the framework suggested by Spengler, in which a distinction is drawn between 'aggregative' economic impacts and 'substitutive effects'; those experienced in particular sectors and by individual groups. ('Effects Produced in Receiving Countries by Pre-1939 Immigration', in *The Economics of International Migration*.)

In these circumstances the impact of immigration on output and on output per head can be usefully considered in two extreme situations: first, where new immigrant workers are employed in combination with the existing stock of 'productive' capital, implying a fall in capital per man; and secondly, where there is a proportionate rise in the stock of industrial capital to maintain capital per man at its previous level. The two situations are depicted in chart 9.

Clearly, total output, X_2, is higher when the quantity of capital rises along with the supply of labour than the output achieved, X_1, when only employment rises. Our concern, however, is with output per head— average product. In the situation where capital per man remains unchanged, the corollary—with the type of production function specified —is that immigration leaves average product unchanged. Where there is no enlargement of the capital stock and capital per man in consequence falls, the contribution to output of additional immigrant workers approximates to the marginal product of labour in the economy, thereby reducing average product.[1] Therefore, in the circumstances we have postulated, the impact of immigration on national productivity depends essentially on the nature of the consequent changes in capital per man.

A study by E. J. Mishan and L. Needleman points to a decline in the capital-labour ratio and (especially when returns to scale are left out of account) to a fall in output per head.[2] Certainly New Commonwealth immigrants, whilst contributing significantly towards the British labour force, have not been accompanied, personally or indirectly, with capital resources which might have been used, for instance, to import additional productive assets. Whilst large movements of personal capital have probably never been a feature of the major migratory flows, it is well established that, in the nineteenth and early twentieth centuries, migratory and capital movements were positively, if indirectly, related in time and direction:[3] such a movement is out of the question in the case of migration from developing Commonwealth countries to Britain.

Unfortunately, whatever other purpose the Mishan-Needleman study serves, it helps little in determining the *actual* impact on the British capital-labour ratio of recent New Commonwealth immigration. For the study was directed essentially to a hypothetical situation of 'large scale net immigration' at a 'constant rate of inflow of half a million

---

[1] That is, for small increases in the labour force. For large additions to the labour force, the immigrant worker's contribution to output falls below the pre-existing marginal product.

[2] E. J. Mishan and L. Needleman, 'Immigration: Some Long Term Economic Consequences (Part A)', *Economia Internazionale*, vol. xxi, no. 2, May 1968, pp. 281–300. See also E. J. Mishan and L. Needleman, 'Immigration: Long-Run Economic Effects', *Lloyds Bank Review*, no. 87, January 1968, pp. 15–25.

[3] Thomas, *International Migration and Economic Development*, pp. 10 et seq.

a year, equal to about 1 per cent of the present United Kingdom population';[1] that is, about five times the rate of total immigration in the period 1961–6, about eight times the rate of New Commonwealth immigration and as much as fourteen times the rate of net immigration (immigration less emigration) in the same period. This assumption, when taken in conjunction with the Mishan-Needleman hypothesis that immigrants' social capital needs are met entirely from new capital formation within a year of arrival, the residual (if any) going to the industrial sector, suggests that not only the size, but also the direction of the relevant impact (change in the capital-labour ratio) cannot be identified with actual immigrant repercussions in this period. Since the Mishan-Needleman model assumes these initial social capital requirements of immigrants are of the same order as those of the indigenous population,[2] and that this entails a deduction from industrial capital investment equivalent to 1.2 times their first year contribution to output, it is hardly surprising that the model yields, for some years, a stock of industrial capital less in absolute amount than that which would have existed in the absence of the assumed immigration.   Our own conclusion was that the industrial capital needs of immigrants are likely to be met first and their social capital requirements, in so far as they come out of new capital formation, delayed.[3]

The Mishan-Needleman model is 'dynamic' in the sense that some of the calculations take account of the possibility of increasing returns to scale and provide for an exogenous growth factor.   However, Mishan and Needleman are dubious about the presence of the former and their assumption about the latter, $1\frac{1}{2}$ per cent per annum, appears for our period to be on the small side.[4]   We return below to these dynamic aspects of the Mishan-Needleman model.

In another article where they considered the shorter-term, possibly inflationary, impacts of mass immigration—discussed more fully in the following chapter—Mishan and Needleman made some very different assumptions about capital.[5]   They postulated that all immigrant capital needs, industrial and social, are quickly met—within two years of arrival. In this model, additional industrial capital needs were related to the 'primary increase in national income . . . resulting from the immigrant inflow' by means of the average capital-output ratio, after allowing

---

[1] 'Immigration: Some Long Term Economic Consequences (Part A)', loc. cit. p. 287.

[2] More precisely, it is assumed that the 'social capital requirements for immigrants bear the same proportion to their income as do those of the indigenous population' (ibid. p. 288).

[3] See chapter 7.

[4] See below, p. 136.

[5] E. J. Mishan and L. Needleman, 'Immigration, Excess Aggregate Demand and the Balance of Payments', *Economica*, vol. xxxiii, no. 130, May 1966, pp. 129–47.

for pre-existing excess capacity.[1] This built in constancy in the capital-output ratio need not necessarily imply an unchanged capital-labour ratio. But because, in this model, the authors identify immigrant labour's contribution to national output with its average product— wages plus profit margins—an approximation to a constant capital-labour ratio is implied.[2]

Reder has drawn attention to the fact that any reduction in the capital-labour ratio as a result of immigration will be limited by a consequent rise in the rate of return to capital and a greater inducement to invest.[3] Moreover, to the extent that low population growth has been inhibiting investment, it is not inconceivable that a wave of immigration would induce so much new investment that the capital-labour ratio actually rises. However, induced investment of this sort would be more likely to occur where spare capacity was available than where resources were fully employed. The United Kingdom hardly fell into such a category in the early 1960s.[4] It is more realistic to assume (as Mishan and Needleman did in their longer-term model) that the supply of new capital in the United Kingdom depends on the community's propensity to save. From the data surveyed in chapter 5, it seems probable that, even when remittances abroad (not all of which return as export demand) are left out of account, the propensity to save of New Commonwealth immigrants is, initially at least, higher than that of the indigenous population.

Another possibility, for some years countenanced wherever migratory movements were discussed, is that: 'Immigrants and their descendants do not really augment an immigrant receiving country's population, but instead displace natives and/or their descendants by inducing them, together with their descendants, to make their net reproduction rates lower than they otherwise would have been.'[5] The effect of this would

[1] Though they believe the marginal investment responses to be near to unity, implying that there is little excess capacity (ibid. pp. 140–1).

[2] It is difficult to pin down the Mishan-Needleman model more closely on this point because of the asymmetry of treatment involved. It makes use of the national capital-output ratio for gauging capital requirements but uses, in effect, sectoral average labour productivities to measure the impact of immigrant labour on output (ibid. pp. 137–8).

[3] M. W. Reder, 'The Economic Consequences of Increased Immigration', *The Review of Economics and Statistics*, vol. xlv, no. 3, August 1963, pp. 221–30.

[4] A disadvantage commonly attributed to immigration is that in its absence 'a greater amount of capital would have been invested in labour saving machinery', (Peach, *West Indian Migration to Britain*, p. 94). If, in fact, the economy's resources are underemployed, immigration should provide an incentive to invest more; if resources are fully employed, immigrants may raise investment via a higher propensity to save. Therefore, this alleged disadvantage probably reduces to the fact that immigration is conducive to investment in equipment with a capital saving bias rather than labour saving techniques—a likely result if immigration raises the ratio of capital returns to wages.

[5] Spengler, 'Effects Produced in Receiving Countries by Pre-1939 Immigration', in *The Economics of International Migration*, p. 22.

be to dampen any tendency for immigration to reduce the capital-labour ratio, and thereby output per head. But it is now fashionable to discount such an impact, especially the relationship, at least in the direction indicated, between immigration and indigenous fertility rates.[1]

However, allowance should be made for two factors. First, largely as a result of the sharp rise in the rate at which average weekly hours of work were reduced,[2] but also on account of the extension of annual holidays (37 per cent of manual workers had more than two weeks' basic holiday in 1966, compared with less than 3 per cent in 1961), the expansion of British labour supplies in the period 1961–6 was less than that recorded for the period 1956–61, and also below that experienced in the period 1951–6. The slackening, almost to the point of standstill, in the expansion of British labour supplies would tend to create a situation in which external supplies of labour would be absorbed without any fall in the capital-labour ratio. Part of this slackening would have been because emigration from the United Kingdom continued throughout the period 1961–6 at a rate equal to about half that of total immigration,[3] and this would liberate industrial, as well as social capital for immigrant workers. Moreover, any tendency for the capital-labour ratio to fall as a result of immigration would be moderated to the extent that the fall in average hours reflected an increase in shift working—a factor which we know to have been important in the textile industry to which many coloured immigrants went as shift-workers.

Secondly, it seems fairly clear that, although the occupational and industrial distribution of New Commonwealth immigrants has not been such that they have filled gaps in the British labour force, in terms of time and place of arrival they have made a contribution.[4] In short, they have tended to arrive at times when, and gone to places where, industrial capital has afforded jobs for which there were no indigenous takers.

Among such uncertainties, it is a fact that the 'productive' capital-labour ratio and output per man both rose substantially during the period—the former by 18 per cent, the latter by 14.6 per cent.[5] Whether

---

[1] See, for example, Thomas, *International Migration and Economic Development*, p. 49.

[2] The rate at which average weekly hours worked decreased in the period 1961–6 was six times as fast as the rate in the period 1951–61. (See also chapter 3, p. 37.)

[3] OECD, *Labour Force Statistics, 1956–1966*, Paris, 1968. This source gives the following series of net immigration rates for the United Kingdom, derived as the difference between the natural and total increases in the population—1961:2.6 per thousand; 1962:1.7; 1963:0.8; 1964:−0.1; 1965:−0.5. The average rate for this five-year period, 0.9 per thousand, compares with the estimated gross immigration rate of 1.9 per thousand in the inter-censal period 1961–6 (see table 1), implying emigration at the rate of about 1.0 per thousand per annum.

[4] See chapter 2, pp. 9–14 and chapter 4, pp. 82–4.

[5] Derived from productive capital stock, productive output and labour force indices of, respectively, 122.1, 118.6 and 103.5 (see table 10, p. 37 and table 37, p. 147).

or not the capital-labour ratio would have risen even more in the absence of New Commonwealth immigration, it is impossible to say with certainty. Nevertheless, the foregoing paragraphs suggest that any unfavourable impact on this ratio would be cushioned from several directions, even neglecting the much longer-term contribution to industrial assets resulting from the fact that social capital requirements of immigrants in man-years are below those of the indigenous population.[1] Nor have we yet taken into account the possible dynamic effects of immigration which must be set against any unfavourable impact on output per head caused by adverse repercussions on the capital-output ratio. Before proceeding to consider these more dynamic elements however, we shall try to show that, even on the basis of pessimistic assumptions about immigrant induced developments in the capital-labour ratio, the indigenous population taken as a group should suffer little either in terms of lower actual incomes per head or even of improvements forgone.

Regardless of the impact of immigration on the capital-labour ratio, in the absence of any '. . . divergence between marginal private and marginal social product, an immigrant will receive no more than his marginal (private) product and will not, therefore, lower either the total income derived from natively owned factor units or the *per capita* income of natives.'[2] In short, if we identify an immigrant family's contribution to extra output with its wages, and if we assume that the family consumes no more resources than are represented by its wages, then the amount of output left for the indigenous population has not been reduced and its income per head has not declined. This does not preclude a fall in the average income per head of the whole population, immigrants and indigenous combined. Certainly, if one is concerned not only with New Commonwealth migrants but also with the children born to them in this country, the evidence suggests that their average income is below the indigenous level.[3] In these circumstances, and in the absence of offsetting factors, the arrival of immigrants could theoretically reduce the average income per head of the total population, whilst leaving untouched the average living standards of the indigenous population.

Even if New Commonwealth immigrants receive a lower income than the indigenous population, no one denies that it is more than they received in their homelands. This emphasises the need also to assess the gains and losses of migratory movements in a wider geographical framework. To the extent that many New Commonwealth immigrants were unemployed prior to their arrival in the United Kingdom,[4] their transfer is accom-

---

[1] See chapter 7, p. 125.
[2] Reder, 'The Economic Consequences of Increased Immigration', loc. cit. p. 223.
[3] See chapter 5.
[4] See chapter 4.

panied by a rise in British production without any offsetting decline in their country of origin implying, within such a wider geographical framework, a clear improvement in output per head.

A major assumption in the above reasoning is that there is no divergence between marginal private and marginal social product. This means, on one level, that should any social costs accompanying immigration—say discomfort caused by new arrivals in an already densely populated country—outweigh any social benefits, allowance for them would need to be made in the calculation. Unfortunately, not only is it difficult to distinguish costs of this nature which arise from numbers as such from those which are really associated with colour not numbers, but also they are, by nature, extremely difficult to quantify. On another level, the above condition requires that net transfers of resources to immigrants are not such that their total consumption exceeds their earnings; for this would imply that they more than exhaust their own contribution to output and make inroads into the incomes of the indigenous population.

When considering this point in the context of immigration to the United States, Reder believes that, despite what he (probably errone-ously) thought to be above-average demands on the social services, the arrival of immigrants allows certain public expenditure (for instance on defence) to be spread over a larger population in such a way that the net effect is that immigrants make no inroads into indigenous incomes. This conclusion is strongly reinforced in the case of recent New Common-wealth immigrants to this country by our own finding that their demands per head on the social services are significantly below the national average. Indeed, in the case of newly arrived immigrants—with relatively few children—the difference is even more pronounced.[1] Whilst it was not practical to estimate the relative tax contribution of immi-grants, chapter 6 suggests that the difference, even if it favours New Commonwealth immigrants, is unlikely to outweigh their smaller share of the social services.

However, whilst even a fall in the capital-labour ratio is unlikely to reduce the average indigenous income per head, immigration could have a redistributive effect that leaves some members of the indigenous population worse off and others better off. Two types of redistributory effect can be distinguished. Should immigration in fact reduce the capital-labour ratio, then there will be a tendency—under the static conditions assumed in this section—for the return on capital to rise and wage rates to fall, with obvious redistributory implications for the indigenous population. Secondly, regardless of developments in the capital-labour ratio, there may be a tendency for the wages of workers

---

[1] See chapter 6.

that are a close substitute for immigrants to decline, or their increase to be retarded. In the face of rather general agreement on this score, our examination of the evidence in chapter 9 suggests that occupations containing above-average concentrations of New Commonwealth immigrants enjoyed wage rises between 1961 and 1966 that were, in general, relatively high in relation to both other occupations and other periods.

One possible explanation of this paradox derives from the fact that the New Commonwealth immigration occurred in a period when employment was full. As a result there has been some tendency—though not a very pronounced one—for immigrants to be channelled into occupations that have experienced special difficulty in recruiting workers, and therefore where wage rises might be expected to be above average. In times when full employment was not assured, it was these redistributive effects—not only in terms of rates of pay but also as manifested in unemployment—which triggered off demands, often through trade unions, for restrictions on immigration. Repercussions on average income per head, whilst the subject of considerable academic debate, appear never to have been a major practical issue. There is little evidence of a negative impact on the standard of living as a consequence of New Commonwealth immigration in the early 1960s.

As far as the impact of New Commonwealth immigrants on social living standards of the indigenous population is concerned, chapter 7 suggests that it is not very probable that the amount of social capital available for the indigenous residents of Britain has been materially affected by New Commonwealth immigration. Indeed, it appears that, in the case of housing, the most important form of social capital, the arrival of the New Commonwealth immigrants may actually have been a factor in accelerating the improvement in indigenous standards, by stimulating the urban-suburban movement of population. In the case of schools and hospitals too, a general deleterious effect seems improbable, though it is possible that some indigenous children may find themselves not in modern buildings but in older schools which, in the absence of immigration, would have been demolished.

GROWTH IMPACTS IN DYNAMIC CONDITIONS

We must now take account of additions to output which can be attributed to causes other than changes in the inputs of labour and capital of given quality. We must now admit the possibility, indeed probability, that the aggregate production function resembles the following form rather than that assumed in the previous section:

$$X = aL^k C^j e^{rt}$$

K

In this form, the function permits output to change as a result of gains from scale of operation (where $k+j> 1$), and from all those considerations which, together, make up 'technical change' or 'progress'—an element designated by the term e^{rt} since such gains are assumed to be a function of time (t). A rough impression of the relative contribution of these factors to British growth between 1961 and 1966 can be obtained by calculating for this period the familiar, and simple, total factor productivity index.[1]

Between 1961 and 1966, the gross domestic product of the United Kingdom rose in real terms by 17.6 per cent, the economically active population by 3.5 per cent, and the total gross capital stock by 19.5 per cent. If we combine these changes on the basis of a base year labour contribution of £18.5 thousand million[2] and a capital contribution taken to be the difference between this and the 1961 gross domestic product (at factor cost) of £24.1 thousand million, we obtain a rise in total productivity of 9.7 per cent—about 2 per cent per annum. Expressed differently, the calculation attributes only 14 per cent of the rise in aggregate output between 1961 and 1966 to the increase in labour supplies, 26 per cent to the increase in capital and as much as 60 per cent to the residual factors.

Such a calculation needs to be treated both conceptually and in its application with great caution.[3] But any errors would have to be very large to negate the conclusion: that what might for convenience be termed the 'direct' contribution of labour to the growth of output in this period was minimal, and that, if the labour force in general and immigrant workers in particular made a substantial contribution to growth, it would have to be via their effect on the residual, and most important, productivity improvement.

The last few years have in fact witnessed two major attempts, by Professor C. P. Kindleberger and Professor N. Kaldor, to establish theoretically and empirically just such a link between the elasticity of and

[1] The calculation consists of deriving an index of total factor productivity as a quotient from the index of aggregate output and a weighted factor input index in which the capital and labour indices are weighted by means of their base year returns. In effect this means that the contributions to output of additional units of capital and labour are identified with, respectively, the base year return per unit of capital and the average wage; the residual increase in output over the period being attributed to all the multiplicity of causes embraced by the terms 'increasing returns to scale' and 'technical progress'. That is, the total factor productivity index reflects the difference between the actual percentage rise in output and that which would have obtained with the given changes in labour and capital inputs had they been of constant quality and the production function of the form $X=aL^mC^{1-m}$.

[2] Taken as income from employment and self-employment and, therefore, to the extent that some capital returns are included in the latter, an overstatement.

[3] For instance, the identification of capital contribution with the difference between, on the one hand, gross domestic product and, on the other, employed and self-employed income.

growth in industrial labour supplies, and improvements in total pro-ductivity.[1] Both authors ascribe the United Kingdom's relatively poor postwar growth and productivity performance to a lack of elasticity in labour supplies. If such a relationship is at all valid, the potential con-tribution to British growth and living standards of New Commonwealth immigration between 1961 and 1966 could have been substantial.

Kindleberger and Kaldor have, in this context, the same empirical point of departure: growth data and observed relationships of postwar development experience in industrialised economies, probably first brought to light in a study by the United Nations Economic Commission for Europe.[2] The ECE found a tendency among European countries, 'for relatively high rates of increase of labour force to be associated with relatively high rates of growth of labour productivity.'[3] Both Kindle-berger and Kaldor, in their theses, lean rather heavily on earlier theories: respectively, the Lewis model of growth and 'Verdoorn's law'.[4] There the similarities end. For the causal sequences with which the two authors link elastic labour supplies and productivity growth are quite different.

In Kindleberger's view the Lewis growth model with unlimited supplies of labour not only portrays British and United States development in the last century and contemporary growth in the less developed world, but also helps a great deal to explain the current inter-country pattern of western European growth. Essentially the Lewis model envisages growth in the industrial sector being sustained by a continuous transfer of labour from the agricultural sector.[5] Industrial wages remain constant at the level needed to induce this transfer and thus, while this reservoir of labour lasts, profit margins in the industrial sector are undiminished, thereby yielding investment funds and investment on a continuous basis, to match which, in a self-perpetuating process, labour supplies from the agricultural sector continue to appear. By this account, Britain has not recently performed as well as other western European countries because it possesses, for one reason or another, fewer labour supplies on which to

[1] C. P. Kindleberger, *Europe's Postwar Growth: The Role of Labor Supply*, Harvard University Press, 1967; and N. Kaldor, *Causes of the Slow Rate of Economic Growth of the United Kingdom*, Inaugural Lecture, Cambridge University Press, 1966.

[2] UNECE, *Economic Survey of Europe in 1961*, Part 2—*Some Factors in Economic Growth in Europe in the 1950's*, Geneva, 1964.

[3] Ibid. p. 13. This relationship was reflected in a regression equation derived from data relating to 22 'west' European countries, developed and less developed:

$$Y = 3.12 + 1.39X,$$

where Y represents the rate of growth of output and X the growth of the labour force.

[4] P. J. Verdoorn, 'Elements ruling the development of labour productivity', *L'Industria*, no. 1, 1949, pp. 45–53.

[5] W. A. Lewis, 'Development with Unlimited Supplies of Labour', *Manchester School*, vol. xxii, no. 2, May 1954, pp. 139–91. The above interpretation is that which Kindleberger places on the Lewis model.

draw. As a result, periods of expansion have been quickly followed by wage increases, a consequent narrowing of profit margins and a falling away of investment and thereby embodied technological improvements.

Whilst this explanation is quite a convincing one, Kindleberger's case is not helped by his attempt to force the development sequence experienced by some western European countries into the framework of the Lewis model. For all the similarities between the latter and postwar conditions in these economies, by no means can it be said to fit these situations on all fours. In relatively few western European countries did their industrial labour forces grow primarily because their agricultural labour forces contracted. Apart from the United Kingdom Belgium and Scandinavia, a natural population increase was the stronger factor in the Netherlands; in West Germany, France and Switzerland immigration was very important. Even where agricultural labour supplies played a significant role as in Italy, France and West Germany, marginal labour productivity in agriculture hardly approached zero as in the strict Lewis model. And, whilst macro-productivity improvements result, in the Lewis model, essentially from the structural employment shift from low productivity agriculture to the high productivity industrial sector, productivity gains in western Europe have derived mainly from improvements within each sector. Finally, whilst during certain periods industrial wages in West Germany, Italy and France may have risen rather less rapidly than in other western European countries, there has been no approximation to the constancy of industrial wages postulated in the Lewis growth model.

Kaldor, at the outset, draws attention to the positive postwar relationship, found among the industrialised countries of western Europe, North America and Japan, between 'the overall rate of economic growth and the *excess* of the rate of growth of manufacturing output over the rate of growth of the non-manufacturing sectors':[1] a relationship which Kaldor interpreted as revealing the manufacturing sector as the engine room of growth. And, since differences in growth rates are largely due to contrasts in productivity change, Kaldor sought the crucial link in this relationship in the association between manufacturing output and productivity—an empirical relationship previously noted by Verdoorn.[2]

---

[1] Kaldor, *Causes of the Slow Rate of Economic Growth of the United Kingdom*, p. 6. Kaldor obtained the following regression equation for the growth of G.D.P. (Y) on the growth of manufacturing output (X):

$$Y = 1.153 + 0.614X.$$

[2] Also, during the 1950s at Cambridge: see W. E. G. Salter, *Productivity and Technical Change*, Cambridge University Press, 1960 ; also W. B. Reddaway and A. D. Smith, 'Progress in British Manufacturing Industries in the Period 1948–54', *Economic Journal*, vol. lxx, March 1960, pp. 17–37.

The economic explanation of this relationship proposed by Kaldor[1] is the realisation and importance of economies of scale—interpreted in an essentially dynamic sense as those derived from more or less rapid output expansion, rather than the usual static interpretation, the absolute level of output. It is an explanation which, incidentally, finds an echo in this more conventional sense in the longer-term Mishan-Needleman model where, although the authors doubt the presence of significant economies of scale, they point out that: 'What does emerge with great clarity, however, is that ... the most sensitive parameter is the scale effect.' More precisely, a scale factor of 1.2 or more would 'seriously modify' any otherwise adverse productivity impacts of immigration.[2]

The climax of Kaldor's theory, with its special implications for British growth, is contained in the following: '[Verdoorn's law] suggests that a higher rate of growth of manufacturing output breeds higher rates of productivity growth, but not enough to obviate the need for a faster rate of growth of employment.'[3] 'In postwar Britain periods of faster growth in manufacturing industry invariably led to severe labour shortages which slowed down the growth of output ... All this suggests that a higher rate of growth could not have been maintained unless more manpower had been made available to the manufacturing industry.'[4] Like Kindleberger, Kaldor emphasised, in this context, the United Kingdom's very small labour reserves in the agricultural sector. Also like Kindleberger, he views an elastic supply of labour as vital for supporting growth. But, whilst Kaldor sees labour's role in its instrumentality in the release of economies of scale, for Kindleberger the function of the supply of labour is to avoid wage rises and the narrowing of profit margins, and thus prevent the falling off of investment.

It is easy to be convinced, and very enthusiastic, about the importance of labour supplies in promoting growth and productivity when such a conclusion is suggested by lines of economic reasoning that differ so much in their mechanics. And whilst the growth implications of immigration in such circumstances are clearly favourable, some words of caution are necessary.

[1] Kaldor's calculations suggest that in western Europe in the period 1953–4 to 1963–4, the relevant regression equation was:
$$P = 1.035 + 0.484X$$
where P represents changes in productivity in the manufacturing sector and X changes in manufacturing output.

[2] 'Immigration: Some Long Term Economic Consequences (Part A)', *Economia Internazionale*, May 1968, p. 296.

[3] Kaldor's regression equation of the rate of growth of manufacturing employment, E, on the rate of growth of manufacturing output, X, is: $E = -1.028 + 0.516X$. (*Causes of the Slow Rate of Economic Growth of the United Kingdom*, p. 12.)

[4] Ibid. pp. 25 and 26.

First, it would seem that neither the Kindleberger nor the Kaldor explanations, both being essentially in the factor-supply category of growth theory, make any allowance for the observations of a not inconsiderable number of economists who regard poor demand management—too much, too little or too unstable—as the root cause of Britain's poor growth and productivity performance. Both theories implicitly assume that demand is somehow enlarged in such a way that it draws the available labour resources into the industrial sector at the required rate. But the Kindleberger thesis, at least, directly implies that a flexible labour supply makes the management of demand easier by allowing it to expand faster without giving rise to inflationary wage rises.

Secondly, both theories attach very little direct weight to capital as a harbinger of productivity improvements. This omission, which is repugnant to intuition, is perhaps more apparent than real; both theories in fact allocate roles, if somewhat secondary ones, to capital. For Kindleberger, the enlargement of industrial capacity (presumably not excluding the embodiment of improved technology) plays a role even if, in the last analysis, it is one that is allowed by the acquisition of labour from other sectors and an absence of wage rises. Kaldor believes that the contrasting investment performance of western European countries explains their departure from the growth performance which, on the basis of available manufacturing labour supplies, would have been anticipated.[1]

Thirdly, some doubt has been cast upon the common departure point—the empirical relationship between employment and productivity improvements. Beckerman has drawn attention to the fact that, whilst this relationship may be detected on the basis of the ECE data (upon which Kindleberger drew heavily) relating to twenty-two 'west' European countries, a restriction of the analysis to the thirteen industrialised western European economies virtually destroys the relationship.[2] These ECE data related to European countries only, over the period 1949 to 1959, whereas Kaldor was able to discern the required positive relationship in the case of the industrialised countries of western Europe, North America and Japan in the period 1953-4 to 1963-4. However, Wolfe has reminded us of the statistical and methodological limitations of the type of cross-country regressions upon which Kaldor largely

---

[1] Professor J. N. Wolfe has criticised, *inter alia*, Kaldor's treatment of capital ('Productivity and Growth in Manufacturing Industry: Some Reflections on Professor Kaldor's Inaugural Lecture', *Economica*, vol. xxxv, no. 138, May 1968, pp. 117–26). In reply, Kaldor claims that, even when the role of capital is taken into account, the basic relationship between growth and employment remains undisturbed ('Productivity and Growth in Manufacturing Industry: A Reply', *Economica*, vol. xxxv, no. 140, November 1968, pp. 385–91).

[2] Beckerman and Associates, *The British Economy in 1975*, p. 22.

relies.[1]   Obviously the empirical relationship between employment and productivity changes must be the subject of further investigation before it can be wholeheartedly endorsed.

Table 36.   *New Commonwealth contribution to total and manufacturing industry labour force changes, 1961–6*

	1966 index	Change, 1961–6
	(1961 = 100)	*(Thousands)*
Total employed		
Indigenous[a]	102.8	652.4
New Commonwealth	160.3	182.1
Total labour force	103.6	834.5
Manufacturing		
Indigenous[a]	99.3	−61.1
New Commonwealth	185.4	102.0
Total labour force	100.5	40.9

SOURCE: Table 10.
[a] Total labour force less New Commonwealth.

This limitation must be kept well to the fore when considering the implications of table 36.   It is clear that, if the Kindleberger-Kaldor view of labour's role in economic development is basically valid, New Commonwealth immigration between 1961 and 1966 must have made an appreciable contribution to the rise in Britain's productivity: within the framework of immigration legislation, the arrival of New Commonwealth immigrants seems to have been keyed, above anything else, to the British employment situation and developments in the British labour force.[2] For not only did the new arrivals contribute something of the order of one to two-fifths of the increase, in this period, in the British labour force[3]— thereby helping to retard the deceleration in its growth—but also, the contribution to the growth of employment in the manufacturing sector was even more pronounced.   Table 36 shows that, while the number of indigenous manufacturing workers declined by 0.7 per cent, the number of New Commonwealth manufacturing workers increased by 85 per cent and, as a result, so did that of total manufacturing workers, by 0.5 per cent.

---

[1] 'Productivity and Growth in Manufacturing Industry: Some Reflections on Professor Kaldor's Inaugural Lecture', loc. cit.
[2] See chapter 2.
[3] See chapter 3.

Such a beneficial productivity impact takes no account of any structural improvements that derive from the arrival of New Commonwealth workers. A theme of this study has been that such benefits are probably less important than is usually thought: that the bulk of immigrant work rs are by and large fairly evenly spread over the various economic activities.

CHAPTER 9

IMMIGRATION, INFLATION AND THE BALANCE OF PAYMENTS

It is a widely held view that net immigration into a full-employment economy will contribute to inflationary forces. The reason cited for this is that, even if immigrants should have a propensity to consume which is below the level of that of the indigenous community, the additional resources made available for new investment are by no means sufficient to cover the immediate capital needs of the new members of the population. There can be no doubt that in certain circumstances the threat is real, and sometimes the inflationary contribution of immigration can be substantiated. Since 1964/5 the Swiss authorities have restricted the immigration which had contributed so much to growth in the early 1960s primarily because of a suspected inflationary impact.[1] But it seems to the present authors that it is very easy to exaggerate the amount of inflationary pressure in Britain that can be attributed to the immigration from the New Commonwealth which actually occurred during the period 1961–6.

Again, the only attempt to quantify the degree of excess demand arising in this country as a result of immigration has been made by Mishan and Needleman.[2] Their study suggests that over a period of some years large-scale immigration will give rise to excess aggregate demand. Unfortunately this study, too, is a poor guide to the implications of *actual* immigrant flows into Britain in the period 1961–6, since, as the authors stress (and as in the case of their examination of longer-term impacts), it is concerned with the 'effects of a large-scale immigration into any country that might occur under an "open door" policy'; in short, Mishan and Needleman 'were not attempting to analyse the effects of past immigration'.[3] Whilst their results are presented for a standardised unit inflow of immigrants (actually, Jamaicans), the values assumed for some of the basic parameters—the marginal investment responses especially—are strongly influenced by this assumption of mass immigration and so,

---

[1] Kindleberger, *Europe's Postwar Growth*, pp. 41–7.

[2] Mishan and Needleman, 'Immigration, Excess Aggregate Demand and the Balance of Payments', *Economica*, May 1966: also Mishan and Needleman, 'Immigration: Some Economic Effects', *Lloyds Bank Review*, no. 81, July 1966.

[3] See 'Immigration, Excess Aggregate Demand and the Balance of Payments', loc. cit., also L. Needleman, 'The Economic Effects of Immigration', Institute of Race Relations, *News Letter*, February 1967.

therefore, are the final results.[1]

A variety of factors could have helped offset the potentially inflationary impact of New Commonwealth immigration in the early 1960s. First, although in contrast to earlier years the period was one of net immigration, emigration from Britain (the effect of which is excluded in the Mishan-Needleman calculations) continued to occur, and in this period was running at a rate equivalent to about half that of total immigration. Assets, industrial and social, liberated by these emigrants would limit the new capital formation requirements of New Commonwealth immigrants.

Another possibility is that the immigration may simply have served to 'fill in' a dip in the growth of the indigenous population, in which case, again, there would need to be no acceleration in the rate of capital formation to meet the capital needs of the immigrants. The evidence set out in chart 10 points, if anything, to the opposite conclusion: that net emigration from and net immigration to the United Kingdom since the war has introduced irregularities into population changes rather than suppressed them.[2] From the beginning of the 1950s to the middle of the 1960s there was a gradual rise in the natural population increase, from about 0.3 per cent per annum to rather more than 0.7 per cent. Yet in the early part of this period, between 1950 and 1958/9, the country experienced net emigration, and from 1958/9 to 1964 net immigration. Comparable data for France, West Germany, Switzerland and the Netherlands also reveal a tendency for migratory movements to introduce, rather than offset, irregularities in population developments. Indeed, there is an intriguing contrast between this effect which migratory movements appear to have within a country over time, and the tendency emphasised in a recent study by the Economic Commission for Europe, for migratory movements between Western European countries to counteract inter-country differences in rates of population growth.[3]

---

[1] As stated above (chapter 8, p. 130), there is an inconsistency between their examination of the longer-term growth impact of immigration and the shorter-term inflationary impact. Essentially they make, in the growth context, the unfavourable assumption that as a result of immigration the capital-labour ratio will fall and, in the short-term inflationary context, the equally unfavourable, but inconsistent, assumption that immigrant capital requirements are met. In our view some, though not all, the immediate capital requirements are met, implying less of an immediate inflationary impact than in the Mishan-Needleman model, and in the longer term the capital-labour ratio, especially the industrial capital-labour ratio, will not fall to the extent implied in that model, so that, as argued in the previous chapter, the productivity implications of immigration will be more favourable than those suggested by Mishan and Needleman.

[2] In this respect, therefore, there is an interesting contrast with the way in which New Commonwealth immigrants (as workers rather than consumers) have tended to fill in gaps in the growth of the British labour force (see chapter 8, p. 132).

[3] Chapter III, 'Determinants of the Labour Supply in Europe, 1950–80' in UNECE, *Economic Survey of Europe in 1968: The European Economy in 1968*, New York, 1969.

Chart 10. *Natural population increase and net migration in five western European countries, 1946–67*

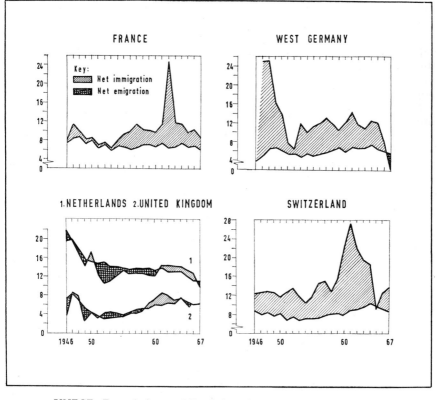

SOURCE: UNECE, *Economic Survey of Europe in 1968.*

A third factor is potentially the most important of all: the existence of spare capital capacity.[1] In the context of a cushioning role of spare capacity, a sharp distinction needs to be drawn between industrial and social capital. In the case of industrial capital, the margin of spare capacity that would have been needed to meet the additional demand derived from the New Commonwealth immigrants is really very small. The 312 thousand New Commonwealth immigrants who arrived between 1961 and 1966 represented only 0.6 per cent of the total British population. Thus, assuming New Commonwealth immigrants' output requirements per head to be identical with those of the indigenous

---

[1] Other than that 'liberated' by emigrants—that is, the above argument applies even in the absence of emigration.

population (see chapter 7) their needs, in terms of spare industrial capacity, would be commensurately small. In the period in question the British economy must be regarded as one of basically full employment of resources, but unless the pattern of immigrant demand differed markedly from the pattern of excess industrial capacity, there must have been some scope for absorbing immigrant demand by means of the activation of spare capacity, at least initially.[1] Moreover, a special way in which additional demand can be met from the existing stock of industrial capital is to expand shift working. The early 1960s witnessed such a development in the United Kingdom.

No one would argue that there is much spare social capital relative to desirable living standa ds Yet the part of this study dealing with immigrant needs for social capital, chapter 7, strongly suggests that there is much elasticity in the absorptive capacity of the existing stock of social capital—elasticity of which immigrants have made full use, especially in the case of housing. The same chapter emphasised that, eventually, the social capital needs of immigrants, along with those of the indigenous population, would have to be met in full.

Similarly, whilst spare industrial capacity might act as a buffer for immigrants' needs in the short to medium term, any consequent fall in the degree of spare capacity below a 'normal' level would need to be made good by means of additional investment in the longer term. A time pattern of events, along these lines, seems to have been experienced in Switzerland, where large-scale net immigration from 1958 onwards (see chart 10) gave rise to inflationary pressures that did not reach a peak until about four years later.[2] It is a sequence which has important implications for policy decisions associated with immigration. For it means that an inflationary situation is not foisted upon the authorities of the receiving countries immediately net immigration occurs on any scale. They are afforded a breathing space in which to plan the required investment and, if necessary, to prepare and implement compensatory disinflationary measures.

An attempt can be made to estimate the magnitude of the impact of New Commonwealth immigration on industrial capital formation in the

---

[1] Mishan and Needleman illustrate the potentially high absorption of spare capacity by showing than an annual inflow of 186 thousand families, much more than actually occurred, would be needed to use up 1 per cent of capital stock. ('Immigration, Excess Aggregate Demand and the Balance of Payments', loc. cit. p. 143.)

[2] The increases in the GDP price deflators for the years 1959 to 1963 were, respectively, 0.2 per cent, 3.6 per cent, 4.4 per cent, 5.7 per cent and 4.7 per cent. Kindleberger writes, in the context of developments in Switzerland: 'After a time, however, with full employment of domestic industrial capital, housing, schooling, hospitals and so on, additional immigration requires capital expenditure to accompany the additional labor and on this account tends to push up investment and costs.' (Europe's Postwar Growth, p. 42.)

Table 37.   *Changes in United Kingdom population and capital requirements^a, 1961–6*

	1961	1966	Change, 1961–6	1966 index (1961=100)
	(Thousands)			
Total population^b	52,709	53,788	1,079	*102.0*
of which: New Commonwealth^c	556	877	321	*157.7*
Indigenous^d	52,153	52,911	758	*101.5*
	(£ thousand millions)			
Gross productive capital stock^e	50.3	61.4	11.1	*122.1*
Productive output	16.6	19.7	3.1	*118.6*
Gross social capital stock^e	40.5	47.1	6.6	*116.3*
	(£)	*(£)*	*(£)*	
Productive output per head	315	366	51	*116.2*
Social capital per head	768	876	108	*114.1*
Capital-output ratio	*3.03*	*3.12*	*3.61^f*	*103.0*

SOURCES: *Annual Abstract of Statistics, 1968,* no. 105; *National Income and Expenditure, 1968;* table 1.

^{a} 1958 prices. ^{b} April of each year.
^{c} Based on table 1, but including an estimate for Northern Ireland.
^{d} Total population less New Commonwealth.
^{e} The published sources do not show industrial assets in textiles and agricultural buildings and vehicles separately from social capital. Data supplied by the Central Statistical Office suggest that a refinement for this would yield for industrial capital an index of *121.6* (absolute change £11,400 million) and for social capital an index of *116.6* (absolute change £6,300 million).
^{f} Incremental capital-output ratio.

period 1961–6,[1] on the assumption that excess capacity afforded no cushion whatever. Table 37 shows developments in the United Kingdom over the period. The period was essentially one in which output grew much faster than the increase in the population (of which New Commonwealth immigrants accounted for about a third), implying a substantial rise in output per head; and the rise in output was accompanied by a parallel, and in fact rather more than proportionate, rise in capital stock.

Table 38 portrays a hypothetical picture of changes in the period 1961–6 on the assumption that no immigration from the New Commonwealth occurred. It also assumes that the output needs per head of those who in fact arrived during the period were equivalent to the average needs

[1] We have preferred to examine capital formation in the five years 1962 to 1966—corresponding to the change in the stock of capital between end-1961 and end-1966—rather than in the five years 1961 to 1965. This automatically allows for some time-lag between the arrival of immigrants and consequent capital formation.

of the indigenous population in 1966; that the capital-output ratio associated with these immigrant output needs was equal to the 1966 average for the economy; and that the aggregate production function is such that, for relatively small departures from the actual 1966 level of output, there are proportionate changes in capital requirements.[1]

Table 38.   *Hypothetical changes in United Kingdom population, industrial output and capital*[a], *1961–6*

	1961	1966	Change, 1961–6	1966 index (1961 = 100)
	(Thousands)			
Total population[b]	52,709	53,467	758	*101.4*
of which: New Commonwealth[c]	556	556	—	*100.0*
Indigenous[d]	52,153	52,911	758	*101.4*
	(£ thousand millions)			
Gross productive capital stock[e]	50.3	61.0	10.7	*121.3*
Productive output	16.6	19.6	3.0	*117.8*
	(£)	*(£)*	*(£)*	
Productive output per head	315	366	51	*116.2*
Capital output ratio	*3.03*	*3.12*	*3.61*[f]	*103.0*

SOURCES: As table 37 and NIESR estimates.

[a] 1958 prices.   [b] April of each year.
[c] Based on table 1, but including estimate for Northern Ireland.
[d] Total population less New Commonwealth.
[e] Excluding textile and agricultural buildings and vehicles.
[f] Incremental capital-output ratio.

The effect of postulating no new immigration in these conditions is to reduce the productive capital stock required at the end of 1966 from £61.4 to £61.0 thousand million, that is by £400 million—or about 4 per cent of the actual net increase in productive capital, £11.1 thousand million during this period.   In terms of the gross capital formation which occurred during this period the effect is even less.   For the sum of gross capital formation over the five years 1962 to 1966 is necessarily larger than the *net* change in the stock of capital recorded between the end of 1961 and the end of 1966, a good slice of new investment being needed to replace scrapped equipment—scrapping which, in the case of industrial

---

[1] If the absence of new immigration would have implied a labour force in the productive sector smaller by about the same proportion as the accompanying lower output requirements, then we have simply assumed that a slightly smaller output could have been achieved with (identical) proportionate reductions in both labour and capital inputs.

capital, we assume is not delayed by immigration. Total gross capital formation over the period was £17.2 thousand million—implying scrappings of £6.1 thousand million (£17.2 less £11.1 thousand million) that would have had to be met whether or not immigrants came—of which £400 million represents a little over 2 per cent.

The discussion of the industrial capital requirements of New Commonwealth immigrants in chapter 7 suggests that a more valid assumption would be identical productive output requirements per head but a capital-output ratio for New Commonwealth immigrants some 15 per cent higher than the indigenous level. The effect of introducing this refinement is almost indistinguishable.[1] It suggests that, in the absence of New Commonwealth immigration, productive capital formation in the period 1961–6 would have been about 2½ per cent less.

The implications of New Commonwealth immigration for capital formation in social assets can be examined along broadly similar lines. The analysis is simpler than that of industrial capital, in the sense that we do not concern ourselves with two types of relationship—needs for output per head and capital-output ratios—but complicated somewhat because of the indications that much of the social capital needs of New Commonwealth immigrants was met by a postponement of scrapping. Indeed, if all their social capital needs had been met in this way, then the assumption of no New Commonwealth immigration would leave gross capital formation in the period, and inflationary pressures from this source, unchanged.[2]

Let us estimate, however, as in the case of industrial capital, what the hypothetical change in social capital would have been in the absence of New Commonwealth immigrants in this period, on the assumption, first, that they had social capital requirements per head equal to the average 1966 indigenous level (£876). The result is that the gross stock of social capital would have risen from £40.5 thousand million at the end of 1961 to £46.8 thousand million at the end of 1966, compared with the actual

---

[1] To be precise, the assumption of identical productive capital requirements per head reduces the end-year stock figure by £370 million. If New Commonwealth productive capital requirements were 15 per cent above the indigenous level, the 1966 capital stock figure would be reduced by £420 million.

[2] This is quite feasible in the sense that the total social capital needs of New Commonwealth immigrants in the period 1961–6 were less than the notional scrappings assumed for this period in the national accounts. Capital formation in social assets totalled £8.2 thousand million in this period and, with a net change in the gross capital stock of £6.6 thousand million, this implies scrappings of about £1.6 thousand million. Even on the assumption that the additional 321 thousand New Commonwealth immigrants (see table 37) needed, per head, £876 of social capital—the 1966 indigenous figure—this represents only £300 million of assets. To the extent that the actual rate of scrappings is overstated in the national accounts, the net rise in the stock of capital and therefore its level at the end of the period will be understated.

1966 level of £47.1 thousand million. Thus, in the absence of New Commonwealth immigration and on the above assumptions, the rise in the gross stock of social capital would have been £6.3 thousand million as opposed to the actual change of £6.6 thousand million—or some 4½ per cent less. A more realistic assumption is that the social capital requirements of New Commonwealth immigrants were about a fifth[1] below the national average. On this basis, the absence of immigration would have meant a rise in the social capital stock from £40.5 thousand million at the end of 1961 to £46.9 thousand million at the end of 1966, a rise of £6.4 thousand million, or some 3½ per cent less than the actual increase of £6.6 thousand million.[2]

Again, in terms of gross capital formation, the relevant concept for gauging the possible inflationary impact, the difference is even smaller than that suggested by these figures. Compared with the net increase in the stock of social capital of £6.6 thousand million between 1961 and 1966, gross capital formation was £8.2 thousand million.[3] Thus, on the assumption that the social capital requirements of immigrants were identical with indigenous needs, gross capital formation would have been some 3½ per cent less in the absence of New Commonwealth immigration, and, on the assumption of immigrant needs equivalent to 80 per cent of the average, gross capital formation would have been some 2½ per cent less.

Two estimates have been obtained for the impact of immigration on industrial capital requirements, according to whether one assumes New Commonwealth immigrants' industrial capital needs are equal to those of the indigenous population or, on the basis of chapter 7, about 15 per cent above the national average. Three results were obtained for social capital on each of the assumptions: all immigrant needs met by delayed scrappings; immigrant needs equal to indigenous needs; and immigrant needs a fifth below the average. Combining these industrial and social capital requirements in various ways suggests an immigrant impact on gross capital formation, between 1961 and 1966, varying from 1.5 per cent at its lowest up to 2.8 per cent. Two of the possible com-

---

[1] To be precise, 19 per cent (p. 125)—though we have rounded this to a fifth in the calculations.

[2] Interpretation of this case is not quite straightforward. As stated in chapter 7, the situation it reflects—especially in the case of the largest social asset, housing—is one where New Commonwealth immigrants obtain old social capital which provides them with four-fifths of the country's average housing usage, in the process displacing some of the indigenous population whose needs are met from new capital. The above procedure, in effect, attributes four-fifths of this new capital to immigrant needs, the balance representing an improvement in the indigenous population's standards.

[3] To the extent that the period was one in which scrappings were delayed, the actual net rise in the stock of social capital is somewhere between £6.6 and £8.2 thousand million.

binations appear especially realistic: industrial and social capital requirements based on the refinements of chapter 7; and the same industrial capital requirements together with the assumption that all immigrant social capital needs were met by delayed scrappings. These yield impacts on gross capital formation of about £600 and £300 million respectively, equivalent to 2½ per cent and 1½ per cent of actual gross capital formation between 1961 and 1966.

Since New Commonwealth immigration was responsible for as much as about a third of the population increase between 1961 and 1966, it might, at first blush, occasion surprise that the assumption of no immigration reduces new capital formation by such a relatively small amount. The explanation of this apparent anomaly is that the period in question was essentially one of capital 'deepening'—a rise in capital per head—not one of capital 'broadening'—an enlargement of the stock of capital to match a rise in numbers. The total capital stock, industrial and social together, increased by 19.5 per cent, of which as much as 17.1 per cent reflected a rise in capital per head, a development needed both to help raise output per head and to improve social living standards: two objectives which the indigenous population would have sought whether or not the period had witnessed immigration from the New Commonwealth.

Some of the capital requirements of New Commonwealth immigrants would be offset by their savings. At 1958 (gross capital formation) prices, savings of the indigenous population were £31 per head in 1961 and £34 in 1966. The information presented in chapter 5 suggested New Commonwealth savings in the range £55 to £67 per head a year.[1] Excluding remittances New Commonwealth savings were not very different from the indigenous level. Assuming that they were the same, £30, and that the 321 thousand new immigrants were evenly spread over the five-year period,[2] New Commonwealth immigrants would have provided, over that period, investment resources totalling £30 million, compared with the additional capital requirements of approximately £300 million or £600 million derived above. Deducting these contributions in terms of investment resources from the postulated additional capital requirements of New Commonwealth immigrants suggests a net impact equivalent to about 1.2 to 2.2 per cent of gross capital formation in the period.

[1] Table 24, which suggests a savings percentage (including remittances) for the New Commonwealth community of at least 16 per cent, yielding on the basis of weekly incomes of 131s. to 162s. per head, annual savings, at 1958 prices, of £55 to £67 per head. By using the incomes and savings propensities of New Commonwealth households inclusive of children born in Britain, the total savings of immigrants will tend to be underestimated.

[2] They were bunched towards the beginning, which means that these calculations may underestimate on this account also the size of New Commonwealth savings in the period, though by no means sufficiently to affect the general conclusion.

L

Whilst the additional capital requirements of New Commonwealth immigrants in this period were very small compared with total capital formation, the extent to which they could have been offset by the savings of immigrants was also small, even when allowance is made for an above-average propensity to save among New Commonwealth immigrants. Thus, judged solely in the context of capital requirements, and assuming no spare industrial capacity which could be used to meet their needs, the arrival of immigrants in this period would have given rise to a greater increase in demand than production and, in consequence, inflationary pressure. How excess demand from this source compares in size with that arising from other causes we do not know. It can only be repeated that, compared with total gross capital formation over the period and, *a fortiori*, with total demand in the economy, it was small.

There are two possible ways in which immigrants may have a dis-inflationary impact on costs, to be set against this excess demand induced by immigrant capital needs. On the one hand are the potential growth and productivity bonuses considered in the previous chapter:[1] on the other are the tendencies, widely canvassed, for immigration to reduce the rate of increase of wages in certain occupations relative to the average or to the past. Use can be made of the data relating to wage rates which were rejected in the context of a static earnings comparison to test this hypothesis.[2] It is less hazardous to assume that the occupational earnings-basic wage pattern shows some stability over time than that, at any given moment, the proportionate disparity between average earnings and the basic wage is the same for all occupations.

Table 39 presents the average annual rate of increase in the basic weekly wage for nineteen manual occupations in which New Commonwealth immigrants formed large concentrations between 1961 and 1966, a period in which the average rise in the basic weekly wage was 4.2 per cent per annum.[3] In as many as thirteen of the nineteen occupations,

---

[1] Confidence in the realism of the Mishan-Needleman short-term study is not heightened by the fact that, in addition to assuming that growth is independent of immigration (even mass immigration), their model is such that for wide and not unreasonable ranges of the marginal investment response, 'the higher the economy's growth rate the longer the initial period and the greater the magnitude of the primary excess aggregate demand'. ('Immigration, Excess Aggregate Demand and the Balance of Payments', *Economica*, May 1966, p. 145.)

[2] See chapter 4, p. 72.

[3] Consideration of this question requires that the selected immigrant occupations be 'matched' with the occupational categories in the Department of Employment and Productivity's, *Time Rates of Wages and Hours of Work*—a source which does not adhere to the standard Classification of Occupations. This 'matching' process revealed that a reasonable degree of correspondence could be achieved for nineteen of the thirty-seven selected manual occupations (that is twenty-six male occupations, plus eleven for females—see chapter 4); separate attention is paid to the four non-manual occupations—male doctors, female nurses, male and female teachers.

the average wage rise was equal to or higher than—in some cases appreciably so—the average rise of 4.2 per cent per annum; the unweighted
average of the nineteen wage increases was 4.6 per cent per annum.
The six occupations which failed to match the average rise were all male
categories—textile workers, tailors, bakers, rubber workers, engineering
labourers and laundry workers.

Table 39.   *Changes in weekly wage rates in manual immigrant occupations,
1961–6*

Census occupation	Equivalent occupation for wage index	Male or female	Wage rise (annual average)	Percentages Wage rise relative to average
071 Press Workers	Press Metal (other)	M	4.2	100
100 Fibre Preparers	⎱ Wool Textile Industry			
184 Textile Labourers	⎰ in Yorkshire	M	3.2	76
	Tailoring			
110 Tailors	Measure Cutters	M	3.8	90
110 Tailors	Cutters	F	4.9	117
112 Clothing Sewers	Machinists	F	4.8	114
120 Bakers	Baking (other)	M	3.1	74
140 Workers in Rubber	Rubber Manufacture	M	4.1	98
Labourers in	Labourers in			
181 Chemicals	Heavy Chemicals	M	4.5	107
182 Engineering	Engineering	M	3.8	90
186 Glass	Glass Containers	M	4.2	100
194 Railway Guards	Railway Guards	M	5.5	131
205 Bus Conductors	Municipal Conductors	M	5.0	119
206 Railway Porters	Railway Porters	M	5.3	126
256 Waiters	⎱			
257 Cooks	Hotels and Restaurants[a]			
258 Kitchen Hands	⎰ Other Workers	M	5.9	140
256 Waitresses	Waitresses	F	5.4	128
264 Launderers	Laundering	M	4.0	95
264 Launderers	Laundering	F	4.5	107
266 Hospital Orderlies	Hospital Orderlies	M	5.0	119
266 Hospital Orderlies	Hospital Orderlies	F	5.3	126

SOURCE: *Statistics on Incomes, Prices, Employment and Production.*

[a] Average of three categories: Unlicensed Place of Refreshment; Licensed Residential
Establishment and Licensed Restaurant; and Licensed Non-Residential Establishment.

The absence of a comparable measure of the average rise in basic
salaries makes a review of salary increases in those professions where
immigrants are important rather more difficult. However, an average
earnings series for salaries is available and, since the disparity between
basic salaries and earnings is likely to be much less pronounced than that
between basic wages and average wage earnings, this figure, which shows
a rise of 5.9 per cent for both males and females between 1961 and 1966,

has been used for comparison.[1] Compared with this average rise in salary earnings, the basic minimum salary of the two medical categories where immigrant hospital doctors are most important, registrars and senior house officers, increased by 5.0 and 5.7 per cent a year respectively. However, it should be noted that these rises were appreciably larger than that enjoyed by the category where indigenous doctors are relatively most important, consultants—their salary increase in the period averaged only 4.1 per cent a year. During the same period male teachers received a 5.9 per cent increase in salaries—equal to the average rise in salary earnings—and female teachers slightly less, 5.4 per cent. The rise in the pay of nurses, more precisely enrolled and staff nurses, was 7.0 per cent, appreciably more than the average.

The evidence suggests therefore that, for the most part, occupations where the numbers of New Commonwealth workers were disproportionately large in 1961, especially manual jobs and those where females are important, tended to enjoy above-average pay increases. It could be argued, however, that these occupations frequently enjoy above-average pay increases and that the entry of New Commonwealth immigrants has restrained the rises below their previous rates. A check on the five-year period 1956 to 1961 shows that this is not the case. In general, the rates by which pay in these nineteen occupations increased between 1956 and 1961 were below those of the later period, both in absolute terms and relative to the average increase.[2] It might still be claimed that had not New Commonwealth workers entered these occupations in such numbers, the rates of pay would have risen by more than in fact they did in the period 1961 to 1966. To the extent that New Commonwealth workers have taken up occupations where the shortage of labour is most marked, it might reasonably be expected that remuneration would have risen even more in the absence of this new supply of labour. But it would be almost impossible to gauge the magnitude of such an effect; and even more its ramifications throughout the labour market on restraining the general level of wages[3]—the route by which, for Kindle-

[1] This series covers administrative and technical grades (including employees with professional qualifications) and clerical and analogous grades. (*Statistics on Incomes, Prices, Employment and Production.*)

[2] In only three of the nineteen manual occupations did wage rates rise more in the period 1956–61 than in 1961–6. And the (unweighted) average of these rises in the period 1956–61 was equal to, not more than, 3.6 per cent per annum, the average rise for all occupations.

[3] Claims have been made that migration into Switzerland had such a general disinflationary impact, in the early stages at least: 'Up to 1962, according to informants, many Swiss thought that foreign workers held down wages and prices. After the winter of 1962/3, and especially in the spring of 1963, this view was altered, and it was thought that the way to preserve stability was to limit the inflow of labor. The change in opinion turned on whether foreign labor was combined with existing capital or gave rise to the need for new capital outlays.' (Kindleberger, *Europe's Postwar Growth*, p. 44.)

berger, elastic labour supplies promote growth and productivity.

However, if it could be demonstrated that New Commonwealth immigrants have not restricted wage rises in certain occupations below rates that would otherwise have been anticipated—and, therefore, have had no disinflationary impact on this score—by the same token they could not be accused of harming the direct interests, in terms of wage increases, of indigenous workers in these jobs.[1] Again we encounter a situation where the disadvantages with which recent immigration has been labelled are essentially alternatives. On the evidence relating to wage increases, it seems that both the disinflationary impact, in this context, of New Commonwealth workers and their redistributory impact on relative wages have been quite small.

Finally, it is instructive to view the possible inflationary impact of immigration to Britain, in the perspective of developments in other European countries. Chart 10 shows that, over the postwar period as a whole, the United Kingdom (along with the Netherlands) has been predominantly neither an immigrant nor an emigrant country. In contrast, France, West Germany and Switzerland have clearly experienced rather large-scale immigration.[2] Moreover, even in the recent period of net immigration to Britain, the rate of net inflow, relative to the growth of the total British population, was much below the rates experienced over the whole postwar period by France, West Germany and Switzerland.[3] Yet between 1950 and 1966, prices in the United Kingdom increased on average by 3.8 per cent a year, more than in West Germany, where the rate of increase was 3.0 per cent, more than in Switzerland, where it was also 3.0 per cent, though significantly below the rate of increase of 5.5 per cent in France.[4] Moreover, British prices in the period 1961–6 rose by 3.4 per cent, a rate below the longer-term increase.[5] Such evidence suggests that, if immigration has had a net inflationary impact, this effect has been more than offset by other factors both between countries and, for the United Kingdom, over time.

Perhaps it is too much to seek anything approaching a precise measurement of the inflationary pressures arising as a result of recent New

---

[1] See chapter 8, pp. 134–5.

[2] Ireland, Greece, Italy, Spain and Portugal have equally clearly been net emigration countries throughout the postwar period, often on a very large scale.

[3] Between 1950 and 1965, net immigration accounted for 50 per cent of the population increase in Switzerland, 46 per cent in West Germany, 37 per cent in France, 27 per cent in Sweden and 22 per cent in Belgium (UNECE, *Economic Survey of Europe in 1968*, p. 231). Between 1959 and 1963 (inclusive) net immigration into the United Kingdom accounted for 20 per cent of the total increase in population; over the period 1951 to 1966 it accounted for only 6 per cent of the increase.

[4] Price deflators for gross domestic product have been used.

[5] For the period 1958–66, the rate of inflation, 2.8 per cent per annum, was lower still.

Commonwealth immigration. This chapter has done nothing to change this view. It does suggest, however, that any inflationary impact resulting from New Commonwealth immigrants' capital needs was probably small, especially in relation to the other forces to which the economy was subject in this period. Moreover, immigration was accompanied by factors that would tend to counteract, if not completely negate, the inflationary impact. Given the small size of the impact and the likelihood that it would have been, in any case, a delayed one, it must surely have been a manageable problem in the sense that it could have been dealt with by appropriate planning. This chapter suggests fairly strongly that possible inflationary consequences of immigration are more properly a reason for policies which take immigration into account than for restrictions.

More than any other effect, an assessment of the immigrant impact on the balance of payments is essentially impressionistic. It is known what special considerations need to be taken into account and fed into the calculation—and these are set out below—but in many cases they consist of the end products of previous assessments, the inflationary and productivity impacts of immigration: effects which, as we have seen, are themselves rather nebulous.

There is first, what might be termed the direct effect of New Commonwealth immigration on the balance of payments, which consists essentially of the direct quantitative impact—exclusive of less direct price and cost influences—on imports and exports. The approximate size of this impact is easier to measure in the case of imports than of exports. Immigrant demand for goods and services will imply additional imports on approximately the same proportionate scale as the demands of indigenous residents. Assuming the income per head of New Commonwealth immigrants to be £520, and the savings proportion (including remittances) to be, say, 15 per cent, consumption per head would be £442 per head per year.[1] It is estimated that the 321 thousand additional immigrants present in 1966 represent an extra 1.06 million immigrant-years in the period 1961 to 1965 inclusive,[2] yielding total additional consumption expenditure by immigrants of £468 million. Adding this to our upper estimate of £600 million for additional gross capital formation induced by immigrants yields a total of £1,068 million. If the import element of this is equivalent to the average for the economy as a whole, 20 per cent (and we have no reason to think that it deviates a great deal in either direction), this suggests additional imports of £214 million—say £200

[1] Tables 22 and 24, pp. 90 and 93. It will be seen that the higher income per head of immigrants less children born in Great Britain has been taken. Import requirements per head in New Commonwealth *households* will be proportionately less than the above.
[2] Spreading the arrival of the 321 thousand immigrants (table 37) over the five-year period, in accordance with the flows shown in table 2.

million. While this figure is of the same order as the total deficit registered over the whole five years from 1961 to 1966 on the current balance
of payments, £271 million, it constitutes only 0.5 per cent of the total
import bill in the period. There will be some offset on the export side,
but it is impossible to quantify this.

Whether or not the arrival of immigrants has a direct impact on the
level of exports depends basically upon whether export orders (at existing
prices) can be met, or met in time, without additional workers. If during
this period labour bottlenecks were a factor preventing the fulfilment of
orders then obviously immigration should have helped to boost exports.
Whilst one may suspect that such situations occurred, it is impossible to
quantify the effect. It is clear, however, that failure to make any
allowance for benefits from this source would show immigrants as having
an adverse impact on the balance of payments.[1]

A similar statement can be made about the remittances abroad of New
Commonwealth immigrants. There is a clear liability here on the British
balance of payments, estimated to be—if we accept a remittance rate of
7 per cent and a New Commonwealth income per head of £520 per
annum—about £40 million over the period 1961–6. However, some of
this—the amount is very uncertain, but is unlikely to be very high—
will return as export demand.[2]

Apart from any direct quantitative effects on imports and exports,
immigration may affect these flows indirectly, via its impacts on costs
and prices. Two major channels for these impacts exist: one unfavourable, the other favourable. First, to the extent that New Commonwealth
immigration was responsible for any net inflationary impact on the
economy, a part of it would be reflected in the substitution of cheaper
imports for domestic products, and another repercussion would be a
switch of foreigners' demand away from the now more expensive British
export goods. We have noted that any such inflationary effect, if it
existed at all, would have been unlikely to be large. But to the extent
that any adverse impact on the balance of payments did arise—as a result
of this factor or the direct quantitative immigration effects referred to
above—and was partially responsible for the 1967 devaluation of sterling,
the repercussion becomes translated into an adverse movement in
Britain's terms of trade.

The adverse impact of such a development on Britain's real income
would, in turn, need to be set against the potential large-scale productivity
gains which, we have noted, may well have accompanied New Common-

---

[1] Taken alone, an immigrant boost to exports would, of course, accentuate domestic
inflationary pressures.

[2] When considering immigrant capital requirements, a deliberately high assumption, a
return of half in the form of export demand, was made (chapter 7).

wealth immigration. However, not only should this factor be set against any possible adverse developments in the terms of trade, it is also one which could well prevent such an unfavourable impact. By improving productivity and reducing costs, domestic demand could be diverted from imports and at the same time the competitiveness of exports improved. As a result, New Commonwealth immigration could have had a net beneficial impact on the balance of payments, the extent of which is unfortunately unknown because of the uncertainty which attaches to this possible productivity bonus.

CHAPTER 10

CONCLUSIONS

This study has been concerned with the macro-economic impact of recent-immigration to this country. More precisely, it has attempted to evaluate some of the economic effects on the receiving country of largely—but not entirely—coloured immigration from the New Commonwealth. Attention has been focused on immigration and changes which occurred in Britain between the years 1961 and 1966. These are years for which we have most information in the censuses, and they also cover a period identified largely, if not precisely, with the recent influx of New Commonwealth migrants to this country.

A feature of the study has been the frequency with which the alleged disadvantages for Britain of recent immigration are revealed, on closer scrutiny, to be *alternative* impacts. At times, both high and low rates of unemployment have been claimed as features of the New Commonwealth labour force and, moreover, both have been seen as disadvantageous in that they represent, respectively, a burden on the social services and a contribution to racial tension. In fact, the evidence suggests that at times of generally low unemployment there is little difference between indigenous and immigrant rates, and whilst New Commonwealth unemployment might increase disproportionately with a rise in general unemployment, this means that immigrants bear much of the strain of deflationary fluctuations, without giving rise to a cost effect that weighs heavily on the social services.

Secondly, immigration has been labelled, at one and the same time, as provoking inflationary processes in the economy and adversely affecting workers in some occupations as a result of a restraining influence on certain wages. This paper suggests that, in the case of this pair of alternative impacts, the former is probably the more important. There is no way of assessing any restraint on wage rises as a result of high concentrations of immigrants in some jobs, and therefore neither adverse redistributory nor welcome disinflationary influences from this source can be identified.

Thirdly, immigrant needs for social and industrial capital have been thought of as both inflationary and injurious to the living standards of the indigenous population. But again, there exists a 'trade-off' relationship between these two impacts. If immigrant capital requirements have been met in full by means of potentially inflationary capital expenditure, indigenous living standards can hardly have been adversely affected in this respect. The study suggests that, in all probability, indigenous living standards have not suffered as a result of immigrants' capital needs—indeed they may have marginally improved—but that, for various reasons, the amount of inflationary capital expenditure required has been relatively small.

A consideration of the capital requirements of immigrants and their possible inflationary impact provides a useful starting point for a review of the findings of this study. Since in principle it is concerned with the impact of new immigrants in the period 1961–6, and excludes implications attributable to children eventually born to them in this country, any long-term evaluation of the capital requirements per head of immigrants would almost certainly reveal that they are lower than those of an indigenous inhabitant who has spent all his life in this country. For the essence of immigrant flows is that normally—and recent New Commonwealth migration to this country was no exception—they consist of individuals who have just entered upon their working life. A narrowly economic inspection of such inflows reveals the acquisition of workers who will contribute, like indigenous workers, to capital formation, but in whom much capital, social and industrial, has already been embodied, the cost of which the recipient country has been spared.

However, this study has been concerned with the more immediate economic impacts of immigration. It suggests that the requirements of new immigrants on arrival in this country are rather higher than those of the indigenous population in the case of industrial capital, rather lower in the case of social capital and, taken all round, are probably not much different. In terms of the additional capital formation required, however, the needs of new immigrants are really quite small, probably not more than about 2½ per cent of total capital formation in the period 1961–6, despite the fact that New Commonwealth immigration was responsible for almost a third of the increase, during this period, in the British population. There are two reasons for this. First, many of the social capital needs of immigrants have been met from delayed scrappings. Whilst this has substantially reduced the potentially inflationary new capital formation required by immigrants, it would be wrong to suppose that it is a solution devoid of any economic cost. For although the opportunity-cost of buildings due for slum clearance may be negligible, that of the land on which they stand is often high. Secondly, capital formation (like many other economic variables—the balance of payments for instance) has been keyed not so much to changes in the size of the population as to changes in living standards, and whilst, during the period in question, the former, even inclusive of immigration, was not very large, the latter continued to rise at an appreciable rate. Between 1961 and 1966 whereas the rise in gross domestic product was 17½ per cent, the increase in the population was only 2 per cent, so that the difference represented a rise in real incomes per head. The evidence suggests that, compared with the extent to which British aspirations, individual and collective, for higher living standards were responsible for inflation in this period, the role of immigration was minimal, especially when account is taken of certain disinflationary influences that also accompanied it.

On the other hand, the discussion and evidence presented in chapter 8, whilst by no means conclusive, suggest fairly strongly that immigration did much to allow these aspirations for higher living standards to be realised. Certainly it seems improbable that, as some have feared, immigration has restrained indigenous living standards below the level which, in its absence, they might have attained. Among other evidence which points to this conclusion, special mention should be made of those sections of the study that indicate demands on the social services below those of the indigenous population, and an impact on the housing market which may well have helped, marginally, to raise the standards at which the indigenous population, on average, lives.

The more positive, potentially large, impact on productivity growth and improvements in British living standards stems from the impact of immigration on the labour force. Yet this impact does not appear to have been derived from the essentially 'structural' benefits which New Commonwealth workers are widely supposed to have brought to the British economy. Contrary to popular belief, only a minority of recent immigrants to Britain have facilitated growth by contributing to structural changes in the British economy either specifically, in the form of a 'replacement' labour force in declining sectors, or as a boost to labour force supplies in expanding jobs and industries. Rather has immigration substantially mitigated a fall in the rate at which the indigenous labour force was increasing, at a time when economists were beginning to identity inelasticity in the total labour supply as a cause of poor growth and productivity performances. In these circumstances, the contribution of New Commonwealth immigration to improvements in British living standards could well have been large. With the techniques at our disposal, however, it is not measurable, and for this reason it is impossible to gauge with any confidence the direction, let alone the size, of any immigration impact on the balance of payments.

The study has been solely concerned with the economic impacts of immigration in the recipient country. Paradoxically, a study that also embraced effects in the countries of origin would in many ways have been conceptually easier though statistically more difficult. A calculus of productivity changes accompanying migration would point even more positively to net gains if one were to take into account the fact that the marginal productivity of New Commonwealth workers in their countries of origin was frequently very low.[1] But the fact that migration to this country has benefited individual members of the New Commonwealth community should certainly not be taken to mean that it is preferable to, say, either the donation of more aid to the developing world, or the adoption of a more liberal import policy.

Within its relatively narrow terms of reference, the study was intended to be descriptive rather than prescriptive. Yet it would be foolish to pretend that its contents, if valid, hold no lessons for British economic and social policy. Three, in particular, stand out. First, if the discussion of the impact of immigration on British growth and productivity gains is substantially correct, then the economic cost of an unduly restrictive immigration policy could well be high—especially since the natural demographic forces in this country are such that, certainly up to 1980, the rate of increase of the labour force will be even less than the small expansion experienced between 1960 and 1965.[2] Secondly, whilst the economy has probably already experienced most of the benefits,[3] especially the productivity boost, accompanying immigration, some of the costs are still to be met, particularly delayed capital expenditure to raise immigrants' living standards to those of the indigenous population. Minimising the inflationary impact of this expenditure will require appropriate planning and policies on the part of the authorities. More generally, the potentially inflationary impact of immigration is less a reason for restricting immigration than for anticipating it. Thirdly, there would seem to be no great economic loss involved in a policy for dispersing the location of immigrants in this country. Such a policy could well help to ease the social problems of immigration, to the solution of which it is hoped this study will contribute.

---

[1] Doctors and nurses are a special case.

[2] 'Determinants of the Labour Supply in Europe, 1950–1980', in *Economic Survey of Europe in 1968*, pp. 65–6.

In this respect, the United Kingdom is in the company of Sweden, Switzerland and West Germany. The ECE comments: 'These are the countries in which it may most plausibly be expected that labour shortages will result either in raising activity rates, or in immigration, if the momentum of economic growth is to be kept up.' (ibid. pp. 65–6.)

[3] The benefit implied in immigrant demands on the social services that are below the indigenous level will persist for some years.

APPENDIX A

OCCUPATION AND INDUSTRIAL DISTRIBUTIONS

It is possible to make some assessment of the relative contributions of indigenous-immigrant differences in occupational distributions, and of differences in their occupation-industry matrices, to the observed variations in the industrial distributions of the indigenous and New Commonwealth labour forces. This can be done by calculating the hypothetical industrial distribution of the New Commonwealth labour force from its actual occupational distribution, on the assumption that it was allocated among industries in accordance with the indigenous occupation-industry matrix. The resulting hypothetical industrial distribution for New Commonwealth males and females together, in 1961, on the basis of the total labour force matrix for England and Wales,[1] can then be compared with the actual industrial distributions of the indigenous and New Commonwealth labour forces. Proximity of the hypothetical New Commonwealth industrial distribution to the actual indigenous industrial distribution would suggest that differences between indigenous and immigrant occupation-industry matrices did more to shape the differences between the industrial distributions of New Commonwealth and of indigenous workers than differences between their occupational distributions. Proximity of the hypothetical New Commonwealth industrial distribution to the actual New Commonwealth industrial distribution would indicate that the indigenous and immigrant matrices were very similar, and that observed contrasts in their industrial distributions could be traced largely to occupational differences. If the occupation-industry matrices for indigenous and New Commonwealth workers were identical, the matrix-standardised New Commonwealth industrial distribution would coincide with the actual New Commonwealth industrial distribution.

The results show that, in 1961, the mean deviation between the actual indigenous and the matrix-standardised New Commonwealth industrial distributions was 0.85, and between the latter and the actual New Commonwealth industrial distribution was 0.96. Since the two mean deviations are of the same order, it would seem that the occupational and matrix contributions to differences between the industrial distributions of the indigenous and New Commonwealth labour forces were of a similar order of magnitude, though neither of them are very large, because there is, in any case, relatively little difference between the indigenous and New Commonwealth industrial distributions.

[1] General Register Office, *Census 1961, Industry Tables, Part I*, H.M.S.O., London, 1966, table 7.

164

LOCATION AND INDUSTRIAL DISTRIBUTIONS

Locational contrasts would have had an important influence on differences between the indigenous and immigrant industrial distributions if, as one might be excused for expecting, there existed: (a) sharp differences between the conurbation and national industrial distributions of the indigenous labour force and (to a lesser extent given the preponderance of conurbation workers in the New Commonwealth labour force) between the conurbation and national industrial distributions of the New Commonwealth labour force; but (b) rather less distinction between the industrial distributions of indigenous and immigrant workers in the conurbations. In these circumstances the relative concentration of New Commonwealth workers within the special industrial framework of the conurbations could have contributed substantially to indigenous-immigrant industrial contrasts at the national level.

These expectations were not borne out in 1961. Indeed an opposite effect is found. The differences between the indigenous and New Commonwealth industrial distributions in the conurbations (1.6 for males, 1.9 for females and 1.6 for males and females), are no narrower than those at the national level (1.6, 1.8 and 1.6 respectively); while conurbation-national differences are appreciably smaller in the case of both indigenous (1.1, 0.5 and 0.9) and New Commonwealth (0.8, 0.7 and 0.7) workers.[1] For both indigenous and New Commonwealth workers, public administration activities were relatively underrepresented and transport activities relatively overrepresented in the conurbations. There the similarities end. In the case of indigenous workers the other activities appreciably underrepresented in the conurbations were agriculture and mining; and those overrepresented, engineering and finance. For the New Commonwealth workers the other principal underrepresented activity was professional services (mainly medical) and the over-represented activity, clothing. Obviously urban location does much to restrict mining and agricultural activities for immigrant workers but, equally clearly, in the circumstances revealed by these data, it is not too

---

[1] Moreover, the mean deviations presented for the conurbation-national differences will tend to overstate the true distinction. For whilst indigenous-immigrant differences within the conurbations have been measured between two distributions adjusted for bias, the con-urbation-national differences are between distributions which are, respectively, adjusted and unadjusted (see pp. 47–8). The error introduced may be appreciable in the case of the New Commonwealth group where the conurbation factors are rather large, and for which, also, the conurbation and national definitions do not coincide.

surprising that the contribution of the special features of New Commonwealth workers' locational pattern to general differences in their industrial distribution appears to be small.

APPENDIX C

TABLES

Appendix table 1. *The regional distribution of immigrants, 1961 and 1966*

Regions[a]	All immigrants		New Commonwealth		India and Pakistan		British Caribbean		Other New Commonwealth		*Percentages* Total population	
	1961	1966	1961	1966	1961	1966	1961	1966	1961	1966	1961	1966
Northern	2.0	1.9	1.9	1.6	2.7	2.1	0.4	0.4	2.3	2.3	6.3	6.2
North Western	9.1	8.9	5.5	6.3	6.2	7.8	4.7	5.4	5.6	5.5	12.8	12.6
Yorkshire, Humberside and East Midlands[b]	10.2	10.3	9.1	10.6	11.1	14.8	9.1	9.3	6.6	6.9	15.1	15.2
West Midlands	9.5	10.3	11.6	13.2	13.3	17.8	16.4	15.5	4.7	5.4	9.3	9.4
South Eastern[c]	56.3	56.8	61.8	59.8	54.5	49.2	65.2	65.5	67.1	66.6	34.6	34.8
South Western	5.1	5.0	5.3	4.6	5.9	4.1	2.8	2.6	7.2	7.1	6.6	6.8
Wales	2.3	2.0	1.5	1.2	1.5	1.0	0.8	0.7	2.1	1.9	5.2	5.1
Scotland	5.4	4.8	3.4	2.7	4.8	3.2	0.6	0.5	4.4	4.3	10.1	9.9
All regions	100.0	100.0	100.0	100.0	100.0	100.0	100.0	100.0	100.0	100.0	100.0	100.0
Total (*thousands*)	2221.8	2603.2	541.1	850.6	197.9	315.5	172.9	270.1	170.3	265.0	51,283.9	52,303.7

Conurbations[a]												
Tyneside	1.1	1.0	1.0	0.9	1.9	1.5	0.2	0.1	1.2	1.2	5.1	5.1
West Yorkshire	5.7	6.2	5.0	6.7	8.9	12.9	3.8	4.0	2.4	2.8	10.2	10.5
S.E. Lancashire	8.7	8.8	4.5	5.7	5.4	7.2	4.1	5.1	4.2	4.7	14.5	14.7
Merseyside	3.4	2.9	1.9	1.5	2.4	1.5	0.8	0.8	2.9	2.5	8.3	8.2
West Midlands	11.1	12.2	14.3	15.9	17.8	23.0	18.3	17.2	4.5	5.3	14.2	14.5
Greater London	69.9	68.8	73.3	69.3	63.6	53.9	72.8	72.7	84.8	83.5	47.7	47.0
All conurbations	100.0	100.0	100.0	100.0	100.0	100.0	100.0	100.0	100.0	100.0	100.0	100.0
Total *(thousands)*	*1158.6*	*1361.2*	*330.9*	*529.5*	*103.5*	*178.4*	*135.5*	*208.8*	*91.9*	*142.3*	*16,746.3*	*16,327.4*
Conurbations	52.1	52.3	61.2	62.3	52.3	56.5	78.4	77.3	54.0	53.7	32.7	31.2
Other areas	47.9	47.7	38.8	37.7	47.7	43.5	21.6	22.7	46.0	46.3	67.3	68.8
TOTAL	100.0	100.0	100.0	100.0	100.0	100.0	100.0	100.0	100.0	100.0	100.0	100.0

SOURCES: *Census 1961, Birthplace and Nationality Tables* and *Commonwealth Immigrants in the Conurbations; Sample Census 1966, Commonwealth Immigrant Tables.*

[a] Corresponding to 1966 definition of regions and conurbations.

[b] The former East and West Ridings and North Midlands, less Peterborough.

[c] The former London and S.E., Eastern and Southern, plus Peterborough; currently the South Eastern and East Anglian regions.

Appendix table 2.1. *The occupational distribution of the immigrant labour force, 1961 and 1966 (males)*

Occupation	All immigrants 1961	All immigrants 1966	New Commonwealth 1961	New Commonwealth 1966	India and Pakistan 1961	India and Pakistan 1966	British Caribbean 1961	British Caribbean 1966	Other New Commonwealth 1961	Other New Commonwealth 1966	Percentages Total labour force 1961	Percentages Total labour force 1966
I Farmers	2.62	1.87	1.04	0.50	1.48	0.48	0.27	0.22	1.32	0.94	5.44	4.75
II Miners	1.90	1.23	0.37	0.25	0.32	0.15	0.55	0.49	0.21	0.09	3.24	2.33
III Chemical Workers	0.83	0.84	0.90	0.88	0.86	0.90	1.29	1.19	0.44	0.38	0.80	0.80
IV Glass Workers	0.49	0.42	0.41	0.44	0.35	0.48	0.55	0.49	0.33	0.26	0.44	0.43
V Metal Workers	1.42	1.70	1.57	2.47	1.21	2.91	2.80	2.95	0.53	0.91	1.42	1.24
VI Electrical Workers	1.81	2.17	2.37	2.52	2.44	1.95	2.35	2.88	2.25	3.11	2.95	3.30
VII Engineering Workers	11.66	13.75	11.91	14.85	11.80	13.50	14.96	19.11	7.97	11.37	14.67	15.40
VIII Woodworkers	2.35	2.70	2.84	3.29	0.85	1.58	6.23	6.69	1.67	1.76	2.74	2.85
IX Leather Workers	0.47	0.44	0.57	0.62	0.22	0.31	0.52	0.67	1.26	1.15	0.57	0.45
X Textile Workers	1.30	2.05	1.56	3.84	2.70	7.65	1.05	0.89	0.28	0.60	1.04	1.01
XI Clothing Workers	1.17	0.98	1.28	1.37	0.42	0.94	0.82	0.94	3.39	2.86	0.57	0.53
XII Food Workers	1.46	1.57	1.36	1.73	0.86	1.40	1.79	2.14	1.63	1.79	1.81	1.74
XIII Paper Workers	0.71	0.80	0.74	0.85	0.77	0.90	0.67	0.93	0.77	0.61	1.37	1.39
XIV Other Manufacturing	1.61	1.94	2.02	2.78	1.51	2.89	3.38	3.67	1.07	1.27	1.14	1.29
XV Construction Workers	3.57	3.97	0.86	1.16	0.57	0.63	1.20	1.94	0.91	1.06	3.51	3.70
XVI Painters	1.75	1.82	1.28	1.45	0.51	0.72	2.23	2.83	1.32	0.91	1.99	1.95
XVII Crane Drivers, etc.	2.12	2.46	1.51	2.00	0.96	1.68	2.59	3.01	1.00	1.16	1.91	1.97
XVIII Labourers n.e.c.	14.45	13.42	13.84	15.32	10.28	16.79	24.21	19.92	5.95	5.78	7.66	7.48
XIX Transport Workers	6.22	6.85	8.76	8.49	8.53	7.06	11.42	12.62	5.56	5.36	8.52	8.34
XX Warehousemen	2.82	2.96	2.94	3.16	2.66	2.75	3.50	3.56	2.67	3.40	3.23	3.34
XXI Clerical Workers	5.44	5.37	7.99	6.32	11.02	7.44	3.13	2.58	9.35	9.52	7.00	6.96
XXII Sales Workers	5.11	4.58	4.28	3.44	6.56	4.79	0.77	0.79	5.09	4.63	7.88	7.70
XXIII Service Workers	8.07	8.57	8.44	7.71	5.08	4.49	4.43	3.44	19.67	20.22	5.06	5.43
XXIV Administrators	3.19	3.26	2.74	1.92	4.27	2.68	0.48	0.41	3.16	2.61	3.71	4.43
XXV Professional Workers	9.94	10.21	12.01	9.95	16.87	12.28	3.25	3.22	15.51	15.09	7.88	9.16
XXVI Armed Forces	5.07	3.44	3.25	1.80	4.29	1.88	1.27	1.26	4.16	2.41	1.95	1.49
XXVII Inadequately Described	2.46	0.63	3.15	0.89	2.61	0.77	4.29	1.16	2.53	0.75	1.50	0.54
Total Economically Active	100.0	100.0	100.0	100.0	100.0	100.0	100.0	100.0	100.0	100.0	100.0	100.0
(*Thousands*)	890.5	1112.1	226.3	353.3	91.8	157.6	83.3	115.7	50.7	80.1	16,235.6	15,993.8

SOURCES: *Census 1961, Occupation Tables and Industry Tables; Sample Census 1966, Economic Activity Tables,* vol. III.

Appendix table 2.2. The occupational distribution of the immigrant labour force, 1961 and 1966 (females)

Occupation	All immigrants 1961	All immigrants 1966	New Commonwealth 1961	New Commonwealth 1966	India and Pakistan 1961	India and Pakistan 1966	British Caribbean 1961	British Caribbean 1966	Other New Commonwealth 1961	Other New Commonwealth 1966	Percentages Total labour force 1961	Percentages Total labour force 1966
I Farmers	0.50	0.48	0.37	0.22	0.70	0.44	0.06	0.03	0.45	0.38	1.14	1.18
II Miners	—	—	—	—	—	—	—	—	—	—	0.01	—
III Chemical Workers	0.16	0.17	0.12	0.22	0.19	0.21	0.13	0.30	—	0.08	0.20	0.20
IV Glass Workers	0.14	0.15	0.13	0.15	0.27	0.10	0.03	0.22	0.11	0.08	0.47	0.40
V Metal Workers	0.14	0.17	0.23	0.26	0.08	0.10	0.41	0.45	0.11	0.05	0.14	0.14
VI Electrical Workers	0.99	1.26	1.05	1.60	0.85	1.49	1.48	1.94	0.56	1.02	0.72	0.98
VII Engineering Workers	3.93	4.91	4.22	6.80	1.86	3.29	7.75	10.97	1.35	2.16	3.50	3.46
VIII Woodworkers	0.10	0.13	0.16	0.17	0.08	0.15	0.25	0.19	0.11	0.13	0.15	0.15
IX Leather Workers	0.58	0.57	0.76	0.71	0.39	0.15	1.17	1.11	0.56	0.51	0.84	0.72
X Textile Workers	2.43	2.15	1.09	1.49	0.54	1.34	1.80	2.05	0.62	0.54	3.82	2.75
XI Clothing Workers	5.65	5.73	9.96	10.47	2.47	3.37	11.73	10.11	17.68	18.64	5.02	4.32
XII Food Workers	1.10	1.25	1.25	1.85	0.85	0.85	1.73	2.73	0.95	1.13	1.31	1.38
XIII Paper Workers	0.82	0.70	1.11	0.65	0.62	0.59	1.80	0.74	0.62	0.51	1.46	1.28
XIV Other Manufacturing	1.60	1.70	1.99	2.36	1.24	1.39	3.22	3.31	0.90	1.48	1.58	1.45
XV Construction Workers	—	0.04	—	0.02	—	0.05	—	0.01	—	—	0.01	0.02
XVI Painters	0.13	0.13	0.13	0.19	—	0.08	0.32	0.32	—	0.03	0.17	0.12
XVII Crane Drivers, etc.	0.03	0.02	0.03	0.02	—	—	0.03	0.04	0.06	—	0.04	0.04
XVIII Labourers, n.e.c.	1.65	1.42	2.32	2.28	0.77	1.70	4.32	3.28	1.01	0.89	1.26	1.07
XIX Transport Workers	1.43	1.53	1.59	1.59	1.86	1.70	1.70	1.84	1.01	1.00	1.90	1.85
XX Warehousemen	3.31	3.64	3.59	4.77	2.51	3.35	5.45	6.19	1.85	3.42	3.87	3.71
XXI Clerical Workers	17.27	17.88	21.07	18.01	38.59	34.91	6.62	7.60	21.38	21.12	25.35	25.83
XXII Sales Workers	6.67	7.04	3.75	3.38	6.19	6.64	0.98	1.25	5.16	4.20	12.99	12.99
XXIII Service Workers	28.32	27.79	17.19	19.14	13.19	14.35	20.62	22.11	16.89	18.26	21.51	23.96
XXIV Administrators	0.63	0.69	0.56	0.42	1.08	0.98	0.06	0.08	0.67	0.51	0.52	0.65
XXV Professional Workers	19.82	19.56	23.53	22.13	23.39	21.89	22.92	21.91	24.80	22.81	10.15	10.27
XXVI Armed Forces	0.20	0.21	0.29	0.16	0.46	0.33	0.22	0.05	0.17	0.19	0.16	0.14
XXVII Inadequately Described	2.40	0.68	3.51	0.94	1.82	0.57	5.20	1.17	2.98	0.86	1.71	0.94
Total Economically Active	100.00	100.00	100.00	100.00	100.00	100.00	100.00	100.00	100.00	100.00	100.00	100.00
(Thousands)	424.4	597.1	91.0	150.1	28.4	38.9	44.9	74.1	17.7	37.1	7780.3	8862.6

SOURCES: As appendix table 2.1.

Appendix table 2.3. *The occupational distribution of the immigrant labour force, 1961 and 1966 (males and females)*

Occupation	All immigrants 1961	All immigrants 1966	New Commonwealth 1961	New Commonwealth 1966	India and Pakistan 1961	India and Pakistan 1966	British Caribbean 1961	British Caribbean 1966	Other New Commonwealth 1961	Other New Commonwealth 1966	*Percentages* Total labour force 1961	Total labour force 1966
I Farmers	1.93	1.39	0.85	0.42	1.33	0.47	0.16	0.15	1.09	0.76	4.05	3.48
II Miners	1.29	0.80	0.25	0.17	0.25	0.12	0.39	0.30	0.14	0.06	2.19	1.50
III Chemical Workers	0.62	0.61	0.66	0.68	0.75	0.76	0.93	0.84	0.27	0.28	0.60	0.59
IV Glass Workers	0.38	0.33	0.31	0.35	0.33	0.41	0.39	0.38	0.27	0.20	0.45	0.42
V Metal Workers	1.00	1.16	1.20	1.81	0.91	2.35	1.94	1.97	0.41	0.64	1.00	0.85
VI Electrical Workers	1.54	1.85	2.02	2.24	2.00	1.86	2.10	2.51	1.77	2.45	2.23	2.47
VII Engineering Workers	9.16	10.66	9.71	12.45	9.40	11.48	12.43	15.93	6.14	8.45	11.05	11.14
VIII Woodworkers	1.62	1.80	2.05	2.36	0.67	1.30	4.12	4.15	1.23	1.25	1.90	1.88
IX Leather Workers	0.51	0.49	0.63	0.65	0.25	0.28	0.70	0.84	1.09	0.95	0.66	0.55
X Textile Workers	1.67	2.09	1.42	3.14	2.25	6.40	1.32	1.34	0.27	0.58	1.94	1.63
XI Clothing Workers	2.62	2.64	3.78	4.09	0.91	1.42	4.66	4.52	7.50	7.86	2.01	1.88
XII Food Workers	1.35	1.46	1.32	1.76	0.83	1.29	1.79	2.37	1.50	1.58	1.65	1.61
XIII Paper Workers	0.75	0.77	0.85	0.79	0.75	0.84	1.09	0.86	0.68	0.58	1.40	1.35
XIV Other Manufacturing	1.60	1.86	2.02	2.65	1.50	2.60	3.34	3.53	1.09	1.34	1.28	1.35
XV Construction Workers	2.42	2.59	0.60	0.82	0.42	0.51	0.78	1.19	0.68	0.72	2.38	2.39
XVI Painters	1.22	1.23	0.94	1.08	0.42	0.60	1.55	1.85	0.96	0.63	1.40	1.30
XVII Crane Drivers, etc.	1.44	1.60	1.07	1.41	0.75	1.34	1.71	1.85	0.68	0.79	1.30	1.28
XVIII Labourers n.e.c.	10.32	9.23	10.53	11.43	7.99	13.80	17.25	13.42	4.50	4.23	5.59	5.19
XIX Transport Workers	4.68	4.99	6.68	6.44	6.90	6.00	8.08	8.41	4.23	3.98	6.37	6.03
XX Warehousemen	2.97	3.20	3.15	3.64	2.66	2.87	4.12	4.59	2.46	3.40	3.44	3.47
XXI Clerical Workers	9.26	9.74	11.75	9.81	17.55	12.88	4.35	4.54	12.69	13.19	12.94	13.69
XXII Sales Workers	5.61	5.44	4.13	3.42	6.49	5.15	0.78	0.97	5.18	4.50	9.54	9.59
XXIII Service Workers	14.61	15.28	10.97	11.12	7.07	6.44	10.10	10.73	18.96	19.60	10.39	12.04
XXIV Administrators	2.36	2.36	2.11	1.47	3.49	2.34	0.31	0.29	2.46	1.95	2.68	3.08
XXV Professional Workers	13.13	13.47	15.32	13.58	18.39	14.18	10.10	10.52	18.15	17.54	8.62	9.55
XXVI Armed Forces	3.50	2.31	2.43	1.31	3.33	1.58	0.93	0.79	3.00	1.71	1.37	1.01
XXVII Inadequately Described	2.44	0.65	3.25	0.91	2.41	0.73	4.58	1.16	2.59	0.78	1.57	0.68
Total Economically Active	100.00	100.00	100.00	100.00	100.00	100.00	100.00	100.00	100.00	100.00	100.00	100.00
(Thousands)	1314.9	1709.1	317.3	503.4	120.2	196.4	128.7	189.8	68.4	117.2	24,015.9	24,856.5

SOURCES: As appendix table 2.1.

Appendix table 3.1. *The industrial distribution of the immigrant labour force, 1961 and 1966 (males)*

Percentages

Industry	All immigrants 1961	All immigrants 1966	New Commonwealth 1961	New Commonwealth 1966	India and Pakistan 1961	India and Pakistan 1966	British Caribbean 1961	British Caribbean 1966	Other New Commonwealth 1961	Other New Commonwealth 1966	Total labour force 1961	Total labour force 1966
I Agriculture	2.23	1.55	0.97	0.45	1.40	0.45	0.15	0.15	1.29	0.88	4.85	4.17
II Mining	2.10	1.48	0.55	0.42	0.45	0.34	0.64	0.64	0.60	0.26	4.47	3.48
III Food	2.79	2.83	3.00	3.31	2.07	2.75	3.78	4.07	3.62	3.32	2.75	2.88
IV Chemicals	1.87	1.78	1.88	1.57	2.01	1.43	2.02	1.95	1.49	1.27	2.36	2.28
V Metals	3.53	3.96	4.90	6.60	4.85	8.73	7.56	6.94	1.46	1.85	3.54	3.31
VI Engineering	9.68	10.40	11.36	11.77	13.78	13.41	11.24	11.55	7.27	8.78	9.68	10.28
VII Shipbuilding	0.56	0.53	0.64	0.34	0.54	0.28	0.37	0.21	1.19	0.64	1.44	1.08
VIII Vehicles	4.74	4.92	4.52	4.70	5.60	5.00	4.49	5.96	2.68	2.29	4.64	4.49
IX Metals n.e.s.	2.31	3.09	3.05	4.66	2.49	5.28	4.84	5.42	1.64	2.34	2.25	2.46
X Textiles	2.63	3.38	3.10	5.63	4.91	10.56	2.36	1.91	0.89	1.16	2.32	2.25
XI Leather	0.33	0.35	0.32	0.46	0.24	0.34	0.37	0.74	0.40	0.32	0.23	0.22
XII Clothing	1.53	1.31	1.97	1.93	0.92	1.37	1.72	1.39	4.15	3.85	0.96	0.89
XIII Building Materials	1.84	1.72	1.54	1.86	1.40	2.17	2.02	2.16	1.14	0.80	1.59	1.64
XIV Timbers	1.31	1.24	1.79	1.64	0.89	1.01	1.18	2.83	1.29	1.19	1.61	1.57
XV Paper and Printing	1.60	1.69	1.63	1.74	1.97	2.04	3.35	1.52	1.64	1.47	2.59	2.64
XVI Other Manufacture	1.90	2.19	2.46	3.23	1.92	3.27	3.85	4.55	1.54	1.25	1.17	1.30
XVII Construction	13.90	14.42	5.90	6.87	3.61	4.03	10.16	12.02	4.29	5.09	9.77	11.45
XVIII Gas and Electricity	1.42	1.45	1.23	1.18	1.17	0.81	1.53	1.71	0.92	1.13	2.14	2.31
XIX Transport	8.58	8.68	13.71	12.22	13.04	10.26	18.39	17.20	8.66	8.94	9.23	8.67
XX Distribution	7.37	6.58	6.61	5.69	7.23	5.87	4.71	3.78	8.04	8.10	10.73	10.18
XXI Finance	1.49	1.64	1.78	1.44	2.42	1.72	0.47	0.43	2.41	2.36	2.15	2.33
XXII Professional Services	7.63	7.79	8.43	7.43	10.57	8.04	3.31	3.57	11.47	11.78	5.35	5.98
XXIII Miscellaneous Services	13.46	11.89	11.39	9.77	7.95	5.75	7.13	5.42	23.08	24.09	6.88	7.35
XXIV Public Administration	5.20	5.13	7.27	5.09	8.57	5.09	4.36	3.88	8.84	6.84	7.30	6.79
Total Economically Active (Thousands)[a]	100.00 848.2	100.00 1069.4	100.00 212.0	100.00 338.4	100.00 87.5	100.00 152.2	100.00 77.0	100.00 110.1	100.00 47.5	100.00 76.2	100.00 15,675.4	100.00 15,534.6

SOURCES: *Census 1961, Industry Tables*; *Sample Census 1966, Economic Activity Tables*, vol. III.

a Excluding 'industry inadequately described'.

Appendix table 3.2. The industrial distribution of the immigrant labour force, 1961 and 1966 (females)

Industry	All immigrants 1961	1966	New Commonwealth 1961	1966	India and Pakistan 1961	1966	British Caribbean 1961	1966	Other New Commonwealth 1961	1966	Percentages Total labour force 1961	1966
I Agriculture	0.57	0.54	0.39	0.29	0.68	0.54	0.07	0.06	0.53	0.49	1.26	1.33
II Mining	0.06	0.05	0.06	0.06	0.12	0.11	—	0.01	0.06	0.09	0.27	0.23
III Food	3.26	3.42	4.02	4.64	2.81	3.30	5.93	6.24	2.52	2.89	3.60	3.45
IV Chemicals	1.21	1.22	1.39	1.23	2.25	1.44	1.10	1.18	0.65	1.11	1.71	1.62
V Metals	0.58	0.70	0.84	0.99	0.40	0.52	1.47	1.67	0.41	0.17	0.94	0.86
VI Engineering	6.82	7.31	6.80	8.24	7.70	9.12	7.95	9.17	3.52	5.49	6.80	6.87
VII Shipbuilding	0.06	0.07	0.03	0.06	0.04	0.19	—	—	0.06	0.03	0.15	0.12
VIII Vehicles	1.24	1.32	0.97	1.28	1.04	1.08	0.99	1.76	0.82	0.54	1.46	1.30
IX Metals n.e.s.	2.05	2.30	2.58	3.58	1.44	2.17	4.56	5.41	0.88	1.49	2.28	2.10
X Textiles	3.50	3.21	2.09	2.42	1.64	2.17	2.84	3.07	1.47	1.40	5.64	4.32
XI Leather	0.37	0.34	0.53	0.48	0.28	0.16	0.96	0.68	0.18	0.40	0.33	0.29
XII Clothing	5.63	5.54	10.86	10.56	2.69	2.87	14.11	10.99	17.24	17.84	5.22	4.40
XIII Building Materials	0.43	0.44	0.53	0.52	0.44	0.35	0.58	0.73	0.59	0.29	0.96	0.87
XIV Timbers	0.48	0.50	0.55	0.52	0.48	0.65	0.65	0.54	0.47	0.34	0.70	0.65
XV Paper and Printing	1.76	1.64	2.04	1.62	2.29	2.14	2.19	1.47	1.41	1.37	2.63	2.41
XVI Other Manufacture	1.47	1.62	1.71	2.36	1.64	2.06	2.12	3.00	1.11	1.43	1.49	1.46
XVII Construction	0.58	0.76	0.60	0.51	1.24	1.08	0.10	0.26	0.53	0.40	0.90	1.17
XVIII Gas and Electricity	0.22	0.33	0.32	0.30	0.64	0.70	0.10	0.13	0.23	0.23	0.55	0.62
XIX Transport	2.76	2.92	3.71	3.73	4.77	3.95	4.32	4.10	1.11	2.75	3.00	3.06
XX Distribution	11.51	11.78	8.01	7.80	11.78	11.99	3.15	4.47	10.79	9.92	19.93	19.42
XXI Finance	1.98	2.22	2.49	2.04	4.49	3.57	0.34	0.73	3.22	3.00	3.11	3.43
XXII Professional Services	27.06	27.52	31.05	29.44	29.06	27.26	33.32	32.09	30.09	26.54	16.95	18.33
XXIII Miscellaneous Services	24.11	21.25	14.71	13.86	16.47	16.49	11.20	10.10	18.12	18.47	16.38	17.58
XXIV Public Administration	2.29	3.00	3.72	3.47	5.61	6.09	1.95	2.14	3.99	3.32	3.74	4.11
Total Economically Active	100.00	100.00	100.00	100.00	100.00	100.00	100.00	100.00	100.00	100.00	100.00	100.00
(Thousands)a	408.5	570.9	85.5	140.6	27.3	36.9	41.4	68.7	16.8	35.0	7554.7	8365.8

SOURCES: As appendix table 3.1.
a Excluding 'industry inadequately described'.

Appendix table 3.3. *The industrial distribution of the immigrant labour force, 1961 and 1966 (males and females)*

Percentages

Industry	All immigrants 1961	All immigrants 1966	New Commonwealth 1961	New Commonwealth 1966	India and Pakistan 1961	India and Pakistan 1966	British Caribbean 1961	British Caribbean 1966	Other New Commonwealth 1961	Other New Commonwealth 1966	Total labour force 1961	Total labour force 1966
I Agriculture	1.69	1.20	0.77	0.40	1.22	0.47	0.09	0.11	1.02	0.76	3.68	3.16
II Mining	1.43	0.99	0.44	0.31	0.35	0.29	0.42	0.40	0.44	0.21	3.11	2.33
III Food	2.94	3.03	3.29	3.70	2.27	2.86	4.56	4.90	3.34	3.19	3.03	3.08
IV Chemicals	1.66	1.58	1.75	1.47	2.09	1.43	1.77	1.66	1.16	1.22	2.15	2.04
V Metals	2.57	2.83	3.73	4.95	3.75	7.12	5.41	4.92	1.16	1.32	2.69	2.44
VI Engineering	8.75	9.33	10.05	10.73	12.38	12.58	10.05	10.64	6.25	7.75	8.74	9.07
VII Shipbuilding	0.39	0.37	0.44	0.25	0.44	0.26	0.25	0.13	0.87	0.45	1.02	0.74
VIII Vehicles	3.61	3.67	3.50	3.70	4.53	4.24	3.21	4.35	2.18	1.74	3.61	3.36
IX Metals n.e.s.	2.23	2.81	2.92	4.35	2.27	4.67	4.73	5.42	1.45	2.07	2.26	2.33
X Textiles	2.91	3.32	2.82	4.69	4.18	8.92	2.53	2.35	1.02	1.23	3.40	2.99
XI Leather	0.34	0.35	0.40	0.47	0.26	0.30	0.59	0.72	0.29	0.34	0.26	0.24
XII Clothing	2.87	2.78	4.54	4.46	1.31	1.66	6.08	5.08	7.99	8.25	2.35	2.14
XIII Building Materials	1.38	1.28	1.28	1.46	1.13	1.81	1.52	1.61	1.02	0.64	1.39	1.36
XIV Timbers	1.04	0.98	1.45	1.31	0.78	0.94	2.45	1.95	1.60	0.93	1.31	1.24
XV Paper and Printing	1.66	1.67	1.71	1.71	2.00	2.06	1.52	1.50	1.45	1.44	2.60	2.56
XVI Other Manufacture	1.76	1.99	2.25	2.98	1.92	3.04	3.29	3.95	3.20	1.30	1.27	1.36
XVII Construction	9.57	9.66	4.37	5.00	3.05	3.45	6.59	7.50	0.58	3.62	6.89	7.80
XVIII Gas and Electricity	1.03	1.06	0.97	0.92	1.05	0.79	1.01	1.10	1.02	0.85	1.62	1.70
XIX Transport	6.69	6.68	10.85	9.73	11.07	9.03	13.51	12.17	6.54	6.99	7.21	6.67
XX Distribution	8.71	8.39	6.99	6.31	8.28	7.07	4.14	4.04	8.87	8.67	13.72	13.47
XXI Finance	1.65	1.84	1.98	1.62	2.88	2.08	0.42	0.54	2.62	2.56	2.46	2.72
XXII Professional Services	13.94	14.66	14.92	13.89	14.91	11.79	13.77	14.53	16.71	16.42	9.12	10.37
XXIII Miscellaneous Services	16.93	15.15	12.33	10.97	10.03	7.85	8.53	7.22	21.66	22.32	9.97	10.99
XXIV Public Administration	4.25	4.39	6.25	4.62	7.85	5.29	3.55	3.21	7.56	5.73	6.14	5.84
Total Economically Active	100.00	100.00	100.00	100.00	100.00	100.00	100.00	100.00	100.00	100.00	100.00	100.00
(Thousands)[a]	1256.7	1640.3	297.5	479.0	114.8	189.1	118.4	178.8	64.3	111.1	23,230.1	24,100.4

SOURCES: As appendix table 3.1.

[a] Excluding 'industry inadequately described'

Appendix table 4. *Coverage of New Commonwealth income and expenditure surveys*

	House-holds	Persons				Economically active		
		Child-ren	Adults		Total	Male	Female	Total
			M	F				
Manchester survey								
New Commonwealth[a]	199	297	182	156	635	158	94	252
West Indies	160	244	127	136	507	113	87	200
Birmingham survey								
New Commonwealth[b]	920	966	1,093	530	2,589	..	..	1,161
India and Pakistan	618	582	723	309	1,614	..	..	709
West Indies	302	384	370	221	975	..	..	452

SOURCES: See text.

[a] West Indies, India and Pakistan, Africa.
[b] West Indies, India and Pakistan.

PUBLICATIONS OF THE
NATIONAL INSTITUTE OF ECONOMIC
AND SOCIAL RESEARCH
published by
THE CAMBRIDGE UNIVERSITY PRESS

Books published for the Institute by the Cambridge University Press are available through the ordinary booksellers. They appear in the four series below.

ECONOMIC & SOCIAL STUDIES

    *I   *Studies in the National Income, 1924–1938*
        Edited by A. L. BOWLEY. Reprinted with corrections, 1944. pp. 256. 15s. net.
   *II   *The Burden of British Taxation*
        By G. FINDLAY SHIRRAS and L. ROSTAS. 1942. pp. 140. 17s. 6d. net.
  *III *Trade Regulations and Commercial Policy of the United Kingdom*
        By THE RESEARCH STAFF OF THE NATIONAL INSTITUTE OF ECONOMIC AND
        SOCIAL RESEARCH. 1943. pp. 275. 17s. 6d. net.
  *IV *National Health Insurance : A Critical Study*
        By HERMANN LEVY. 1944. pp. 356. 21s. net.
   *V *The Development of the Soviet Economic System : An Essay on the Experience of Planning in the U.S.S.R.*
        By ALEXANDER BAYKOV. 1946. pp. 530. 45s. net.
  *VI *Studies in Financial Organization*
        By T. BALOGH. 1948. pp. 328. 40s. net.
 *VII *Investment, Location, and Size of Plant : A Realistic Inquiry into the Structure of British and American Industries*
        By P. SARGANT FLORENCE, assisted by W. BALDAMUS. 1948. pp. 230. 21s. net.
  VIII *A Statistical Analysis of Advertising Expenditure and of the Revenue of the Press*
        By NICHOLAS KALDOR and RODNEY SILVERMAN. 1948. pp. 200. 25s. net.
  *IX *The Distribution of Consumer Goods*
        By JAMES B. JEFFERYS, assisted by MARGARET MACCOLL and G. L. LEVETT. 1950. pp. 430. 50s. net.
   *X *Lessons of the British War Economy*
        Edited by D. N. CHESTER. 1951. pp. 260. 30s. net.
  *XI *Colonial Social Accounting*
        By PHYLLIS DEANE. 1953. pp. 360. 60s. net.
 *XII *Migration and Economic Growth*
        By BRINLEY THOMAS. 1954. pp. 384. 50s. net.
*XIII *Retail Trading in Britain, 1850–1950*
        By JAMES B. JEFFERYS. 1954. pp. 490. 60s. net.
 *XIV *British Economic Statistics*
        By CHARLES CARTER and A. D. ROY. 1954. pp. 192. 30s. net.
  XV *The Structure of British Industry : A Symposium*
        Edited by DUNCAN BURN. 1958. Vol. I. pp. 403. 55s. net. Vol. II. pp. 499. 63s. net.
 *XVI *Concentration in British Industry*
        By RICHARD EVELY and I. M. D. LITTLE. 1960. pp. 357. 63s. net.
*XVII *Studies in Company Finance*
        Edited by BRIAN TEW and R. F. HENDERSON. 1959. pp. 301. 40s. net.
XVIII *British Industrialists : Steel and Hosiery, 1850–1950*
        By CHARLOTTE ERICKSON. 1959. pp. 276. 45s. net.
  XIX *The Antitrust Laws of the U.S.A.: A Study of Competition Enforced by Law*
        By A. D. NEALE. 2nd edition, 1970. pp. 548. 80s. net (also in NIESR Students' Edition).

*At present out of print.

OCCASIONAL PAPERS

*At present out of print.

*XIX   *Post-war Investment, Location and Size of Plant*
      By P. SARGANT FLORENCE. 1962. pp. 51. 12*s.* 6*d.* net.
 *XX   *Investment and Growth Policies in British Industrial Firms*
      By TIBOR BARNA. 1962. pp. 71. 12*s.* 6*d.* net.
  XXI   *Pricing and Employment in the Trade Cycle : A Study of British Manufacturing Industry, 1950–61*
      By R. R. NEILD. 1963. pp. 73. 15*s.* net.
 XXII   *Health and Welfare Services in Britain in 1975*
      By DEBORAH PAIGE and KIT JONES. 1966. pp.142. 21*s.* net.
XXIII   *Lancashire Textiles : A Case Study of Industrial Change*
      By CAROLINE MILES. 1968. pp. 124. 21*s.* net.

STUDIES IN THE NATIONAL INCOME AND EXPENDITURE OF THE UNITED KINGDOM

Published under the joint auspices of the National Institute and the Department of Applied Economics, Cambridge.

  1   *The Measurement of Consumers' Expenditure and Behaviour in the United Kingdom, 1920–1938*, Vol. I
    By RICHARD STONE, assisted by D. A. ROWE and by W. J CORLETT, RENEE HURSTFIELD, MURIEL POTTER. 1954. pp. 448. £10 net.
  2   *The Measurement of Consumers' Expenditure and Behaviour in the United Kingdom, 1920–38*, Vol. II
    By RICHARD STONE and D. A. ROWE. 1966. pp. 152. 90*s.* net.
  3   *Consumers' Expenditure in the United Kingdom, 1900–1919*
    By A. R. PREST, assisted by A. A. ADAMS. 1954. pp. 196. 55*s.* net.
  4   *Domestic Capital Formation in the United Kingdom, 1920–1938*
    By C. H. FEINSTEIN. 1965. pp. 284. 90*s.* net.
  5   *Wages and Salaries in the United Kingdom, 1920–1938*
    By AGATHA CHAPMAN, assisted by ROSE KNIGHT. 1953. pp. 254. 75*s.* net.

NIESR STUDENTS' EDITION

  1   *Growth and Trade* (an abridged version of *Industrial Growth and World Trade*)
    By A. MAIZELS. 1970. pp. 312. 21*s.* net.
  2   *The Management of the British Economy, 1945–60* (unabridged)
    By J. C. R. DOW. 1970. pp. 443. 22*s.* net.
  3   *The Antitrust Laws of the U.S.A.* (2nd edition, unabridged)
    By A. D. NEALE. 1970. pp. 548. 28*s.* net.

*At present out of print.